GUERRILLA
INVESTING

GUERRILLA INVESTING

Winning Strategies for Beating the Wall Street Professionals

PETER SIRIS

LONGSTREET
Atlanta, Georgia

Published by
LONGSTREET PRESS, INC.
A subsidiary of Cox Newspapers,
A subsidiary of Cox Enterprises, Inc.
2140 Newmarket Parkway
Suite 122
Marietta, GA 30067

Printed in the United States of America

1st printing, 1998

Library of Congress Catalog Card Number: 97-76264
ISBN: 1-56352-467-8

Jacket and book design by Jill Dible

To my mother, Elaine Winik, who taught me how to think, and my father, Burt Siris, who taught me how to invest.

ACKNOWLEDGMENTS

I would like to thank my grandfather, Sam Kappel, and my father, Burt Siris, who taught me about the stock market when I was a young boy. I guess the lessons must have amounted to something after all. And I would like to thank my mother, Elaine Winik, who taught me the value of learning, even if I was not the easiest student. You always said if I could not find work, I could always write a book. This makes two. Now you need to write one more and we will be even.

I would also like to acknowledge some of the people whom I have worked with on Wall Street. David Keidan and David Goldsmith of The Buckingham Research Group run one of the finest boutique brokerage firms on Wall Street. While quality work may not be the hallmark at many firms, it is at Buckingham. Much of my success I owe to David and David and the rest of my former partners at Buckingham. I am fortunate to have spent seven years working with such fine individuals.

Mark Suvall, Andy Rodman, and Charlie Frumberg of UBS Securities are three of the smartest and most charismatic people on Wall Street. They took an almost dormant brokerage firm and built it into a power, and they did it without compromising either quality or morality. It was an honor to have worked for them.

I would like to thank Linda Wachner, the chairman of both Warnaco and Authentic Fitness, for giving me the opportunity to work for her. In my years on Wall Street, I have known many of the most successful executives in American industry. Linda is, quite simply, the smartest. She also has a dedication to her work and a will to win that few have ever matched.

I would like to thank all the people at Keim-Wilson for helping me over the years. Stud Hoffman, a legendary trader, and Mark Erman, a top researcher, kept me continually informed about all the critical events I was missing while I was working on this book. Dick Keim and David Wilson provided me with both good friendship and good counsel. (They also have done a superb job managing some of my money.)

Special thanks to Leigh Curry, who not only kept me up-to-date on research, but also read the manuscript and provided me with excellent inputs. Some of the better lines in this book belong to Leigh. (Leigh's lines are easy to spot. They are the ones with the Texas drawl.) Also thanks to Stephen Cohen, a true guerrilla investor, for his inputs, and to Peter Levinson for his constant support.

I would like to thank my agent, Carol Mann, and all of the people at Longstreet, especially my editor Suzanne De Galan and her assistant Sherry Wade. They worked tirelessly on my manuscript and greatly enhanced the quality of this book. Their perspective has been invaluable.

Finally, I would like to thank my loving wife, Barbara Wyckoff, and my children, Alex and Tracy, for putting up with me while I wrote this book, especially during crunch time. Having a husband or a father who is sitting up in a study typing away until the middle of the night is probably not their idea of fun. But I greatly appreciate their love and support.

Despite the advice from a wide range of friends and associates, all of the opinions in this book are mine. This book is designed to show individual investors how the professionals play the game of investing, and how individuals can compete against them. In writing the book, I have referred to specific companies, executives, brokerage firms, and analysts. All of the references are for illustrative purposes only. There is no intent to recommend or criticize any particular stocks, brokerage firms, or analysts. Nor should any comment, taken out of context, be used as a judgment of the overall quality of a particular individual or firm. Every analyst and brokerage firm makes mistakes. I know I certainly have. My intention is not to take a cheap shot at anyone, but rather to explain how the investing game is played. My hope is that this book will help individual investors understand more about how to win.

PETER SIRIS
New York, New York

TABLE OF CONTENTS

—

GUERRILLA INVESTING

INTRODUCTION

When I was a young boy, I would go to my grandparent's house. While we watched the Brooklyn Dodgers on television, my father would read the market quotes to my grandfather and they would talk about the stocks. I can still remember most of the stocks my grandfather owned, even though many of the companies have long ceased to exist. It was the early 1950s, and most Americans were learning how to invest. Later, I took the money that I had earned delivering newspapers and bought my first stock: American Motors. (I liked the little Nash Rambler, whose horn went "beep, beep, beep.") Even though that company also no longer exists, my first investment worked out well. From then on, I have always been fascinated by the market.

For many years, few shared my interest. After all, the market was lower in 1982 than it had been in 1969. Smart investors were putting their money in real estate, commodities, gold, impressionist paintings, antique furniture, and even baseball cards. Five cards had come with a piece of bubble gum for a nickel, but they were now worth hundreds of dollars. (Of course, my mother had thrown out my collection when I was away at camp. She thought they were junk. She obviously did not realize that I was counting on them for my retirement.) Why should anyone gamble in the stock market when they could invest in baseball cards? Besides, with bonds and money funds paying more than 10 percent, who needed a dead stock market?

Even after the stock market began to advance, few individuals were interested. The increase seemed a temporary aberration. When the crash came in 1987 and the stock market dropped 500 points in one day, it confirmed what everyone already knew: investing in stocks was for fools. My friends, who knew I worked on Wall Street, called to console me. Some offered to lend me baseball cards, and one even offered me a job as a waiter. (I was hoping for a job as a taxi driver, but in New York, my ability to speak English worked against me.) Fortunately, for me, the market did shrug off the crash and begin to rally. Soon, individuals started to take an interest in Wall Street. Their interest may have been stimulated by the fact that real estate had collapsed, or by the fact that everybody knew someone who was making serious money in the market.

As the advance continued and everyone started to make money, stocks supplanted real estate as the investment of choice and subject of the cocktail party conversations. People stopped asking questions and started giving advice. Now everyone has hot stocks. My friends in real estate have hot stocks. So does my doctor, my lawyer, my cable TV man, my plumber, and my auto mechanic. The cable man loves media stocks, and the plumber loves biotechs. And my garage mechanic is constantly bemoaning the fact that he missed the move in auto stocks. *"I drive these American cars every day. I could see that they were getting better,"* he tells me when I come in for a repair. *"So how was I so stupid to miss it?"*

DOWNSIZED TO RICHES

The reason for the resurgence of stocks is very simple. As the Baby Boomers approached middle age, they hit a crisis. The 20 percent increases in pay they were accustomed to receiving were now trimmed to the cost of living. Promotions stopped as millions clogged the few openings at the top of the pyramid. There were too many competing for too few top management jobs. Something had to give, and it was the Baby Boomers. Worse, companies started to downsize. Now it was the turn of the white-collar, not the blue-collar, workers to lose their jobs. Where once Baby Boomers figured on huge annual increases, they were now praying that they would keep their jobs. To make matters worse, real estate, the primary underpinning of their wealth, had begun to flatten. With corporate downsizing and real estate in a funk, the Baby Boomers suddenly found that they were approaching middle age with little saved for their retirement. More than half of their working lives was now behind them. Things were not getting better and the clock was ticking. They had to accumulate money and they had to do it quickly.

Fortunately, the Baby Boomers had already bought most of the things they would ever need. After all, they had spent almost three decades acquiring every imaginable material good, and there had never been a generation better at spending. But the one thing they needed most, financial security, was the one thing they lacked. They had saved little for their retirement, and as they looked at the world and realized that they could live for another fifty years, they started to worry. They knew that they had to build up a nest egg quickly.

Ironically, the Baby Boomers' problems also became their solution. Corporate downsizing, a flattening of the real estate market, and somewhat lower spending led to a sharp decline in inflation. Bonds, which had once yielded over 10 percent, were now yielding 6 percent. Money market funds were now yielding 4 percent. Real estate was dead. Gold was selling for less than half its all-time high. Even baseball cards stopped appreciating. There was no choice but to invest in stocks.

Money flowed from bonds into stocks, from money funds into stocks, from real estate into stocks, from collectibles into stocks, and from spending into stocks. The flow of funds pushed up prices of stocks. At the same time, the very downsizing that had jeopardized the Boomers' future made companies more efficient and led to higher earnings. With lower interest rates, investors were willing to pay more for the same stream of earnings. So the combination of better earnings and higher price-earnings ratios propelled the stock market upward.

The Dow Jones Industrial Average was over 1,000 in 1968, but by 1982, it had declined to below 800. For almost fifteen years, no one had made any money in the market. But then the boom began. Between 1982 and 1987, the Dow almost quadrupled. Then came the crash of 1987. The market dropped more than 500 points in one day and 1,000 points from its top. But the crash did not last long. With interest rates declining, the market resumed its surge. By 1997, the Dow had surpassed 8,200, more than ten times its level in 1982. In fifteen years, the market had jumped by more than 1,000 percent, a compound rate of 20 percent per year—an increase virtually without precedent!

THEN REALITY HITS

But nothing goes up forever. Just as real estate boomed in earlier decades only to flatten in the 1980s, just as gold went from $32 to $800 an ounce only to drop below $300, just as collectibles have had boom and bust cycles—so the market will do the same. There is no way to know when the market will flatten out and when it will decline. But this much is certain: No class of assets, not stocks, not real estate, not paintings, not even baseball cards, can grow at a compounded rate of 16 percent per year forever. The huge run in the market over the past fifteen years has given many of the Baby Boomers financial security, and it has made the game look easy. When the stock market stops going up, many new investors will face a flat or even a down market for the first time. Most were not investing in 1987. To them, October 19 was just a date in history. They did not have to sit and watch as their net worth was slashed before their eyes. Fewer still can remember the slow death of the stock market in the 1970s, when, for thirteen years, the market went sideways and valuations dropped. A flat or a down market will be a new experience for most investors, and it will most likely separate the strong from the weak.

WHY YOU NEED THIS BOOK

It would be nice if individuals could choose to invest only in bull markets, but such an alternative is not possible. The only effective way to stay ahead of the game is to try to outperform the averages in all markets. A successful investor can make more money than the average in an up market, make some money in a flat market, and lose less money than the average in a down market.

To outperform the market, you must beat the competition. If you cannot beat the average investor, you cannot win. But, against conventional wisdom and every investor's hopes, the average investor is not a widow in an old-age home selling off an estate. Nor is the average investor an orphan whose only goal is to protect an inheritance. Instead, the average investor is usually a well-trained professional, who wants to win as much or more than you do and will use every tool at his disposal to defeat you.

The individual, however, is not without weapons. The Internet has put information at the fingertips of everyone. Now, with a click, people can monitor their portfolios, receive quotes, utilize charts, follow the earnings estimates and recommendations of leading analysts, stay abreast of the news, and study in-depth financial reports from the companies themselves and trade at prices equal to or below those available to professionals. The challenge for the individual investor is to learn how to use this new powerful resource.

To win, individual investors must find ways of gaining advantages against the professionals. For those with limited time, this may mean nothing more than buying good stocks and holding them, and thus avoiding the trading games of the professionals. But for those with more time and resources, *Guerrilla Investing* will present a number of more action-oriented strategies that will enable the individual to gain an edge.

Guerrilla Investing is written for the serious amateur investor who wants to compete against the professional in good markets and bad. However, it does not offer any magic bullets. It will not tell you how to strike it rich. Few ever strike it rich in the stock market. The competition is just too tough. This book will not provide you with ten secrets to success that guarantee a profit. Profit is never guaranteed and if there were such secrets, someone would have discovered them long ago. Nor will this book give you specific stock tips. The market is too dynamic. Any Buy and Sell recommendations would be out of date before you could read them. In fact, change is really the only certainty in the stock market. Industries come in and out of favor. Stocks go up and down. Those investors who can anticipate the changes will win, while those who cannot anticipate the changes will lose.

This book will provide the amateur investor with the tools to understand the dynamics of the market and anticipate the changes in it. It also provides specific information about on-line investing tools. The computer icon in the margin of the page will alert you to look for information about the Internet. Guerrilla Investing is a strategy that uses both the latest technology and time-tested, common-sense techniques to allow the amateur, against all odds, to win. It will also give the investor the weapons he needs to compete with the professionals and outperform the market.

The Battle Plan

CHAPTER ONE

Understand the Field of Battle

- Have you ever listened to Wall Street professionals talk about their performance and wondered why you were not doing as well?
- Have you noticed how the professionals always seem to have news ahead of time?
- Have you watched as the professionals took every share of a hot new issue?
- Have you ever received a report from your broker only to notice that the stock had already gone up by 25 percent?

As an individual investor, you are playing in a game that is rigged against you. The professionals get better information from salesmen, analysts, traders, and from the managements of the companies. They have more capital and better systems. They can act quickly, completing their trades before the individual even knows what is happening. **Individual investors typically lose because they try to take on the professionals on their own turf.** Individuals do not have the resources or the information that the professionals have. But there is a way for the individual to defeat the professional.

Think of investing as a war and the professionals as a well-trained army. The individual cannot attack the professionals head-on. The individual does not have the weapons, but the individual can fight the professionals in much the same way as a guerrilla force fights a mechanized army: attacking the professionals' weaknesses, avoiding the professionals' strengths, fighting on local terrain, finding niches that the professionals miss, and using the individual's smaller size as an asset rather than a liability. We call this Guerrilla Investing. If individuals can think of themselves as guerrillas and plot a strategy of competing against a well-entrenched professional the way a guerrilla force would against a well-entrenched army, they have a strong chance of winning.

INVESTING IS LIKE WAR

As an investor, just like a military strategist, you are trying to defeat your enemy and outperform the market, while your enemy is trying to defeat you. Each investment is like a battle, and the sum of the battles makes up the war. If you do not win most of your battles, you will never win the war. In *The Art of War*, the Chinese philosopher Sun Tzu stated his most important rule, "Know yourself, know your enemy. In one hundred battles, there will be one hundred victories." If this is the first rule of warfare, it is also the first rule of investing. In order to win in the market, investors must know their strengths and weaknesses and those of their enemies.

In investing, the enemy is anyone on the opposite side of a trade. You do not have a picture of your enemy on your wall with a bullet through his heart. In fact, it may be difficult to think of a mild-mannered portfolio manager from a bank or a charismatic CEO of a corporation as the enemy, but the fact remains that if they are selling while you are buying, they are your enemy, and only one of you will win.

When looking at a stock, the investor must ask:

> *"What does my enemy know that I do not?"*
> *"Why is my enemy selling when I am buying?"*
> *"How can I get an edge that will enable me to defeat my enemy?"*

To most people, investing does not seem like war. If you buy a stock and it goes up, you were right. If you buy a stock and it goes down, you were wrong. Most people are thrilled when the market goes up and frustrated when it goes down. Right now, most people are thrilled. But giant bull markets, like the current one, occur only once in a generation. The previous comparable market occurred in the late 1960s. Once it ended, investors had to wait thirteen years before stocks began to recover. Because there is no way to predict the market, investors should train themselves to defeat their enemies and beat the averages in all markets. To achieve these ends, each investment should be looked at as a military deployment. If investors can figure out how to win most battles, they will ultimately win the war.

IN EVERY TRADE 50 PERCENT OF INVESTORS ARE WRONG

Every time a trade is made, the buyer is saying, *"Of all the things that I could do with my money, owning this stock is the best,"* while the seller is saying, *"Of all the things that I could do with my money, owning this stock is the worst."* If the stock goes up, the buyer will have been right. If the stock goes down, the seller will have been right. It is impossible for both of them to be right at the same time.

It is critical that every investor understands this rule of combat. **Investing is not a win-win game. It is a win-lose game.** Everyone who plays the game is in the stock market to win. They are not in the stock market to make the world a better place or to help your net worth. They are in the stock market to make as much money as they can for themselves. If you buy stock that a professional or a company insider is selling, only one of you will end up being right. In such a contest, the professionals and the insiders have substantial advantages. As a guerrilla investor, you must be extremely careful not to get suckered into fighting stronger enemies on their own turf.

"SMART MONEY" LOSES, TOO

Many people believe that there is "smart money" in the market and that smart money usually wins. The financial institutions are obviously the "smart money." Their portfolio managers and analysts are paid hundreds of thousands or millions of dollars, so they must be smart. Fidelity Investments is obviously the smartest of the smart, because it is the biggest. When Fidelity buys or sells, the market often takes notice. I have often heard salesmen whisper, *"Fidelity is buying,"* in a voice that reverently conveyed the idea that anything Fidelity was buying must be a great stock. But if Fidelity is always right, then the person or institution on the other side of the trade must, by definition, always be wrong.

Think for a moment about the other side of the transaction. If Fidelity is buying 2,000,000 shares of a stock, who is selling? Do you think that there are 20,000 orphans, each selling 100 shares they were given at birth? How about 200 widows, each selling 10,000 shares that their husbands left them? Of course not. When Fidelity buys 2,000,000 shares of a stock, the seller is probably another financial institution.

Fidelity spends millions on research, but so does the financial institution on the other side of the transaction. Fidelity has skilled portfolio managers, analysts, and traders and receives superb inputs from the Street, but so does the firm on the other side of the transaction. There are millions of dollars of salaries on each side of the transaction, but only one of the institutions and its experts will be right.

Many will dispute this characterization. They will claim that people have different investment styles and that these styles create the trades that are mutually beneficial for all concerned. A value investor, for example, would buy a stock that had collapsed and was selling at a discount to its enterprise value. As the stock appreciated, the value investor would in turn sell it to a moderate growth investor, who would own it from a level slightly under "fair" market value to a level somewhat above "fair" market value. The moderate growth investor would in turn sell the stock to a momentum investor, who would seek to buy stocks that have high earnings growth and relative strength. In these cases, one

6

could claim that all sides were winners because each owned the stock during a period in which it conformed to his or her investment style.

There are obviously instances in which a stock goes up so much that everyone can feel like a winner. In January 1995, an associate of mine, Annie Erner, and I recommended CompUSA at $7. (The stock had previously declined from about $21, so the people who sold at $7 were not happy.) But at $7, CompUSA was a perfect candidate for value players, betting on a turnaround. New management had come in. The controls were improving, and insiders were buying. When the stock reached $14, some value investors started to sell. Moderate growth investors started to invest, as it became clear that the business was getting better. Management continued buying the stock. Earnings surprised on the upside. The stock reached $28. Momentum players piled in. By May 1996, CompUSA reached $45.

When a stock goes from $7 to $45 in sixteen months, it is difficult for anyone to think of himself as a loser, except, of course, for the person who sold the stock at $7. Each group of investors could be satisfied with the fact that they doubled their money in six months. The problem is that they could also second-guess themselves. The value investors who sold at $14 must have watched as the stock raced to $45 and had second thoughts about their decision to sell. The moderate growth investors could have second-guessed themselves on both sides of the transaction. They could have bought at $10 instead of at $14, and they could have sold at $40 instead of at $28. In doing so, they could have quadrupled, rather than doubled, their money. The momentum investors could also have moved in sooner, rather than waiting until the stock had more than tripled.

Even with second-guessing, each of these investor groups should have been thrilled. But what happens in a more normal case? A stock is selling for $20. Earnings are going to be reported the next day. Someone buys the stock, expecting good earnings. Someone else sells the stock, expecting bad earnings. If the earnings are above plan and the stock goes up, the buyer was right. If the earnings are below plan and the stock goes down, the seller was right. If the stock is unchanged, both were wrong, because both had to pay transaction costs. The reality is simple: this is a war. Each trade is a battle, and in each trade, only one of the sides will be right.

STOCK PRICES: A STAND-OFF BETWEEN COMPETING FORCES

No general would ever commit troops to an attack without first surveying the battlefield and understanding the forces as they are currently arrayed. The same is true in the stock market. To defeat your enemies, you must understand the current position of the market, because it is this point around which change will occur.

Prices reflect the collective wisdom of all participants at a particular point in time. This is a simple truism but one that is critical to investing. There is no absolute right price for a stock or for the market. The prices, at any point in time, reflect the stand-off between competing forces. Brokers are constantly calling with great pieces of advice concerning the market and individual stocks. How many times have you heard someone say,

> *"This stock is much too cheap. Buy it now!"* Or
> *"This stock is much too expensive. There is no way that it can keep going up."*

It is extremely tempting to believe that the broker actually *knows* something. Brokers, analysts, and strategists all have opinions, but opinions are all that they have. No matter what they personally think, the reality is that at any instant, a stock is neither cheap nor expensive. It is only cheap or expensive in your broker's mind. This is not to impugn your broker. But if your broker thinks that a particular stock is "undervalued," then someone else must think that it is "overvalued." Otherwise there would never be a seller to match up with the buyer. Only when there is a balance of buyers and sellers can the stock actually trade, and when the stock does trade, it will trade at the price that reflects the collective wisdom of all participants at that point in time. There is no such thing as underpriced or overpriced. There is only one person's view relative to the rest of the world.

If the Dow Jones is selling at 8,000, that is the price that the sum of all investors have determined is appropriate at that point in time. Some investors may believe the Dow is overvalued. They will be sellers. But if the Dow is selling at 8,000, then other investors must believe it is undervalued, and they will be buyers. Investors trade one billion shares every day. The sum of their collective wisdom is the price of the market.

The same is true of individual stocks. It is tempting to look at a stock and say that it is overvalued or undervalued. Have you ever watched a stock drop from $50 to $20 and thought that it was now too cheap? Well, it may be too cheap in your view, but the fact that it has dropped $30 does not mean that it will suddenly turn and go back up. If the stock is trading at $20 per share, that price reflects the collective wisdom of all investors.

Investors have been hotly contesting the valuation of the new Internet stocks. Netscape, Yahoo, Amazon.com, E*Trade, and other Internet companies have been characterized by some analysts as being extremely overvalued. But for every investor who has been selling one of these stocks, there is another who has been buying. For everyone who believes that the Internet is a fad, there is someone else who believes that it is the wave of the future. While 50 percent of these investors will be right, the other 50 percent will be wrong.

So it is not reasonable to say that the market or a stock is too cheap or too expensive. It is only reasonable to say that some individual has these opinions. At any point in time, the market reflects the best of everyone's expectations. It is critical for investors to understand this rule. Understanding the current level of the market is like understanding the field of battle. Before you can attack, you must know who your enemy is and how your enemy is positioned. While future movements are the key to the market, you cannot understand them unless you understand the current positions.

INVESTOR EXPECTATIONS CHANGE THE BATTLEFIELD BALANCE

Since the market at any point in time is selling at a level that reflects the collective expectations of all investors, prices can only change when investors change their actions. If a stock is trading at $30 without moving up or down, it does so because there is a balance of buyers and sellers. The price will change only when the balance is changed. If more people take action on the buy side, the price of the stock will go up. If more people take action on the sell side, the price of the stock will go down.

Changes in expectations cause people to change their behavior toward the stock. The price of the stock itself can cause changes in expectations. As a stock moves up, people often believe that their risk/reward ratio has changed. An investor bought IBM at $90. As IBM reached $105, that investor decided that there was now more risk and less reward, and that it was time to take profits.

While the appreciation of a stock often causes people to sell, it sometimes causes people to buy. There are investors who believe that when a stock has broken through a "resistance" level, it will move higher. Those investors may look at a chart and believe that if IBM reaches $105, it will soon go to $115. As a result, those investors will be waiting for IBM to reach $105 in order to buy.

COMPANY ANNOUNCEMENTS CHANGE EXPECTATIONS

Changes in expectations can come from actual events, such as an earnings announcement. On October 27, 1997, Oxford Health Plans reported that it would take a loss in its September quarter because of lower-than-expected revenues and higher-than-expected write-downs. The news shocked investors. With new lower expectations, many rushed to sell, but no one wanted to buy. The stock, which had closed at $68 3/4, opened at $38 3/4, a loss of 44 percent. The price of $38 3/4 reflected the new level of expectations for the company. Unfortunately for Oxford's shareholders, the level did not hold for long. As the day continued and the news was evaluated, the stock declined to $25 13/16 for a loss of 62.5 percent in one day.

The announcement of a merger also involves changes in expectations. When Staples and Office Depot announced that they were going to merge, the stock of Office Depot jumped from $14 to $20, while the stock of Staples declined from $23 to $19. The reason for the change in expectations related to the terms of the merger in which the holders of Office Depot were to receive more than one share of Staples for each share of Office Depot. Since the stock price of Office Depot had been much lower than the price of Staples prior to the announcement, it went up. The stock of Staples, on the other hand, went down because investors believed that the merger would lower its earnings. After the government rejected the merger as being anti-competitive, the stocks moved back in the opposite direction.

Changes in expectations can come from comments by analysts. As analysts follow companies, they can often sense that business is better or worse than plan. Sometimes the impetus comes from their own research, while sometimes it comes from the company itself. As analysts raise or lower their earnings estimates, some investors will modify their own expectations.

ECONOMIC DATA CHANGES EXPECTATIONS

A piece of economic data can cause expectations to change. At any point in time, the pricing of the market reflects a specific level of activity in the economy. When measures such as the Producer Price Index (PPI) or the Consumer Price Index (CPI) are reported, economists immediately attempt to decide how the new information impacts the economy. The policy of the Federal Reserve Board also changes expectations. If the market expects the Fed to lower interest rates by twenty-five basis points and the Fed does just that, the action will probably have no impact on prices. The market will have already discounted the change. However, if the Fed lowers interest rates by fifty basis points, the market will probably rally, because the change was more positive than the expectations, while if the Fed does not lower rates, the market will probably go down, because investors had been expecting a reduction.

PUBLICITY CHANGES EXPECTATIONS

Sometimes changes in expectations occur because a brokerage firm or a commentator publicizes a particular company. Other times a company may appear on television or at a conference sponsored by a brokerage house. Sometimes the company conveys a piece of hard information, but in many instances the changes in expectations relate to the quality of the presentation. For example, if management tries to avoid answering questions, or if the key people come off looking like jerks, investors will lower their expectations. If the management tells its story in a convincing way, investors may raise their expectations. The reason that the stock will go up or down is that investors are reevaluating their judgment of management's ability to run the company.

IT'S THE EXPECTATIONS THAT COUNT

It is critical to recognize that it is not whether the news is good or bad, but whether the news is good or bad relative to expectations that impacts the prices of stocks. Virtually every investor has seen instances in which a company reported excellent earnings and the stock went down, or in which a company reported a major write-off and the stock went up. These actions seem contrary to logic. But they are not. Good earnings are never enough to push up the price of the stock. The earnings must be good relative to the expectations. Similarly, weak earnings are not enough to lower the price of the stock. They must be weak relative to expectations. If the earnings were not as weak as people expected, the stock might even go up.

In May 1997, Mecklermedia, a pioneering Internet company with a great management and an excellent record, announced a much better than expected quarter. But on the conference call, management cautioned that the next quarter would have a loss because of a change in timing of one of its trade shows. From management's point of view, this was a non-issue, but investors panicked. The stock, which had been up $1, plunged by $7 within the next hour as expectations turned negative.

When investors expect terrible news, the stock sometimes goes up once the news is announced and the negative expectations are removed. A number of years ago, Fruit of the Loom went on an acquisition spree, but the acquisitions were a disaster. Fruit's earnings plunged and its debt ballooned. At the end of 1995, Fruit announced that it was writing off most of the acquisitions. The stock immediately jumped, and within the next year, it had almost doubled. While the write-off may have highlighted the mistakes of management, it also allowed the company to eliminate its money-losing acquisitions and focus on its profitable underwear business. Once the money losers had been written off, analysts could raise their estimates, and the stock price could increase.

At any point in time, if more people increase their expectations, a stock or the market will go up, while if more people lower their expectations, the stock or the market will go down. The critical variable is not whether the company reports good news or bad news, but whether the expectations of the majority of people in the market change for the positive or the negative. The trick for the investor is to figure out whether the new information raises or lowers expectations.

THE EXPERTS AS A GROUP ARE ALWAYS WRONG!

Because expectations rule the market, a funny thing happens when there is relative consensus on any issue. All the experts will be wrong. If all the experts expect the market to go up, it will go down. If all the experts expect the market to go down, it will go up. There is not much that is guaranteed in life. But this is.

If all the experts think that the stock market can only go up, they will all be fully invested. If every expert is fully invested, there will be no more cash to buy stocks. Without buying, the market can no longer go up. Further, if everyone is already bullish, expectations can no longer change for the positive. Many investors can remain bullish, but even if only a few lower their outlook, expectations will change for the negative. A negative change will create selling, which will push down the price of stocks. Thus, even if most investors are still bullish, the stock market will go down, because on balance, expectations are changing for the negative.

This pattern works equally well if all of the experts are bearish. In such a situation, they will all be sitting with large amounts of cash, expecting the worst. If the news is not quite as bad as some had expected, expectations will change modestly for the positive. With large amounts of cash on hand and little appetite for more selling, stocks will begin to go up.

What works for the market also works for individual stocks. You might expect that a stock that was loved by all analysts would significantly outperform the market, while one that was hated by all analysts would significantly underperform the market. You would be wrong. If a stock is loved by everyone, the valuation and expectations will be very high, and even a small disappointment can send it plunging. If a stock is hated by everyone, the valuation and expectations are likely to be very low, and even neutral news can push the stock up.

Consensus is often difficult to find, but when it does occur, the experts will almost always be wrong and the individual can win by betting against them. In Guerrilla Investing, one of the best techniques is to bet against the consensus of professionals. Wait until the consensus has taken a position and then act against it. Any investor who can understand this rule has an excellent chance of outperforming the market. In Chapter 5, we will show you how to win by betting against the pros.

INFORMATION IS THE CURRENCY OF WALL STREET

If changes in expectations drive changes in prices, the easiest way to defeat your enemy is to have perfect intelligence and be able to act on that intelligence before your enemy does.

- If you knew the FDA was going to approve a new wonder drug, you would buy stock in its manufacturer.
- If you knew that a takeover was going to be announced, you would buy stock in the target company.
- If you knew what stocks were going to be featured in Saturday's *Barron's*, you would buy them on Friday.
- If you knew that a company was going to report sharply disappointing earnings, you would short it.

If you had perfect information about future events, you would be in a commanding position against your enemies. Because you knew what was going to happen, you could analyze the impact of your information on the expectations of the market and act before your enemies knew what was happening.

The key to investing on Wall Street is to acquire as much "inside information" as possible. If you *knew* that one company was *secretly* planning to make a tender offer on another, you would have a big advantage against your enemies. Having certain knowledge of the future is always a guaranteed way to win. There is only one problem: trading on this type of inside information is highly illegal.

There is a fine line between what is illegal and what is legal. The difference involves certainty. If you know that some material event will definitely occur, you have inside information, but if you merely guess that the event is likely to occur, you are not in possession of inside information.

Analysts curry favor with executives of companies so that they will get signals about earnings per share. *"I know I can't ask what you are going to earn,"* the analyst says, *"but I'm checking to see if my estimate of $.26 is OK?"* While companies cannot tell analysts what they are going to report, most will give some guidance.

"You won't be disappointed," the chief financial officer might respond. If the analyst trusts the CFO, the analyst will now believe that the earnings will be good and reiterate a buy on the stock. Often analysts may call other executives in the company to double-check the hints from the CFO. They will pit the information from one executive against that from another, looking for a hole that will give them an edge. They may also talk to customers and competitors. Analysts will gossip and trade information with only one goal in mind—to get guidance on the earnings that can enable them to scoop other investors.

Virtually everyone on Wall Street spends a major portion of his or her life attempting to obtain as much legal inside information as possible. With huge sums of money at stake, the ability to gain small advantages in information can yield substantial returns. Just as armies will use spies and satellites to gain an advantage over their enemies, so investors will attempt to use any type of intelligence to gain an advantage over their competition. **Information is the currency of Wall Street. The people with the best**

information usually win, while the people with the worst informa-tion usually lose.

The Professional Advantage

Advantage 1: Time. If information is the currency of Wall Street, the professionals have always had a huge advantage over the amateurs. The professional devotes full time to investing. While the amateur is running his business, taking care of patients, or handling clients, the professional is usually watching a computer screen when news breaks and is able to act before the amateur even knows that something has happened.

Information often has a limited shelf life. The investor has to find out the information and act on it in a very short period of time. A company announces that it is planning a restructuring and that it will have a conference call. Professionals who have the time to watch the news and participate in the conference call have an obvious advantage over individuals who do not. Plus, some investors want to try to get more of an edge to defeat their competition, so between the time of the announcement and the conference call, they phone the company, hoping to get some inside guidance. Companies return phone calls in a particular pecking order, taking care of their friends first. If there are two calls, one from Fidelity and one from John Doe, who do you think will get the call? If someone can obtain exclusive information and act on it before the rest of the world knows what is going on, that person will almost always win.

Advantage 2: Financial resources. The professional also has the financial resources which the individual cannot match. With commission dollars, the professional pays to meet with managements and analysts, purchase technical packages, and develop computer systems.

Advantage 3: "Trickle-down" information flow. With the trickle-down flow of information, the professionals usually have a head start over individuals. Financial information typically flows from companies, through professionals, to individuals in a manner that looks like an inverted funnel. When a company announces earnings, it often issues a terse press release and then gives the details to a small number of analysts and portfolio managers. The analysts tell their institutional salespeople and key clients. The institutional salespeople then call other clients. The analysts write First Call notes, which are disseminated to other institutions and to the brokers in the analysts' firm. When the brokers receive the notes, some might call a few clients, but most are too busy. After the calls and the notes are finished, the analysts will write a report, which will be mailed out to more clients. If individual customers are lucky, they might receive a monthly update from their brokerage firm with a list of reports written by each analyst. If individuals see a report of interest, they can call their broker and ask to have it sent to them. By the time they receive the report, the information could be two months old, an eternity in the stock market.

Advantage 4: New technology. Over the past decade, new technologies have been created to speed delivery of information to the professionals. Through the information distribution company First Call, the professional instantly receives earnings estimates, commentary, and rating changes from analysts. With conference calls, professionals can talk directly to the companies when key news is released. Bloomberg, Bridge, and other systems all provide professionals with elaborate packages of technical tools. Other proprietary systems are able to identify gaps in market valuations and generate computer-driven trading programs.

As professionals have gained more access to instant information, the pace of trading has changed. Turnover has increased. Professionals can respond instantly whenever they see an opportunity. For many, the long term has ceased to exist. The game is to beat your opponents by acting first. But the individuals traditionally did not have access to these tools. They were still locked into using the telephone and waiting for the newspaper, and the gap between the individuals and the professionals widened significantly.

THE NEW WALL STREET BATTLEFIELD

But now the technology changes that gave the professional a huge advantage are swinging in favor of the individual. New delivery systems are being created that are rapidly leveling the playing field. With the

Internet and the financial television networks, individuals now have access to information that, while not quite on a par, is not far behind that available to the professional. Even the process of communicating information has changed. Instead of trickling down over an extended period of time, it is now instantly transmitted.

EVEN THE PROS WATCH TV

The first major change came with the creation of the financial television networks, such as CNBC, CNNfn, and Bloomberg. These networks give individuals access to a ticker tape, analysis of markets and stocks, commentary from top analysts and portfolio managers, interviews with corporate executives, and full coverage of major news stories. Key events, such as the release of government statistics, actions by the Fed, mergers and acquisitions, surprise earnings announcements, or major price swings in stocks are communicated on these networks. Reporters and industry experts are on hand to discuss the immediate impact of these events. As a result, the networks are able to communicate the information to all investors faster and more effectively than can most brokerage houses. In fact, traders and salespeople at most brokerage houses get fast-breaking news from television rather than from their own analysts. If you go into the trading rooms of Wall Street at 8:30 A.M., the time many government statistics are released, you will see traders and salespeople intently watching CNBC.

As these networks have grown, they have become the medium of choice for many companies to deliver their messages. Because companies can reach a universal audience and because television avoids the legal risk of selective dissemination, executives often choose the networks as the place to make major announcements and almost always appear on them after a major corporate event. For example, when two companies announce a merger, the CEOs of both companies usually appear on the financial networks. For professionals as well as amateurs, it is much better to look the managers in the eye, see how they relate to each other, and watch how they answer questions than it is to read a selection of First Call notes. As a result, when major events occur, the professionals often sit glued to their sets watching the financial networks.

But when the professionals watch television, they have no special advantage over the amateurs. They do not have their own private network feed. The information is not coming through a narrow channel of communication, such as a conference call, in which only a limited number of people can participate. Instead, it is being disseminated universally, and the professional does not learn about it any quicker than the amateur does.

Further, since professionals have much larger amounts of money to deploy and since they also often have to deal with investment committees within their own organizations, individuals may actually now have an advantage in terms of timing. If individuals watch an interview with a manager who appears to be credible, they can move as fast or faster than the professionals.

While the development of the business news networks has partially leveled the playing field, they can only take the individual part of the way. The financial networks can discuss major stories, but they cannot focus on all stories. They can show quotes on the most volatile stocks, but they cannot show quotes on all stocks, unless you are prepared to spend the day squinting at the ticker tape. They can offer interviews with managements, but they cannot offer interviews with all companies on demand. They can present the views of analysts and portfolio managers, but they cannot allow the individual to choose which analyst and portfolio manager.

THE INFORMATION REVOLUTION: THE INTERNET

The true challenge to the private information networks of the professional is the Internet. With the Internet, the individual investor now has access to services that had previously been available only to the professional. The change in the information flow is nothing less than a revolution. The old model of giving information to the insiders and professionals and then allowing it to trickle down is beginning to disappear. It is being supplanted by instant and universal dissemination. In political terms, it is a change from an oligarchy to a democracy. The individual still has to learn what to do with the information and still has to overcome the experience of the professionals, but the process of information gathering, and the balance of power, is rapidly shifting in favor of the individual. With the Internet individuals can:

- receive real-time quotes at the same time and in the same detail as can professionals.
- utilize sophisticated portfolio management software, which allows them to monitor stocks, track their performance, and link to rapidly breaking news.
- access the same news stories as can the professionals.
- receive notice of and participate in conference calls along with the professionals.
- receive all legal SEC filings, such as 10Ks and 10Qs, at the same time as the professionals.
- gather information through the companies' own websites.
- obtain on-line charts and other technical tools that are comparable to those that the professionals use.
- access earnings estimates and ratings changes from the major brokerage houses within a relatively short period of time after the changes are made.
- receive financial analysis and commentary from a wide variety of sources in real time.
- follow the actions of professionals through the websites of mutual funds.
- control their own trades and often receive better execution than the professionals receive.
- have a lower trading cost than the professionals have. (Professionals pay an average of $.05 per share, while individuals can pay less than $.01 per share.)

Professionals still receive some information faster than individuals do. Changes in analysts' estimates or ratings reach professionals an hour or two before they reach the Internet. This gives the professional a substantial head start, but one or two hours is a much narrower window than the professionals have traditionally enjoyed. Professionals have hard-wired systems that work very efficiently, but with faster modems and new telephone lines, the difference is becoming less significant. This is not to say that the advantages of the professionals have been eliminated. The professionals still have experience and knowledge. They have the time to study the market and direct access to corporate executives, analysts, technicians, strategists, and company meetings. But some of the advantages in terms of information gathering that had rigged the game in their favor are starting to disappear, and the tides of technological change are turning strongly in the direction of the individual investor.

A DAY ON THE WEB

As an analyst, I have always had an office with all of the most up-to-date professional equipment and services. I am especially partial to First Call and Bloomberg. These and other services cost thousands of dollars each month. As I became more involved in writing this book and as I traveled to see companies, I was often unable to go into the office or access the professional equipment, and instead, was forced to rely on the Internet. At first, I worried about missing key information, but to my surprise, utilizing the Internet was not as much of a detriment as I had first feared it would be. In fact, much of the information on the Internet was as good and as easy to access as the information on my professional equipment, and the cost was extremely modest: only about $25 per month, excluding my Internet access charges.

I especially appreciate the Internet when I am on the road. I plug my computer into the phone, click on the local number for Netcom, my Internet Service Provider, and all of the information that I need is at my fingertips. I rarely need to call someone in the office to ask what is going on. I can find out all of the information on-line.

In managing my investments, the first thing I do every day is log on to the Internet and check the list of stocks I monitor. I keep my list on My

Yahoo!, but many other sites provide similar information and services. There are sites on the search engines, such as Lycos and Excite; on the major service providers, such as AOL and Microsoft Network; on specialized financial services; and on the on-line brokers, such as E*Trade, Datek, Schwab, DLJ Direct, and others. These sites do not charge for their services.

My monitor list includes all of the stocks I own and all of those in which I have an interest. It is the same as the monitor list I have on the professional machines in my office. (Creating a monitor list will be discussed in Chapter 11.) When I click on My Yahoo!, I immediately see the prices of all of the stocks on my list on the left side of the screen and the recent news stories on these stocks on the right side of the screen. Before the market opens, I check the news on my stocks. This only takes a few minutes. All the stocks on which there is news have an asterisk next to them. I page down through the list, looking at the headlines. When I see a story that interests me, I click on it. In an instant, I have the news.

Then, I go down the left side of my screen and look at the earnings surprises and the analyst's upgrades and downgrades. I check to see whether any other stocks I am interested in, but don't have on my list, have reported earnings or have new ratings.

Next, I open up my Internet mail. Every morning, I receive an e-mail from Zacks.com showing the changes in the analysts' earnings estimates for the stocks in my portfolio as well as the dates on which the companies are expected to report their earnings. When a company reports its earnings, I always compare the actual number with the estimates. This service costs $12.50 per month. It is not as complete or as up-to-date as the First Call services that the professionals receive. But for someone like me who is interested in the fundamentals of companies, it is an excellent service. The fact that Zacks sends you information only on your stocks makes it extremely easy to work with.

If one of my stocks is going to report earnings, I click over to the site of Motley Fool, a free service, to see if there is a listing for a conference call. If Motley Fool does not list the conference call, I might phone the company and ask investor relations for the number.

Each day, I pick a few stocks on my monitor list and check out their charts. I usually do this on My Yahoo! because the charts are so easy to use. I click on the ticker symbol and then "charts." When the big charts come up, I start with a two-year time horizon, and then work down the timeframe spectrum. If I need a longer or a better chart, I might jump to one of the charting websites, such as BigCharts, another free service. (We'll discuss how to use charts in Chapter 7.)

Before the market opens, I will usually look at the headlines on Briefing.com. Briefing.com is a service that costs $6.95 per month. It has excellent synopses of what is going on in the market in general and in active stocks in particular. Briefing.com gives me a good overview of the major market movers, many of which are not on my monitor list. Every few days, I check insider selling and buying on The Financial Center's website. (Watching what the insiders are doing can be very important. See Chapter 10.) This entire process, from the time I log onto My Yahoo! until the time I am finished, usually takes no more than ten minutes.

Next, I look through the morning newspapers. I read the *Wall Street Journal, Investors Business Daily*, and the *New York Times*. Because I have checked the prices on-line, I do not have to spend time paging through the financial tables. Instead, I focus on the news. If I have not been able to get a paper for some reason, I go to the on-line services of these periodicals. (The *Wall Street Journal* service costs $20 per year if you are already a subscriber to the newspaper.) I may also check the on-line brokers I have accounts with to see if they are highlighting any special news on one of my stocks. Some of the Internet brokers have excellent research, while some have none at all. But there is so much research information available on the Web that the broker's research services are not that critical to me. If I see something in the news that requires immediate action, I research it right away. If I see something that has more long-term implications, I clip the article, scan it into my computer, and save it for my evening review.

During a normal day, when I am just monitoring the market, I will usually click back on My Yahoo! every few hours to see what is happening. If I see news, I will always check it out. If a stock is up or down significantly, I will click over to one of the on-line brokers to get a "real-time" quote.

(My Yahoo! has a 20-minute delay on its quotes.) While at the broker, I will usually check out the stock's chart. I might also periodically check Briefing.com for headlines and BigCharts for stocks that have had major changes in price and volume. Normally, this monitoring takes only a few minutes a session.

If I see a stock that I want to buy or sell, I go back to my on-line broker. There I check the prices, then type the stock's symbol, the quantity, and the nature of the trade, then click to complete it. Within a matter of seconds, the trade is done. With new systems for small orders at both the listed exchanges and at NASDAQ, I am often able to get as good or better execution on-line than I get through professional brokers. The cost is less than $10 per trade. Trading on-line is faster and easier than calling the broker, and because I can see the actual prices, I know exactly what I am paying. (If I have a very large or complex trade, I will call my traditional broker.) While I am at my on-line broker, I will often check out the value of my portfolio, which is always priced up-to-the-minute.

At night, I usually set aside some time for serious research. I check the day's closing prices and trading actions of the stocks as well as the day's news. I read articles from the newspapers and from the business magazines, such as *Barron's*, *Forbes*, *Fortune*, and *BusinessWeek*. If I see news on a stock that interests me, I will go to Zacks.com and look at "The Whole Enchilada." This gives me an excellent financial overview of the fundamentals of the company, as well as analysts' ratings and estimates. (Chapter 6 will thoroughly cover company fundamentals, and Chapter 9 contains a discussion of using analyst ratings.)

If I need more specific information, I may go the Edgar website and look through the company's recent filings. Most companies now file their financial documents on-line. Edgar has both a free and a paid site. For most investors, the free site will suffice. At times, I might also click over to the company's own website and check out some of its newest developments.

Before going further, I will review the technicals of the company by going to BigCharts and looking at a number of different technical indicators. Because stocks in an industry tend to move in tandem, I may use the BigChart information to graph the company in which I am interested against a few of its key competitors. I may also look at some of the stock screens on Morningstar.net., a free service. (The interrelations of companies in an industry will be discussed in Chapter 8.) At this point, if I am interested in the new stock, I will go back to My Yahoo! and to Zacks.com and add it to my monitor or portfolio lists.

If there is a particular question that interests me or if the stock has recently had significant volatility, I might take a look at one of the message boards to see what people are saying about it. (Message boards and chat rooms will be discussed in Chapter 4.)

These are the Internet services I use today. They are the ones that I know, that suit my investment style, and that I am the most comfortable with. This is not to say that they will be right for you. Because I own a relatively small amount of high-tech stocks, I do not utilize many of the excellent websites that focus on the high-tech sector, such as Silicon Investor. Because I have many friends who are also professional investors, I spend relatively little time in chat rooms and do not use Street.com, which is an excellent service. Because I tend to be a long-term investor, I am less interested in some of the more active-trading websites. With the current dramatic pace of change on the Internet, I am certain that I will be using new websites before this book even gets to print.

If you are to explore the Internet, you must find the websites that work for you. There are a vast number of excellent sites on the Web, and new sites are being created each day. You could spend the entire day looking at information on the Web, just as you could spend your entire day reading reports from various stockbrokers. For almost everyone, this is overkill. The critical task for each investor is to find those websites that are easy to work with and that fit your investing style and time commitments. Pick one or two to start with. Check out a new website each week. If you find one you like, add it to your bookmarks and remove one you do not like as much. The trick is to get the information you need efficiently. Once you are comfortable with the workings of the Internet, staying on top of your investments should not take you very much time.

Navigating through these tasks on the Internet is no more difficult than navigating through the same tasks on the proprietary systems the professionals use. The task for the individual investor is thus to figure out how to reduce the remaining advantages of the professional. To win, investors must think like guerrillas and find areas in which they have specialized experience and contacts they can use against a stronger enemy. They must find the weaknesses in their more heavily armed opponents. The odds are certainly not in favor of individuals, but winning is possible. Still, there is no chance for winning if individuals do not recognize their own strengths and weaknesses and those of their enemies. **In the words of Sun Tzu, "Know yourself, know your enemy. In one hundred battles, there will be one hundred victories."**

CHAPTER TWO

Know Your Enemy, Know Yourself

When you are buying a stock, someone else is selling. Otherwise, there could not be a trade. While you are betting that the best thing you can do with your money is to buy a stock, someone else is betting that the best thing that he or she can do is to sell the stock. The person on the other side of the transaction is your enemy. Your enemy is betting that you are wrong. It does not matter whether that person is your neighbor, a mutual-fund manager, or the Sultan of Brunei. If you cannot defeat that person, you will lose.

To win, you must understand who your enemy is and what your enemy knows that you do not. If you were fighting a war, you would want to know the strength and tactics of your enemy. The same is true in investing. Before making a trade, the first questions you should ask are *"Who is my enemy?"* and *"What does my enemy know that I do not?"* Is your enemy a professional or an amateur? Does your enemy have better information than you do? Has your enemy heard the same story, but is betting in the opposite direction? If you cannot figure out what advantages you have over your enemy, chances are your enemy will win. The only problem is that in investing, it is often difficult to discern the exact identity of your enemy.

Over the years, the nature of the enemy has changed with professionals becoming far more powerful. Forty years ago, investors comforted themselves with the thought that they were competing against widows and orphans. Conventional wisdom held that one was buying a stock being sold by Aunt Hattie, who had had it in her portfolio for forty years and had no idea of what the company did, or by Grandpa Jones's estate, which was being liquidated by his grandchildren. It was easy to figure that you could defeat Aunt Hattie or Grandpa Jones's estate. After all, you had received a tip from a friend who had a friend who was a stockbroker.

I am not sure that investors forty years ago really did compete against Aunt Hattie or Grandpa Jones's estate, but I am sure that the competition forty years ago was much less intense than it is now. The information flow was much slower and more limited. Conference calls were rare and analysts were few. Options and derivatives were almost nonexistent. Turnover was much lower. Mutual funds were smaller, both in absolute and relative size. Professionals were far less important, and many had preservation of capital, rather than capital gains, as their primary goal. While it might not be completely fair to describe the competition as being Aunt Hattie or Grandpa Jones, the fact is that the game was much easier years ago than it is now. But the days of investing against widows and orphans are long past.

KNOW YOUR ENEMY

One of the problems is that investing is one of the few games in which amateurs compete directly against professionals. In sports, people play against others at the same level. In baseball, there are the major leagues and minor leagues, and then there is the local corporate league in which you play. You can hit .300 in the Lawyers League and think you are a star. You go out after a game, have a beer, and brag to your friends about how well you played. But how would you do if you tried to bat against Randy Johnson? The chances are pretty good that you would be bailing out when a 98-mile-per-hour fast ball came whizzing at your head.

In tennis, you could think of yourself as an "A" player. You might even win the local club championship. But how would you do against Pete Sampras? You would be lucky to win a point. You might suggest that this is not a fair analogy. You should not be judged by your ability to play against Sampras. You are over forty and a cardiac surgeon. You spend your days doing bypasses, while he spends his days playing tennis. It is as ludicrous to suggest that you should compete with him on the tennis court as it would be for him to compete with you in the operating room.

Think about investing. Do you ask the same questions when you seek to compete with the top professionals in the stock market? The portfolio managers at Fidelity are professionals, as skilled in their business as Sampras is in tennis or you are in medicine. They are the best in their game, and, like great athletes, they are paid millions of dollars a year because they can consistently perform at the highest levels.

There is only one major difference. In sports, professionals play against professionals, and amateurs play against amateurs. **But in investing, there is only one league, and it is open to everyone**. Investing does not have a club level. There is no Doctors League, Lawyers League, or Little League. There is only one market, and in that market, most of the action in the market is dominated by professionals. If you want to play, you have to play against the greatest investors in the world.

Would you bet your retirement money in a tennis match against Pete Sampras or a golf match against Tiger Woods? No way! But in investing, you would think nothing of matching wits with Bob Stansky, Will Danoff, and Beth Terrana of Fidelity. You would not think anything of it, because it is the only game in town and because you do not know the exact identities of the people on the opposite side of the transaction. When you go to buy stock, your broker does not say, *"Beth Terrana of Fidelity is selling the stock you are buying."*

The only time you actually know the identity of the seller is in an offering. Then your enemy is the company itself, or worse, the executives of the company, who want to diversify their holdings, build a house, or endow a foundation. Before you participate in the offering, it is useful to remember that the seller knows a lot more about the business than you do.

In most other cases, it is almost impossible to know the exact identity of the person against whom you are competing, but this does not mean that you cannot ask questions to help you understand the identity of your enemy. Your broker calls you with a hot scoop about the earnings of a major company. The story sounds good, but before you buy, remember that most major companies are covered by dozens of analysts, and it is very rare that one will be given special information.

Even in the few instances when your broker has special information, you should question whom the broker has told before you. If your broker received some hot tip, it is likely that the first thing he would do would be to buy the stock for himself. He can make much more in his own account than he can by getting a small commission from you. Next, he would call his best accounts. If you are not at the top of the list, the odds are against you. The question that each investor should ask is, *"How many people received the information before I did?"* And then, *"What did they do about it?"*

In assessing the likelihood that a hot tip will enable you to make money, it is critical to recognize where you fit in the information flow. Let us say that a pharmaceutical company is developing a new drug to cure cancer. The first people who will know about the drug are executives within the company, who start to buy the stock. Then the directors and a few of the largest shareholders start to buy as well. The stock jumps. A few analysts discover the opportunity and issue reports. Brokers see the reports and call their best clients. Finally, after the stock has jumped $15 in three weeks, your broker calls you. *"This drug will cure cancer,"* he says. And it may. If the drug really works, the stock could go to $100. Everything tells you to buy. But before you do, ask yourself, *"Who are the sellers?"*

There is no perfect way to answer this question. It is obviously impossible to call someone on the floor of the New York Stock Exchange and say, *"I'll buy this stock only if the person who is selling it is a widow or an orphan!"* But it is useful to stop and think about who is on the other side of the transaction.

Suppose that your enemy is the portfolio manager at Fidelity. The portfolio manager has direct access to the company, an army of analysts dissecting the data, an army of traders who understand the flow of buying and selling, and virtually unlimited amounts of capital. What advantages do you have?

The professionals would appear to have substantial advantages over the individual. Yet as you will discover, there are many ways for the individ-ual to beat the professional, just as there are ways for the guerrilla to beat the modern army. But you will never be able to devise a winning battle plan if you first do not understand the identity of your enemy.

KNOW YOURSELF, THE GUERRILLA

"Know yourself" is as important in the Sun Tzu philosophy as "know your enemy." In fighting a war against a much stronger enemy, the gen-eral of a guerrilla force faces significant obstacles. This does not mean that the general cannot devise a winning strategy, but to do so the general must understand the strengths and weaknesses of his troops. If he sees that the enemy has greater strength but his owns troops have greater quickness, he should use the quickness in making a battle plan. If the enemy has more weaponry but his troops have better knowledge of the local terrain, he should attempt to lure the enemy into the jungle where the superior weapons can be neutralized and the guerrilla's knowledge of local terrain can be the key to victory. If a general does not understand the strengths and weaknesses of his army, he will never be able to mount an effective battle plan.

Much the same process occurs in the battlefield of the stock market. To compete against professional investors, individuals must understand their own skills and craft a battle plan that maximizes their strengths and mini-mizes their weaknesses. Individuals have their own unique strengths and weaknesses. Some can make quick decisions. Others like to deliberate. Some enjoy taking risks. Others prefer a defensive posture. Some have extensive time and resources. Others do not. There will be times when the market favors one of these qualities at the expense of the others. But no matter what particular traits the market favors at any point in time, individuals will not win unless they stick to their strengths and avoid their weaknesses.

An individual who is comfortable in a defensive posture cannot suddenly become a risk taker as markets start to overheat. An individual who knows nothing about technology cannot suddenly jump on that group of stocks, just because it becomes hot. To avoid getting suckered into the ebbs and flows of the market, it is essential that you know yourself, and that means knowing what your skills are and how you compete with others.

It is critical to understand how you compete against others. When I step onto the tennis court, I would love to play like Pete Sampras, but I cannot. I am a fifty-three-year-old with an arthritic knee, and I have to find a tennis game that works for me and play within my range of ability. If I try to play like Peter Siris, I can win some of the time. If I try to play like Pete Sampras, I have no chance.

The same is true when competing in other sports. How often have you watched a professional golfer hit a 280-yard wood shot over a yawning lake onto a postage-stamp-size green? The ball hits pin high and stops dead. Then you get out on the course, 280 yards from the green. Remembering the shot from the pro, you think to yourself, I can do that. Well, maybe you can, but I can't. I can't hit a 280-yard drive. I can't ignore a body of water on the golf course, and I can't stop a wood shot dead on the green, except in my fantasies. That does not mean that I cannot play golf. It only means that I cannot play golf pretending that I am a professional.

And so it is with investing. In order to win in the stock market, you have to know who you are and how you like to compete. You must be able to answer four key questions:

- How much money do you have to invest?
- How much time do you have to invest?
- What is your tolerance for risk?
- What weapons do you have that can help you in investing?

1. HOW MUCH MONEY DO YOU HAVE TO INVEST?

In planning a battle, a general must understand the resources at his disposal. In investing, your capital is your army. The amount of money you have to invest matters for two reasons: returns and risk. If you have a small amount of capital, your returns will be limited, even if you are successful. Your payback for the time that you put in may be very small. Buying mutual funds may be a better way to go. But if you want to begin investing, a small amount of capital should not deter you. Everyone has to start somewhere.

Risk is a bigger issue. If you have a small amount of capital, it is harder to diversify. The more concentrated your portfolio, the higher your risk. The higher your risk, the more likely you will be to panic if a stock that is a major percentage of your portfolio crashes. Once you panic, the game is over. When you own many stocks, a disappointing performance from one will have a smaller impact on your portfolio and will probably not shake you up.

If you have limited capital, you have two alternatives. You can put most of your money in a mutual fund, which will minimize your risk, and use the rest to play a few stocks. Or you can buy smaller quantities of a larger number of stocks. While buying round lots (100 shares) is always a little easier, there is no reason why an investor cannot start with smaller amounts. If you want to build a stock portfolio, try to own at least ten stocks and make a commitment to expand the portfolio to twenty when you get more capital. In this way, your portfolio will not be overly affected if one of your stocks is trashed.

2. HOW MUCH TIME DO YOU HAVE TO INVEST?

In addition to knowing the number of troops in his command, the wartime general also has to recognize the commitment of those troops to the battle. The same is true in investing. Investing is a skill. Like most skills, the more you work at it, the better you will become. But investing is much more complicated than most skills because you are not only competing against an enemy, you are also playing in an arena in which the rules are constantly changing.

Positions that worked yesterday may be outmoded today. Change is constant. Companies change. A leader like Apple Computer can suddenly start to struggle. Industries change. Systems like the Internet can emerge and revolutionize people's views of communications. Commodities fluctuate. War breaks out in the Middle East and oil prices surge. Markets change. Less than two years ago, the Dow was under 4,000 and most people were bearish. Today, the Dow is hovering around 8,000, and most people are bullish. Investment tools change. Program trading and index options, almost unheard of a decade ago, are now major factors in the market. It is difficult to stay on top of a world that is changing unless you are willing to devote time and energy.

Think about the time commitment that you are willing to make. Let us say that you are a doctor. You spend all day seeing patients. You perform surgery. You read medical journals. Do you have the time to read brokerage reports and pour over financial statements? Probably not. Do you have the time to watch the tape? Probably not. Do you have the time to take every call from every broker? Probably not.

THE PHYSICIAN INVESTOR

Recently, a friend who is a doctor called. He was quite upset. *"My broker called me three times about this hot stock,"* the doctor said, *"but I was in surgery. By the time I got back to him, it had gone up three points."*

"That's too bad," I replied.

"It was the nurse's fault," the surgeon said, *"I told her that she should interrupt me if the broker has a really great idea. After all, I'm just doing knees. It's not like I'm transplanting hearts or anything."*

I was not sure if the surgeon was serious or kidding, but my guess is that he was somewhat serious. A year ago, I could never have imagined a doctor being willing to be interrupted in surgery by a broker, but this is a bull market and medical cost containment is on the rise. Nonetheless, even if the doctor had been interrupted, he still could not have acted as fast as the professionals. This does not mean that individuals cannot compete, but it does mean that they will be at a disadvantage against professionals, who are devoting themselves to staying on top of the market. It is crucial to recognize this limitation before you set out.

Accepting a limitation as a starting point is often very difficult. You may be a great doctor or a prominent lawyer. You assume that your skills are easily transferable to investing. But the fact that you are very successful in your career does not mean that you can compete on an even playing field with the best of the professional investors. Before you dismiss this concept, think about how you would feel if the positions were reversed. How would your money manager fare if he took a few minutes from each day to do surgery? It would obviously be a disaster.

Make a realistic assessment of how much time you can spend following the stock market, and then decide what you can learn during that period of time. **If you have a limited amount of time, pick a few areas in which you can compete and ignore the rest**. Make sure your investing strategy matches your time commitment. If you only want to spend a little time looking at stocks, a buy and hold strategy will suit you well. If you are willing to spend considerable time investing, you can trade more actively and utilize more of the strategies recommended in *Guerrilla Investing*. No matter how much time you have available, you should always focus on battles that you can win. Avoid those that you must lose.

3. WHAT IS YOUR TOLERANCE FOR RISK?

In making a battle plan, generals must confront their willingness to take risks. The same is true in the stock market. Risk in investing is like risk in war. Some investors are daredevils. They act quickly and make big bets. Other investors are scared of losing money, so they make only the most conservative of investments.

The amount of risk that individuals take should be determined by their psychological predisposition and their financial condition. No individual should ever accept a level of risk that is at variance with his or her own predisposition. You should never bet the rent money, your children's education fund, or your retirement. If you are nervous about your job, have a large mortgage, or a high level of debt, factor that into your investment decisions.

THE BETTING GAME

Play this simple exercise to judge your ability to take a risk. Think carefully about your answers. Pretend that the bets are real. Assume that you are risking 25 percent of your liquid net worth. If you have $400,000 in the market, assume that you are risking $100,000.

Someone offers to flip a coin. If it comes up heads, you get $200,000. If it comes up tails, you get $0. The odds are 50/50. You have an equal chance of making $100,000 or losing $100,000. Do you take the bet? Most people would not, because most people are somewhat risk averse. If you would, you are a risk taker.

Suppose the individual offers you $150,000 if it comes up heads and $0 if it comes up tails. You stand to make only $50,000, but you stand to lose $100,000. It is a sucker bet that few would take. But you would be surprised at how many people will make this type of bet in the stock market because they do not realize that the odds are against them. When amateurs buy options, these are often the real odds with which they are dealing.

Let us change the bet in your favor. Suppose you have a 50/50 chance of making $150,000 or losing $100,000. The risk/reward ratio is in your favor. Do you take the bet?

What if the payoff changes so that you have a 50/50 chance of making $200,000 or losing $100,000? Do you take the bet? Would you take the bet if you had a 50/50 chance of making $300,000 or losing $100,000?

PAYOFFS ON $100,000 BET					
Bet	Winning Payoff	Losing Payoff	Winning Position	Losing Position	Risk Profile
$100,000	$100,000	− $100,000	$500,000	$300,000	Coin Flip
$100,000	$50,000	− $100,000	$450,000	$300,000	Buy a Lottery Ticket
$100,000	$150,000	− $100,000	$550,000	$300,000	Good Investing Profile
$100,000	$200,000	− $100,000	$600,000	$300,000	Invest Conservatively
$100,000	$300,000	− $100,000	$700,000	$300,000	Don't Play

The level at which you take the bet determines your level of risk aversion. If you accept the bet with a possible payoff of $150,000, you are slightly risk averse. This is probably a good position to be in if you are going to invest. If you demand a possible payoff of $200,000, you are moderately risk averse. At this level, you are an individual who should be diversified and invest conservatively. If you only take the bet with a possible $300,000 payoff, you are highly risk averse. If you demand a return of $3 for every $1 of risk, you are probably better off letting someone else manage your money.

You may think that this game is foolish. Investing, you may say, is a win-win game. When the stock market goes up, everyone makes money. As this book has already emphasized, the problem with this argument is that it applies only to a bull market. But if the bull market stops, what now looks like a win-win situation can become a lose-lose situation. Before you decide on your tolerance for risk, remember that the market can go down and your financial security can be jeopardized.

4. WHAT WEAPONS DO YOU HAVE?

In a war, the mechanized army obviously has substantial advantages over a guerrilla force. The army has missiles. The guerrillas have home-made bombs. The army has tanks. The guerrillas have rifles. The army has battalions. The guerrillas have platoons. The army has satellites. The guerrillas have scouting parties.

The guerrillas possess only one real advantage. Because they are native to the war zone, they know their home turf better than the enemy does. Guerrillas can use their knowledge of local terrain to avoid the enemy by advancing through jungles or on mountain paths without being noticed. They can use their knowledge of weather conditions to time their advances and retreats. They can attack from hidden positions. While the guerrillas have far fewer resources than does the invading army, they can often win battles by utilizing their superior knowledge of their own turf.

It is much the same in investing. While the professional has capital, time, training, and excellent sources of information, the individual does have the advantage of home turf. The challenge is to figure out what "home turf" is. People come into contact with public companies in their profession. They view industry trends, deal with suppliers and customers, and analyze their competitors. They also come into contact with public companies as consumers. They shop in stores, eat in restaurants, fly on airlines, stay in hotels, select long-distance carriers, and surf the Net. Finally, they come in contact with public companies in their hometowns or through friends. Because of their own perspective and their knowledge of their own terrain, individuals are often able to gain insights that Wall Street misses. This knowledge of one's home turf gives the individual an edge when competing against a more well-trained and experienced enemy.

Individuals receive different types of information than do professionals. Professionals receive hard, structured, quantitative information. They read reports, study earnings models, listen to conference calls, talk to managements, review charts, and analyze trading patterns. Individuals receive this information, too, especially through the Internet, but they also receive soft, unstructured, qualitative information that comes from their direct experience. While this information does not come neatly packaged, like an analyst's report, that does not make it less valuable.

Information moves the stock market, and the professionals have an advantage in acquiring it. That is why it is so critical for the individual investor to carefully define what he or she knows. The task is simple. Individual investors must know themselves. They must recognize what they know from their home turf that the professionals miss and then they must utilize that information to defeat the professionals.

CHAPTER THREE

Avoid the Enemy's Strengths

If the enemy has 100,000 troops and the guerrillas have 1,000, it would be foolhardy for the guerrilla to mount a frontal assault. If the enemy has 200 airplanes and the guerrillas have two, it would be idiotic to engage in an air war. No guerrilla would ever attack without first analyzing the strength and position of the opposing force, but ironically, individual investors do not do the same. The most glaring error that individual investors commit is ignoring the enemy's strength. While exceptions do occur, there are areas in which the odds are so set against the individual that it is foolhardy to challenge them. These areas include:

- Timing the market
- Aggressive trading
- Trading on earnings announcements
- Actively trading big-cap stocks
- Trying to hit home runs with options
- Mergers and acquisitions
- IPOs, especially when the proceeds go to the insiders
- Businesses that are too complex to understand
- Emerging markets
- Anything too good to be true

Before investing, an individual should look closely at these areas and avoid them whenever possible.

1. AVOID TRYING TO TIME THE MARKET

The last thing that a wise guerrilla commander would do is attempt to fight on all fronts at once. A guerrilla might have a chance of winning a battle by finding the weakness of the much larger army and exploiting it on a limited terrain, but the guerrilla could never win by simultaneously fighting on all fronts. For the individual investor, the analogy to fighting on all fronts would be attempting to predict the market.

Investors love to have opinions on the direction of the stock market. You might hear a strategist say, *"My charts indicate that the market is going to go up by 1,000 points."* You might read a report from a port-folio manager who says, *"The market is way overextended and is going to drop by 1,000 points."* Predictions on the stock market can be extremely seductive. People are looking for easy answers. Reading annual reports, studying stock tables, and doing research is hard work. Investing on a sure market move is easy and much more fun.

The only problem is, no one knows how the market will perform. Experts conduct their analyses and make their predictions. Some are better than others. Some are even right more often than they are wrong. But most experts have the same chance of being right about the market as they do of predicting whether it will be a hot summer or a snowy winter. The only difference is that most people do not bet their life savings on weather predictions.

From time to time, experts have emerged who many thought could predict the market. Joseph Granville was once treated as a guru because he predicted a downturn. But as the market rallied to historic heights, Granville continued to predict a crash.

Robert Prechter gained renown with his Elliot Wave Theory. In the 1980s, Prechter could move markets. If he said the market was going to go up, it went up. But Prechter and the Elliot Wave Theory did not hold up. While a few waves hit exactly as Prechter had predicted, many did not. Over time, the Elliot Wave Theory proved to be only that, a theory.

Elaine Garzarelli used technical indicators to predict the crash in 1987. She was right, and few others had the courage to make this prediction. Garzarelli is a good analyst, but she is not a seer. In 1996, she predicted that the market would drop. Instead, it rallied to historic heights. She used the same inputs that had worked so well in 1987, but the market did not oblige.

No one can predict the stock market because it is both extremely complex and ever changing. A myriad of factors move the market, including interest rates, the federal deficit, corporate profits, worldwide economic conditions, and political confidence. Understanding how these factors fit together to drive the market as a whole is a complex undertaking for even the most skilled professional. For the individual, it is almost impossible.

JUST WHEN YOU FIGURE IT OUT . . .

The problem is compounded because the market is never the same. Different factors always seem to drive stock prices. In the 1980s, investors waited anxiously for money-supply figures to be announced. If they went up more than expected, the market went down. If they went up less than expected, the market went up. Now, no one ever talks about the money-supply figures. For a while, oil prices drove the market. Investors would watch the OPEC ministers, looking for clues to their future actions. Now, no one seems to care what OPEC does.

Government deficits have driven markets, as investors worried about who would pay for our debt. The trade deficit and the level of the dollar have driven markets, as money flowed into and out of the United States. Corporate profits have driven markets, as investors focused on earnings. Mergers, acquisitions, and corporate buybacks have driven markets, as investors focused on intrinsic value. Economic reports, including consumer confidence, housing starts, leading indicators, producer prices, consumer prices, and unemployment, have driven markets, as investors worried about the level of the economic growth. Political factors such as the war in the Middle East and the end of the Cold War have driven markets, as investors worried about international issues. Recently the actions of the Federal Reserve Board have driven markets. Every time the Federal Reserve Board meets or Alan Greenspan speaks, the market holds its breath and looks for clues as to the future direction of rates.

SMALL AND SUBTLE CHANGES CAN ROCK THE MARKET

Seemingly small events are often sufficient to move markets. For example:

- The government reports that new unemployment claims are 250,000. The market had been looking for 200,000. Fifty thousand more unemployed does not mean much in a country of 250 million, but the slightly higher than expected number may convince some that a slowdown is coming.
- The consumer price index comes in at +.5 percent rather than +.2 percent. The difference may be the result of higher cereal and beef prices caused by floods in the Midwest. A .3 percent higher than expected increase hardly means that we are returning to double-digit inflation, but it can be sufficient to spook stock prices.
- Alan Greenspan says something about "irrational exuberance," and the market drops by 250 points.

To most individual investors, the world looks the same as it did the night before. But to the professionals, these can be signals of future directions. When these numbers are reported, strategists and economists spring into action, modifying their expectations.

Even when individuals understand the impact of events, it often takes them longer to act, causing them to miss the window of opportunity. In the week after the election of 1996, the market staged a huge rally because voters had elected a Democratic president and a Republican Congress. Professionals worried that if one party was in control, inflation would increase. They worried that the Democrats would increase spending for social programs, while the Republicans would cut taxes and increase the deficit. They cheered the split between the White House and Congress, because they viewed gridlock as the best hope for less spending and lower deficits. When the professionals saw the results of the election, they plunged into the market. Individual investors saw the same election returns, but they did not instantly understand their impact on the market and did not move as quickly. If the individuals do not move as fast as the professionals with an event whose outcome they understand, what chance do they have when they are faced with far more complex or more distant events?

Professionals have a better understanding of the factors driving the market and can more easily make adjustments. Whatever moves the individual makes will likely be too little and too late. **Timing the market seems like an easy way to invest, but the odds are so set in favor of the professional that the individual investor is almost certain to lose over an extended period of time.**

While timing the market is usually a risky proposition for the individual investor, there is one significant exception to this rule. That occurs if there is a unanimity of opinion among experts as to the direction of the market. When there is, bet against it. The propensity of the experts to be wrong will outweigh the risks to the individual in timing the market. In Chapter 5, we will look at how to invest when all the experts agree.

2. AVOID AGGRESSIVE TRADING

Aggressive trading is fun. Making quick decisions, jumping in and out of stocks, and placing big bets on short-term moves makes people feel as if they are in the middle of the action. You watch the flow of the stock, see a critical piece of news, and make your bet. In a short period of time, you have either won or lost. There is only one problem. Aggressive trading is a professional's game that plays directly into the professional's strength. This is not to say that individuals should buy and hold forever, but most should avoid getting sucked into the most aggressive trading games. The key in aggressive trading is to be able to move instantly when a critical piece of information crosses the tape. In responding to this information, professionals have major advantages over the individual:

- Professionals are working at investing full time and see the information much sooner. In the world of active trading, "much sooner" is an eternity.
- Professionals are bombarded with inputs from analysts, traders, salespeople, and technicians.
- Professionals often receive selective dissemination of information. On June 19, 1996, the Bank of New York told ninety-two analysts and institutional investors on its conference call that it would set aside $350 million to cover expected losses from delinquent credit cards. The call was held at 2:00, but the news was not publicly disseminated until 4:09. For two hours, ninety-two professionals knew something that the rest of the world did not. By the time this information was fully disseminated, the stock had already declined by $1³/₈. While losing 3 percent is not the end of the world, if you are an active trader, 3 percent moves can add up.
- Professionals talk to each other and often know what their counterparts are planning to do. If a small portfolio manager at Fidelity knows that the Magellan Fund is about to unload all auto stocks, that portfolio manager will not rush to buy Ford.
- The institutions can buy and sell after the small investor thinks that the market is closed. Institutions can trade on foreign exchanges on which many American stocks are listed. The London Stock Exchange, for example, opens five or six hours before the New York Stock Exchange. Institutions can also trade in the "aftermarket." This market consists of negotiated trades over electronic systems which are accessible only to brokers and institutions. Price movements in the aftermarket can often be dramatic if there is late-breaking news.

On July 16, 1996, Intel's stock closed at $70 per share.

Shortly thereafter, Intel reported better than expected earnings. The stock traded up in the aftermarket. The next morning, it opened at $74. While the institutions had the ability to buy and sell between $70 and $74, the small investor did not.

The opposite happened to Motorola on July 9. Motorola waited until 5:30 P.M. to announce it had disappointing earnings. There was very active trading in the aftermarket. The next morning, the stock opened at $57⁵/₈, down nearly $9. Once again, the individual investor was shut out.

This is not to say that all of the institutions in the aftermarket made the right trades on Intel and Motorola. As in all trades, 50 percent of the people were right and 50 percent were wrong. But at least they had a chance to play.

• Professionals can more easily utilize sophisticated techniques, such as trading options, to capitalize on short-term opportunities. For example, if Intel reports bad news, the professionals may decide that the entire technology sector could come under pressure and buy Puts on an index. With computerized trading, the major institutions can play trading games that are well beyond the abilities of the individual investor.

Day Traders: Professionals in Action

A wonderful example of aggressive trading involves individuals who are day traders. These individuals have been called the ultimate guerrillas, but they are also professionals. While the market is open, they do nothing but trade. They are not doctors or lawyers who trade during a break from surgery or court. They work full time trading stocks. Watching them in action is a fascinating experience.

Most trading floors hum with activity. Brokers are yelling orders to each other, talking on the phone with customers, and sharing inputs. Analysts come over the loud speaker with constant updates. Jokes and stories make their way around the trading desk, and there is a strong level of camaraderie between the traders.

On the trading floors of the day traders, there is almost complete silence. Hundreds of young traders, most in their twenties, sit in compact rows, glued to their screens, oblivious to the traders on either side. There are no jokes or stories. While the market is open, they do not talk on the phone, read the newspapers, study financial reports, or listen to conference calls. Instead, they watch the signals from their sophisticated software, looking for instant trading opportunities. They are like a room full of kids playing video games. They are not concerned with fundamentals or earnings estimates. They may not even know the businesses of the stocks they own. They are only concerned with finding short-term gaps in the market that can give them a trading opportunity.

When a Buy or Sell signal is indicated, a trader who sees the opportunity and is fast enough clicks a trade. In an instant, the trader has bought 1,000 shares. Market makers change their prices. Another signal hits the screen. The trader clicks again, selling the stock for a profit of $.25 a share. Less than one minute has passed, and the trader has made two transactions. Other day traders may or may not have made the same trade. As in playing a video game, skills and judgment are required. There is a wide difference between the best and the worst of the day traders.

The day traders really are the ultimate guerrillas. Their strategy depends on hitting weaknesses in the professionals' lines and then retreating. Like a guerrilla who stages a lightening attack and then disappears into the jungle, a good day trader may be in and out of a stock in less than one minute and may execute more than seventy-five trades in an average day. In fact, many of the day traders have been called SOES Bandits. SOES (Small Order Execution System) is a trading system implemented by NASDAQ for small orders. These traders have been called bandits because they have acted like guerrillas in taking profits from the professionals. The day traders, however, are not the exception to the rule of aggressively trading against professionals. The day traders are professionals. Anyone who spends full time investing is, by definition, a professional.

3. AVOID TRADING ON EARNINGS ANNOUNCEMENTS

If professionals are at a big advantage in trading stocks, nowhere are they at a greater advantage than in trading on earnings announcements. It is very tempting for investors to make trades based either on expected or on actual reported earnings. The stockbroker calls and tells you that XYZ Systems is going to report before the opening. He is expecting good earnings. You take a flyer and buy some stock. Ignoring the critical question of whether your broker has a clue as to what he or she is talking about, the questions you should ask are, *"Will I be able to evaluate the earnings when they are reported? Will I be on the conference call? Will my broker? Will I receive a fax with all of the financial data? If I do, will I know what to look for?"* If you think carefully about the sequence of events, you will realize that you will be at a significant disadvantage to the professionals in acquiring and analyzing information.

Your broker calls the next morning. XYZ Systems has just reported better than expected earnings. He advises you to buy more:

"Where's the stock?" you ask.

"It's down a buck," the broker replies.

"What's going on?" you ask incredulously.

"More sellers than buyers," the broker mumbles as he looks on his terminal to see if his analyst has written about the earnings. *"I'm expecting a note from the analyst, but it's not on the system yet."* The stock is now down $2 on heavy volume. *"I'll check with her and call you back."*

The broker calls the analyst. *"I need to talk to her,"* your broker tells her assistant.

"She's on the Intel conference call," the assistant responds, *"and I can't interrupt her."*

"Did she say anything about XYZ Systems?" your broker asks.

"She was on the conference call," the assistant replies. *"She's working on a note."*

"What is she going to say?" the broker asks.

"We'll get back to you as soon as we can," the assistant replies politely.

The broker calls you back and recounts his conversation. *"Where's the stock now?"* you ask.

"It's only down $4 now. It was down $6, but it's acting better," your broker explains, certain that you will feel more comfortable.

"I guess someone did not like the earnings," you say forlornly.

"The earnings were good," the broker responds. *"They beat our estimates."*

"Something is wrong," you say, stating the obvious.

"Look, I'll get back to you when I know something," the broker responds and then hangs up.

At 4:10 the broker calls you back. The stock has closed down $7. *"I talked to the analyst,"* he says (although he probably just read the note that she wrote for the system). *"She says that while the quarter was sensational, future orders are a little soft, and next year's earnings might be flat. She also reduced the stock from a strong buy to a hold."*

"What does that mean?" you ask.

"You should dump the stock," the broker replies. You curse and hang up the phone.

Stop for a second and think about the process. When the company reported earnings, your broker called immediately, which is probably more than most brokers would do. But he only knew the earnings-per-share number. He was not on the conference call. He did not know about the weakness in future orders. He did not know that his analyst would be reducing both her estimates and ratings, and he did not know that what looked to be good numbers were really a disaster. Further, he did not get an explanation until the stock had declined by $7 and the market had closed.

While your broker was in the dark, other people obviously knew. They were probably prepped before the announcement, having reviewed the projected earnings, sales, margins, expenses, inventories, and backlogs with the company or with an analyst.

They may have also received information more rapidly. Companies send press releases to the wire services and faxes to key investors and analysts. Although the wire services should receive and post the information first to assure universal dissemination, it does not always work this way. Sometimes the wire services have an overload of information, and sometimes faxes get sent early to the professionals. Last month, a hedge fund manager I know received a fax from a retailer's PR firm indicating that comparable store sales were up 35 percent and that earnings would be above expectations. He checked his terminal. The wire services had not yet picked up the news. He bought the stock for $9.50. Twenty minutes later, the news hit the tape. One hour later, the stock was selling at $11.25. Because he received the fax before the news was broadly disseminated, he was able to make $1.75 per share in just one hour.

The professionals also were on the conference call, talked directly to the company, and probably even got through to your analyst. The assistant, who stonewalled your broker, would not have done the same to a portfolio manager from Putnam. So while the stock was dropping, your enemies had all of the information they needed. You were flying blind.

Analysts are often inundated because companies in the same industry commonly report earnings on the same day. In retailing, for example, five companies host hour-long conference calls on the same morning every quarter. The analysts barely have time to jump from one to the next. While analysts would like to quickly issue a note on the first company that reports, they cannot afford to miss the next call. (I have often wondered whether companies planned calls at the same time so that the analysts would not have too much time to probe.) If five companies report in a morning, a full day can often pass before the analysts can write a note and disseminate it. This does not hurt the professionals, who participate in the calls, but it does hurt the individual investors, who must rely on the analysts for details.

EARNINGS REPORTS ON THE INTERNET

The Internet eliminates some of the advantages of the professionals by providing individuals with instant and detailed information on earnings.

Internet search engines, on-line brokerage firms, and special on-line services such as Zacks.com, Briefing.com, and Motley Fool list the dates on which companies are expected to report earnings, along with analysts' earning estimates. Even if you are a long-term investor, you should check these lists each week for companies in which you are interested. Here's how:

Step One. Check the earnings estimates on sites such as Zacks.com. Watch especially for changes made close to the date of an expected earnings release.

Step Two. Click over to the company itself and go back to the last time it reported earnings. See how much detail it provides on-line. If there is a complete breakdown of earnings and a balance sheet, you will have access to the same information as do the professionals. If there are only sales and earnings per share, you should call the company and ask to be put on a fax list. If you are especially interested, ask how to be included in the conference call. Motley Fool and other sites give the time and phone numbers for some of the conference calls.

Step Three. Check the Web early on the day that the company is supposed to report its earnings. Most report before the market opens. Compare the reported number with the estimates. Look for upside or downside surprises. Read the company's press release. Look at the balance sheet and the income statement to see if there are any problems. Look for commentary on websites, such as the Motley Fool or Briefing.com websites. Many websites summarize conference calls.

Step Four. Look for "Analyst Upgrades and Downgrades" on the Internet. Analysts frequently change their ratings when companies report, and rating changes are updated on the Internet throughout the day. Watch especially for downgrades of stocks that have performed well or upgrades of stocks that have built a strong base. Note stocks in which the analysts are either exceedingly bullish or bearish, because these stocks can have big moves if the analysts change their ratings.

Step Five. Use the Internet to watch the initial trading pattern after the earnings have been released. This is often a critical time for a stock. If a company reports better than expected earnings and the stock goes down, it may be that the earnings were not as good as you thought or the stock has run out of steam. Whatever the reason, the stock is likely to keep going down. If the company reports worse than expected earnings and the stock goes up, it may be that the earnings were actually better than you thought or the stock has bottomed. Whatever the reason, the stock is likely to keep going up. These are often good opportunities to reevaluate a position.

Step Six. Watch the technical pattern of the stock on the Internet charts. If you don't know how to do this, stay tuned. We'll be talking a lot more about this later. Earnings announcements can be powerful catalysts in changing the direction of a stock's price. Because the next earnings announcement will not come for three months, you must respond if significant changes occur in the technical pattern. It can often have long-term implications.

Monitoring earnings announcements and listening to conference calls can be very useful no matter what your ownership horizon. But even with the added information on the Internet, you should not assume that you now have a level playing field with the professionals. You do not. The professionals still have huge advantages. Thus, while the Internet does somewhat level the playing field, you should be cautious in attempting to trade against the professional on earnings announcements.

4. AVOID ACTIVELY TRADING BIG-CAP STOCKS

Don't attempt to aggressively trade the stocks with the largest capitalizations. These are the stocks on which the professionals earn their living. They have hundreds of millions (if not billions) of dollars, as well as their reputations and careers, invested in these stocks, and they will do whatever they can to win. They cover every aspect of these companies as closely as they can. If there is an easy short-term opportunity in these stocks, they are not going to miss it.

Your broker says that Intel will introduce a revolutionary new chip and the stock should jump. It sounds like a good story. But before you buy the stock for a short-term pop, ask what your broker knows compared with

CONFERENCE CALLS

Conference calls can be a very useful tool. Listen to the tone of the management. You can often tell when a management is pleased or when it is trying to hide something. The question-and-answer period is often a good indicator of how business really is. If every analyst says, *"Congratulations on a great quarter,"* before asking a question, you can be reasonably sure that the quarter has been good. (They are also probably patting themselves on the back for having recommended the stock.) If, on the other hand, the analysts sound antagonistic and keep questioning the company about inventory levels or hidden charges, you can be relatively sure that they are not pleased. You should be especially concerned when an analyst who has a Buy on the stock starts to ask tough questions. Because analysts with Buys want the company to look as good as possible, they frequently ask "soft" questions like, *"How do you keep posting such great results?"* If these analysts ask tough questions, it may be a precursor to a ratings change, and you will have something to worry about. On the other hand, if bearish analysts suddenly seem to be getting more bullish and start asking about upside earnings surprises, you should consider buying, because it is a safe bet that some may raise their ratings. **If the attitudes of the analysts are different than you expected, you should act at once.** Most companies replay their conference calls at later times for people who have conflicts with the live call. While the playback may not help you in terms of short-term trading, it will allow you to listen to the management at your leisure.

what other professionals know. Intel is followed by more than thirty major sell-side analysts. It is also followed by hundreds of buy-side analysts and portfolio managers. These people have billions of dollars invested in Intel. They talk to the company, its suppliers, customers, and competitors. They read every bit of news about semiconductors. They hire experts to follow the technology. If Intel is going to announce a revolutionary new chip, professionals probably know about it and have already made their bet. It is unlikely that your broker has an inside scoop, unless his brother happens to design chips for Intel.

The next day, the broker calls and tells you to buy Philip Morris. A decision is about to be made on tobacco litigation, and the broker thinks that the tobacco companies will win. Once again, the story sounds good, and you are tempted to buy Philip Morris for a short-term trade. Once again, you should resist the temptation. Philip Morris is also followed by fifteen sell-side analysts and hundreds of buy-side analysts and portfolio managers, who have billions of dollars invested in the company. They may even have hired lawyers to attend the trial. These lawyers have listened to the arguments, reviewed the legal issues, and watched the body language of the judge and jury. While no one can predict a jury's behavior, they are in a much better position to make a decision than you are. Philip Morris may be a great investment for the long term, but in the short term you will have no edge.

On December 1, 1997, First Call listed the number of sell-side, brokerage-firm analysts with earnings estimates on the following stocks:

Intel	31	Microsoft	27	Wal-Mart	29
Limited	27	Sears	23	Coca-Cola	17
Bristol-Myers Squibb	24	General Electric	35	Merck	29

This list includes only those analysts whose firms subscribe to First Call. The total number of sell-side analysts who follow these companies is thus much larger. In addition, these companies are all closely covered by buy-side analysts and portfolio managers.

Major financial institutions have huge amounts of money invested in these stocks. In order to demonstrate the magnitude of the investments, I checked the filings of U.S. financial institutions and used the closing prices of the stocks on December 15, 1997. On that date:

- **Fifty-two companies owned a total of more than $300 million worth of stock in Intel.** Twelve of these owned more than $1 billion in stock.
- **Seventy-four companies owned a total of more than $300 million worth of stock in General Electric.** Twenty-five of these each owned more than $1 billion in stock. The twenty largest holders of GE are shown in the table at right.
- **Thirty-eight companies owned a total of more than $300 million worth of stock in Coca-Cola.** Fourteen of these each owned more than $1 billion in stock. The investment in Coca-Cola by Berkshire Hathaway, the company controlled by Warren Buffet, was worth more than $13 billion.

Stop and think about the size of these investments. If an institution had over $1 billion invested in a stock, would it be on top of the activities of the company? You can bet on it! If it is managing some of your money, you better hope it is.

Few major institutions can afford to ignore companies like General Electric, Intel, Coca-Cola, IBM, and Merck. Thus, when one of these major companies reports earnings, there are often more than **500 institutional investors and analysts participating in its conference call.** If you are an individual investor, it is difficult to see how you would ever be able to gain an advantage against these professionals.

The same rules do not apply if you are investing for the long term. Then, the short-term movements of a stock are much less important, and the advantages of the professionals are minimized. You may not know how the market will react to Intel's product announcement over the next week, but over the long term, you believe that Intel will outperform the market. If you think that Intel is a good company, buy it for the long term. But trying to outsmart the professionals for a short-term trade is foolhardy. It

GENERAL ELECTRIC

Institution	Number of Shares	Dollar Value	Institution	Number of Shares	Dollar Value
1. Fidelity	116,000	$8,352,000	11. Putnam	24,660	$1,775,520
2. BZW Barclays	91,888	$6,615,936	12. Northern Trust	24,554	$1,767,888
3. Bankers Trust	54,781	$3,944,232	13. Nationsbank	24,450	$1,760,400
4. State Street	44,380	$3,195,360	14. Alliance	20,854	$1,501,488
5. TIAA CREF	37,987	$2,735,064	15. Smith Barney	20,450	$1,472,400
6. Vanguard	33,143	$2,386,296	16. PNC	19,917	$1,434,024
7. Mellon	32,606	$2,347,632	17. University of Cal.	19,419	$1,398,168
8. Fayez Sarofim	31,927	$2,298,744	18. Wellington	18,704	$1,346,688
9. G.E.	31,430	$2,262,960	19. First Security	18,034	$1,298,448
10. Wells Fargo	26,667	$1,920,024	20. Chase	17,715	$1,275,480

would be like a guerrilla force sending its troops directly into the entrenched positions of its enemy. Winning at investing is difficult enough without playing directly into the enemy's strengths.

5. USE OPTIONS AS A HEDGE—NOT TO HIT HOME RUNS

Options are fun! They offer the opportunity for huge profit with minimal risk. Everyone dreams of the big hit with options, and in a bull market it often occurs.

I used to sit next to an institutional salesman. He had loaded up on options in Macy, because he thought the stock was undervalued. One morning trading in Macy was halted. News crossed the tape that there would be a leveraged buyout. The options jumped by $18 per share. In that one instant, he had made a profit of $2 million on an investment of

$100,000. After the shock had worn off, he turned and shook my hand. *"Good-bye,"* he said, *"I'm taking my money, getting out of the rat race, and moving to Florida to play golf."* I thought he was kidding. He was only forty-six. He is still in Florida playing golf and has a 2 handicap.

OPTIONS EXPLAINED

An option is a contract that gives the owner the right to buy (Call) or sell (Put) shares of stock. The essential elements of the option contract are the strike price, premium, and expiration date. The **strike price** is the price at which the underlying security can be bought or sold. The **expiration date** is the date on which the option expires, and the **premium** is the price that one pays to own the option.

Intel, which is currently selling for $93, has an October $100 Call option selling for $4. This means that the buyer would pay $4 for the right to buy Intel at $100 per share any time until the expiration date in October. Options are contracts for 100 shares. They are quoted on a per share basis. If the premium is $4, one option will cost you $400. (Four dollars per share for 100 shares.)

In a Call option, the investor is betting that the stock will go up. In buying a Call, the investor puts up a relatively small amount of money for the right to buy the stock at a specified price at some point in the future. The price of the premium will vary with both the strike price and the expiration date. The chart below shows a variety of Call options for Intel. In a Call option, the lower the strike price, the higher the premium, and the longer the time until expiration, the higher the premium. With more time, the stock has a greater potential to move in price.

INTEL CALL OPTIONS

Option	Premium	Option	Premium	Option	Premium	Option	Premium
Oct $80	$16	Oct $90	$8 5/8	Oct $100	$4	Oct $105	$2 5/8
Jan $80	$19	Jan $90	$13	Jan $100	$7 7/8	Jan $105	$6 1/4
—	—	April $90	$15 1/4	April $100	$10 1/2	April $105	$8 7/8

The key issue with options is the leverage. If the stock does not reach the strike price, your option will be worthless. If the stock moves above the strike price by less than the premium, you will lose money. But if the stock moves up sharply during the option period, the leverage can be substantial. If you were buying 1,000 shares of Intel, you would need $93,000, but you could put that $93,000 into Intel October $100 options for $4 each. You would have an option on 23,250 shares. If Intel went to $110, you would make $139,500 on the options and only $17,000 on the stock. However, the chances of Intel going from $93 to $110 in two months is exceedingly small.

Buying a Put is the opposite of buying a Call. When you buy a Put, you receive the right to sell an underlying security at a specific price. For example, if you buy an Intel October $90 Put option, you have the right to sell Intel at $90 before the option expires. If the stock drops below the $90 strike price, you can buy the stock at the market price, sell it at the strike price, and pocket the difference, less the cost of the option.

Options are much more complicated than most investors believe. There are a huge number of options in each security. Intel currently has over 220 different Call and Put options (including LEAPS—two-year options). Each of these 220 options trades independently, although all trade off the price of the underlying stock. Selecting the most attractive strike price and expiration date can be a daunting task. The professionals have computer programs that track the volatility of the stock, the dividend, the cost of money, and other factors that allow them to choose the best option. With so many options to choose from, the computer programs can often find market inefficiencies that allow professionals to trade one set of options against another with virtually no risk.

Some of the advantages of the professionals can be eliminated by using options calculation tools that are available over the Internet. One of the best is on the website of the Chicago Board Options Exchange (CBOE). With these tools, the individual can calculate the optimum pricing of all options and compare this pricing with the marketplace.

However, in order to do so effectively, the individual must be able to assess the volatility of the stock. Some stocks are reasonably stable, while others are highly volatile. The higher the volatility, the greater the likelihood that the stock will move substantially, and the more expensive the option. Estimating a stock's volatility can be a complex task. If you select the wrong level, your pricing strategies will be wrong.

BUYING CALLS OR PUTS ON INDEXES

If the odds are against the individual in buying options on stocks, they are even more against the individual in buying options on indexes. Most of the major indexes, such as the S&P 100 and 500, the Dow Jones Industrial, the NASDAQ 100, and the Russell 2,000, have options. There are also a variety of sector and international indexes. Index options can be used to make a bet for or against one of these markets. For example, if you believe that the stock market as a whole is going to go up, you can buy a Call on a major index such as the S&P 100. If you think that it is going to go down, you can buy Puts on the same indexes. If you think that technology stocks will outperform, you can buy Call options on the Goldman Sachs Technology Index. If you think that small stocks will underperform, you can buy Put options on the Russell 2,000.

Over the past several years, buying Call options has been the best of all possible investment strategies. Because the returns on index Call options have been so great, many investors believe that they are a sure path to instant wealth.

The problem, however, is that the strategy only works during a bull market. In a normal market, index options work against most individual investors. They not only require the investor to time the market, they also require the investor to time the market with leverage. In timing the market, the odds are against most individuals, and once the leverage of options is added, the odds become tougher. If you have no special ability to time the market, then timing it with leverage is a good way to lose quickly.

— . —

Options are a professional's game. They play to the professional's greatest strengths—timing, inside information, and better systems—and against the individual's greatest weaknesses—greed.

Options have become a core part of most portfolio managers' investing strategies. Professionals use options to facilitate trades, capitalize on imbalances in the market, lock in profits, and insure a portfolio against catastrophic losses. While individuals are using options to make a bet, professionals are using them to change the rules of the game. .

When small investors attempt to play options, they are entering a world with its own rules and with a pace of trading so fast that only the most sophisticated can keep pace. It would be like entering the Indy 500 on a bicycle. As you are pedaling down the back stretch, you could get killed when cars come roaring by at 250 miles per hour.

THE EXCEPTION

There are, of course, some instances when an individual should consider buying options. If you have real home-turf advantage and a solid piece of information that could move the stock, options are worth considering. For example, if you know that a company in your industry is about to receive a huge contract, you may want to buy Calls. However, before you buy, make certain that you have the correct timing on your information. If the contract is delayed by a few weeks, you could lose your investment.

Puts may actually be more useful than Calls because they can also be used as a substitute for shorting stocks. It is much easier to buy a stock you think will go up than it is to short a stock you think will go down. In many instances, a variety of restrictions can make shorting difficult. In these cases, buying a Put may be an easier way to bet against a company. But whether you are buying a Call or a Put, remember that the advantages of the professionals are magnified and that you should play options only if you have a real advantage in terms of home-turf information and timing.

COMPLEX OPTION STRATEGIES

While buying simple Calls and Puts may not be a good bet for the guerrilla investor, ironically some of the more complex options strategies may make sense because they enable the individual to gain some peace of mind. Investors can use a complex options strategy to limit risk in stocks they already own. For example, investors may sell a Call or buy a Put against an existing position. In effect, they now become long and short in the same stock. Their position is hedged. If they buy a "Protective Put," they must pay a little extra money, but they receive the right to sell the stock at a particular price. This is, in essence, an insurance policy against the stock dropping precipitously. If investors sell a "Covered Call," they receive a premium from a buyer. If the stock remains below the strike price, the premium is a windfall profit. If it goes above the strike price, they will be forced to sell it, but the premium will be an added profit. For a fuller discussion of complex option strategies, check out the website of the CBOE.

Investors who own a large amount of stocks in one industry and think that the market will drop can hedge their positions by buying a "Put Option on an Index." For example, if you own many of the major technology stocks, you can buy a Put option on a technology index. If your technology stocks drop, part or all of the drop will be offset by the option. Of course, if the stocks go up, the gain will also be offset. But you will be able to hedge your bets without having to sell your stocks and pay capital gains taxes. However, before buying a Put on a sector, make sure your portfolio is actually representative of the sector. If your collection of stocks is not representative, the index could go up while your stocks go down, and you could lose on both sides. Exercise great caution in buying a Put option on a sector. Consider this as a strategy only if you own many of the major companies in an index, have huge unrealized profits, and are searching for peace of mind.

Trading options is a complex undertaking that plays directly into the strengths of the professional and into the weaknesses of the individual. As a result, you should not buy Call and Put options on individual stocks, unless you have a significant home-turf advantage. But some of the complex option strategies may be of use because they can enable you to limit downside risk, lock in gains, and gain some peace of mind. If options help you look at the market without nervously gulping antacids, they may be worth considering. The rule for options is thus: Avoid the quick fixes of betting on pure Call options for stocks or indexes, but look at strategies that can allow you to lock in your profits and minimize your risk.

6. AVOID PLAYING MERGERS AND ACQUISITIONS

Playing mergers and acquisitions sounds like an easy way to invest. The Acquiring Company has offered to buy the Target Company at $30 a share, but the stock of the Target Company is still selling at $22. The deal should close within a matter of months. You think that this looks like an easy way to make a quick $8 a share. You are wrong. If there is a big return to be made in a relatively short period of time in an already announced deal, something is wrong with the deal. In a second deal, the stock jumps quickly to $32 when the offer is at $30. You decide to sell your stock in the Target Company. After all, you are getting $2 more than the stock is worth. Once again, you are likely to be wrong.

No area on Wall Street is more dominated by professionals than the risk arbitrage. When a deal is announced, the arbitrageurs immediately spring into action. They talk to the company, its competitors and suppliers, as well as to analysts, lawyers, and even government officials. They cover deals so extensively that most professional investors will not even compete with them. This certainly is not a place for individuals.

In order to value the deal, the arbitrageurs must assess the likelihood of the deal being completed and then the risk to the Target Company if the deal falls apart. This can be more complicated than it might seem. In some cases, the Target Company can be mortally wounded by a failed merger. It shares its secrets with a competitor, many of its managers leave, and the company loses momentum.

I learned this lesson a decade ago when a company named Businessland made an offer for MBI Business Systems. Based on the price of the offer, MBI should have been selling at $18, but it remained at $12. I bought MBI, in expectation of the deal being completed. Unfortunately, when Businessland did its audit, it found that MBI had substantial amounts of missing inventory. (It seems that the employees had cannibalized some of the computers.) The deal was called off, and MBI sank to $2 and never recovered. This is a lesson I will never forget.

In addition to looking at the risk, the arbitrageurs must consider the possibility that someone else will enter the bidding. If a second or a third buyer emerges, a bidding war can take the stock well above the original offer. Several years ago, Viacom made a friendly bid for Paramount. Then QVC entered the bidding. By the time the game was finished, the offer for Paramount was raised many times. Anyone who sold the first time that Paramount reached a premium to the offer price missed out on most of the move. If the stock trades at a premium to the original offer, it is a sign that the arbitrageurs expect another higher offer.

If the deal is not friendly, the game becomes far more complex. Arbitrageurs must assess the ends to which management is likely to go to protect its independence. Managements have sold off key assets, created expensive golden parachutes, made acquisitions of their own, or even turned around and tried to buy the Acquiring Company (Pac Man Defense) in order to avoid being taken over. Sometimes their actions push the stock up. Other times, they drive it down.

When the deal is for stock, the game becomes even more complex because the arbitrageurs will trade the two stocks against each other, buying one and shorting the other, and often using options. These games are so sophisticated and played with such speed that it is almost impossible for individual investors to keep pace.

Yet even the best arbitrageurs can end up being wrong. For example, in 1997, British Telecom agreed to buy MCI. Most arbitrageurs assumed that the deal would go through, because British Telecom already owned 20 percent of MCI and the deal had received government approval. But then MCI reported disappointing earnings, and the terms of the deal were changed. MCI, which one month earlier had sold at $42, dropped to $28. Because most arbitrageurs were long MCI and short British Telecom, what had appeared to be a riskless investment became a nightmare, with many of the world's top investors losing billions of dollars. A few weeks later, both Worldcom and GTE made bids for MCI, but by then most of the arbitrageurs had already lost.

The message is simple—if the arbitrageurs, who have studied every aspect of this deal, are losing billions of dollars, what chance does the individual investor have? The answer is none. The best advice for an investor is avoid playing takeover games. If you happen to own a stock that is the subject of a takeover, you should recognize that once the takeover game begins, you are at a significant disadvantage. The longer and more complex the takeover battle, the weaker will be your relative position.

At all costs, do not try to outsmart the arbitrageurs. They will sometimes be wrong, as they were in the case of MCI/British Telecom. However, if they keep the Target stock at a big discount to the offer price, they are saying that the deal may be in trouble. You might consider selling, even if it means walking away from what looks like a solid return. If they take the stock to a premium, you might hang on for a while to see if another bid materializes. But do not overstay your welcome. This is an extremely hard game to win.

7. AVOID IPOs, ESPECIALLY WHEN PROCEEDS GO TO THE INSIDERS

When you ask about the best way to make money, people will invariably tell you about Initial Public Offerings (IPOs). IPOs give investors a chance to get in on the ground floor of the next sensational growth stock. The record of IPOs has been outstanding. Many have opened at twice their offering price, creating instant profits. But when individuals look at the record of IPOs, they are being misled. The charts that track the performance of IPOs may not really be applicable to the individual investor.

Much of the return in IPOs comes from a small number of hot deals that double or triple on the opening. These profits may be tantalizing, but you will not see them. Like having a date with a movie star, you can dream about it all you want, but it is not going to happen to you.

The way you can tell if an IPO is cold or hot is simple. An IPO is cold if your broker tells you that the deal is hot, but there is still stock available. An IPO is hot if your broker laughs at you when you ask for stock. If the deal is hot, there will be no stock available for you.

There are only two exceptions to this rule. First, if you happen to have a special relationship with the company that is going public, you can always call the CEO and ask to be included in the deal. Second, if your brokerage firm is the lead manager of a deal (the name on the far left-hand side of the prospectus), and if your broker has substantial clout, you can sometimes get a small allocation on a good deal. But before you buy, ask your broker why there is stock available for you. Do not place an order unless you get a good answer.

Be especially wary of offerings from third-tier brokerage firms. When companies decide to go public, they shop for an investment banker. Generally, companies start with the best underwriters in their industry and work their way down. Most prefer the major international investment books or national brokerage firms that are specialists in their industries. Some smaller companies may go with regional brokerage firms that understand their particular markets, but if a company cannot find a major national or even regional brokerage firm to do its IPO, there is likely to be something wrong. Avoid any offering in which a third-tier brokerage firm promises you a profit. If someone promises a profit, the market may be rigged, and you could get killed.

Also be cautious of offerings in which all the proceeds go to selling shareholders (such as company management) and not to the company. When the proceeds go to the company, they can be used to spur growth. This is always a good use of capital. But managements sell stock because they want to cash out. They know when their business has peaked and rarely sell when they believe that the stock will suddenly shoot up or the company will suddenly be taken over. If you see a case in which management is selling most or all of its stock, avoid it at all costs.

8. AVOID STOCKS THAT YOU CAN'T UNDERSTAND

If information moves the stock market and if the people with the best information win, then it goes without saying that individual investors should avoid stocks that are too complex for them to understand. This may sound like an obvious comment, but you would be surprised at how many people buy stock in companies where the business is a complete mystery to them. Investors love to play technology stocks. They offer the greatest opportunities for growth. But the problem for individual investors is that the areas that are often the fastest growing are also the most difficult to understand and the ones at which they are at the greatest disadvantage against the professionals. Professionals tend to specialize in a narrow range of stocks. In major brokerage houses, one analyst may follow nothing but Internet software companies, a second may follow Internet service providers and search engine companies, while a third may follow Internet commerce companies. Further, many of these analysts come directly from industry. There are a number of major analysts who were presidents or CFOs of high-technology companies before moving to Wall Street. Thus, when individuals buy stock in a high-tech company, they are not just competing against professionals, they are competing against professionals who have specialized knowledge.

The problem for the individual is simple. If you cannot understand what the company does, how can you judge its prospects? And if you cannot understand the critical pathways in its development, how can you judge whether it is on the right or the wrong track?

How can you decide if the company is too complex for you to understand? The first and easiest way is to look at the company's mission statement or the description in an analyst's report. Below are mission statements from companies or from analyst reports for three high-tech firms.

LARSCOM

Larscom develops, manufactures, and markets a broad range of high-speed global internetworking solutions for network service providers ("NSPs") and corporate users. Larscom's products provide access to fractional T1, E1, T1/E1, frame relay, fractional T3/E3, cannelized T3 services, and Clear Channel ATM ("CCA") inverse multiplexing, with clear channel T3, ISDN, IMA, and ATM under development. . . .
(Source: Larscom Prospectus)

SUGEN Inc.

SUGEN . . . is a biopharmaceutical company focused on the discovery and development of small molecule drugs which target specific signal transduction pathways. Signal transduction is simply the process by which messages from the cell surface to the cell nucleus either activate or suppress genes. . . . SUGEN's expertise is specific to signaling pathways regulated by the receptors in families tyrosine kinases (TKs), tyrosine phosphatases (TPs), and serine-threonine kinases (STKs).
(Source: C. Anthony Butler, Ph.D., Lehman Brothers, 1/13/97)

LANDEC Corp.

Landec designs and manufactures temperature-activated polymer products using a proprietary side-chain crystallizable polymer technology. The company's proprietary Interlimer@ material exhibits novel properties with a wide range of commercial applications. Unlike other polymers, The Interlimer@ polymer can be engineered to change its physical characteristics sharply when heated or cooled through a pre-set temperature switch.
(Source: Jonathan H. Cohen, Smith Barney, 1/28/97)

If you do not understand the mission of the company, you will never be able to track its progress or analyze its investment opportunities. If McDonald's introduces a new burger, you can decide whether it tastes good as easily as a professional can. But if a biotechnology firm announces that it is in the first stage of clinical trials for a new recombinant hemoglobin, you may not understand what recombinant hemoglobin is, how it can be used commercially, or understand the process of clinical trials.

This is a world of rapid technological change. While companies such as Coke and Budweiser sell virtually the same product year after year, technology companies are constantly coming up with radically new products. An individual does not have to lose sleep wondering whether someone will invent a product that makes Bud obsolete, but the same may not be the case for a company in a high-tech field. Does anyone remember Visicalc, the company that invented the first spread sheet, or Wang, the company that developed the first commercial word processor?

This does not imply that individuals should never invest in high-tech stocks. Some individuals have some specialized knowledge through their profession or their daily lives. Computer professionals may know about software or networking companies. Doctors may know about medical services companies. Many of the investors who made the most money in Internet stocks were early participants on the Web. Similarly, many of the most successful investors in biotech stocks were individuals who had come into contact with the products through the illness of someone they knew. When individuals saw a friend or relative cured of a disease because of a biotech product, they often wisely rushed out and bought the stock of the companies that made the products.

If you want to invest in high-tech stocks, you have three good alternatives. You can buy a specialized mutual fund and let someone else pick the stocks. You can find an area of technology in which you have "home turf" (special knowledge because of direct experience) and focus on what you already know. Or you can educate yourself about a particular technological niche and invest in stocks in that niche. But if you do not understand the business that these companies are in and the factors that drive the marketplace, you should avoid them.

9. AVOID EMERGING MARKETS

Foreign stocks are extremely tempting for most individual investors because they offer potentially strong growth and diversification from the U.S. market. Throughout the world, new economies are emerging. Older economies are restructuring. Former Communist nations are turning toward capitalism, and nations are privatizing former government-owned businesses. Investment opportunities have never been more numerous or more exciting.

Despite the great opportunities, however, individual Americans are at a very significant disadvantage in attempting to buy foreign stocks because most have no home turf. A broker may call and tell you an exciting story about a retailer in China or Chile. You are tempted to buy. But stop. Would you think of buying a retail stock in the United States without first checking out the stores? The same rules should apply to retailers in China or Chile. You can count on the fact that the locals who are trading the stocks are visiting the stores.

Home turf is even more of an advantage in foreign markets than it is in the United States. In the United States, solid information is fairly easy to obtain. American companies report every quarter and have relatively full disclosure. Most participate in public forums and communicate with investors. Trading is also open to all investors. In many foreign markets, especially those that are emerging, the same rules do not apply. Companies report much less frequently and in much less detail, and they usually report only in their native language. Most also do not actively communicate with investors, host conference calls, or post announcements on the Web. In such a situation, investors have to rely much more on gossip and friendships that give them insight into the operations of the companies. In such markets, individuals with connections to the companies can have a vast advantage.

Investing in foreign markets is made more complicated because companies in foreign markets operate with their own unique set of rules. If everyone used the same accounting systems, it would be easy to make adjustments, but there are many differences which can lead to significant distortions. European drug companies may look like they are selling for lower multiples than their American counterparts. But when their earnings are adjusted to conform to American practices, it becomes clear that their multiples are actually much higher.

Japanese banks may look like they have attractive price/book ratios, but these banks rarely write down bad loans, and they carry investments in other stocks on their books at the prices at which they were bought. Since many Japanese companies are not paying their loans and since the Japanese market is now selling at half its previous level, the book values of these banks are greatly overstated.

Companies in emerging nations often look as if they have low price/book ratios because they use "inflation accounting." In this practice, companies write up their assets to their current market value to offset the impact of inflation. While this may be appropriate for the local market, it greatly distorts comparisons with American companies.

Trading can also be very different. In the United States, registration is automatic, but in other countries it is not. Companies often register shares selectively. If they do not want you as a shareholder, they may refuse to register your stock. Large numbers of trades are often turned back because companies do not like the buyers. Local tax issues can also present complicated problems.

Emerging markets also tend to have high volatility. In the past year, the market in Portugal increased by 51 percent, while the market in Thailand declined by 77 percent. With high unemployment in Europe and with Thailand developing as a major power, would you have bet on Portugal being the winner and Thailand being the loser?

The volatility is compounded by extremely high stock turnover. Many markets have turnover four to five times higher than in the United States. In Turkey, for example, 70 to 80 percent of stocks are held for one day or less. Talk about active trading! Think about what it must be like to play in a market in which most investors turn over their portfolios every day. Do you think that you could beat the Turks at this game?

International economic factors can often play havoc with foreign stocks. If there is a significant change in the local currency vis-à-vis the dollar, the value of the investments and state of the economy can change overnight. Mexico's devaluation of the peso in 1994 wiped out five years of profits in the Mexican market.

In 1997, the foreign market disasters have included markets most individuals would have considered to be the most promising. In the twelve months ending December 14, 1997, world markets increased in U.S. dollars by 18.5 percent, but many emerging Asian nations were bombed. The Thailand market declined by a shocking 77 percent in U.S. dollars. A thousand dollars invested in Thailand on January 1 would have been worth less then $235 by December. But Thailand was not alone. The Philippine market dropped by 57 percent. The Malaysian market dropped by 70 percent. The Indonesian market dropped by 73 percent, and the South Korean market dropped by 72 percent. These markets, which had been the strongest in the world for most of the decade, lost more than two-thirds of their value in U.S. dollars in less than one year. Other Asian markets were also decimated. The Singapore market dropped by 36 percent, Hong Kong by 22 percent, and the once mighty Japan by 28 percent. Would you have known enough to walk away from Thailand and other markets before the bottom dropped out?

Even something as minor as the hours of the local markets can offer professionals a substantial advantage. The European markets open about six hours before the New York market, while in Asia the entire trading day occurs while you are asleep. Were you up watching at 2:00 A.M. when the Hong Kong market recently crashed?

Political instability may also play havoc with foreign stock markets. When Boris Yeltsin had a heart attack, the Russian stock market dropped by 25 percent. When he was reelected, it doubled.

Political factors can be magnified because many politicians have their hands directly in businesses. Foreign government officials, or their families, often own huge stakes in major industries. In investing in these industries, it is critical to know whether they are correctly aligned politically and whether the government is secure. If you own stock in a company that is controlled by a dictator's son, that company may thrive so long as the son retains good relations with his father and the father remains in power. But if there is a coup, your company is in serious trouble. (Much of the current mess in Indonesia has been caused by the fact that President Suharto's family owns major stakes in many of the country's largest industries. Note the Bre-X story that follows.)

Most significantly, you may never have a clue when a disaster is about to strike. In 1990, I was sitting in a friend's office at a Swiss bank. *"Something is very strange,"* he said to me. *"Billions of dollars are pouring from the Gulf into Switzerland. I don't know what's going on, but a lot of people are in a big hurry to get their money out of the Mideast."* Two weeks later, Saddam Hussein invaded Kuwait. The U.S. government was shocked. Our allies were shocked. In fact, everyone was shocked, except for those people who had previously moved tens of billions of dollars to Switzerland. The people in the Gulf knew that a war was about to erupt, even if no one else did. If your opponent knows that a war is about to erupt and you do not, you are at a serious disadvantage. The problem is that in emerging markets, wars, coups, and other upheavals can occur with some regularity. As a result, the individual should never underestimate the value of local intelligence.

HOW TO INVEST SUCCESSFULLY IN INTERNATIONAL MARKETS

While the odds are dramatically against an individual investor, this does not mean that you should avoid all international markets. International markets offer strong opportunities for growth and excellent diversification. The challenge for the individual investor is to minimize the advantages of the professionals and the locals. There are a number of ways to accomplish this end.

Individual investors can purchase diversified international mutual funds. These funds are run by professionals who understand the local markets. Most portfolios should have some of these funds. As an individual investor, however, you should resist the temptation to make short-term bets on specific country funds unless you have a real edge. If you would not have bet for Taiwan and against Thailand in the past year, stay away from making short-term bets on specific countries.

In some cases, individuals may actually have some home-turf advantage in other countries. When this occurs, they should capitalize on it. You may be in an international business and travel frequently to another country. In your profession, you may deal with a company that has opened branches in the United States, or you may buy products produced by foreign companies. Many Americans purchased stock in Nokia and Erickson after they bought cellular phones made by those companies.

The Internet has excellent research on companies that have ADRs (American Depository Receipts). ADRs minimize some of the problems of owning foreign stocks. They represent shares in foreign companies, but they actually trade in the United States. Just as you can with American companies, you can use your on-line investing site to get earnings estimates, upgrades and downgrades, and analyst reports. You can also visit the websites of the foreign companies. All this is a huge plus, since other countries have much less rigorous reporting requirements, making it difficult to acquire information. If you look at these investments as long term, buying a group of ADRs will probably hold you in good stead.

The critical issue is to avoid aggressive trading in foreign markets unless you really have some special home-turf advantage. Because foreign markets are much more volatile, have different economic systems, and have far less available information, the odds are set heavily against the individual American investor.

10. AVOID THE HYPE

It is always tempting for individual investors to chase gold mines, whether real or imagined, because people want to believe that there is some easy way to get rich. In most cases, the biggest schemes are the most exotic. The reason is simple. The further investors go from their home turf, the less they know and the easier it is to pull the wool over their eyes. It is difficult to convince people that a fruit-flavored beer will put Budweiser out of business, because they can taste the beer, but it is not difficult to convince people that a biotech company has discovered a new gene that can stop aging, because people know little about genetics. The more removed a story is from an investor's own experience, the harder it is to separate myth from reality.

Hyped stories tend to involve dramatic new technologies, ventures in emerging markets, or both. People play the lottery because they dream they will be winners, even though they know the odds are against them. It is much the same in investing. The problem is that most of the time the hyped stories prove to be only hype, and investors lose all of their capital. If a story seems too good to be true and if it is too far removed from your home turf for you to be able to understand what is going on, walk away from it, no matter how tempting it seems.

EVERY STOCK IS NOT A GOLD MINE—EVEN IF IT IS ONE

No company in recent memory holds more cautionary tales for the individual investor than Bre-X, the Canadian gold-mining company. Bre-X was founded in 1988 by David Walsh, the son and grandson of Canadian stockbrokers, who had spent most of his career vainly trying to push oil and mining investments. Bre-X struggled for many years. In the 1991 annual report Walsh even wrote, *"Yes, we are still in business."* Hardly a bullish statement.

By 1993, Bre-X had five employees. Walsh had been convicted for mishandling a stock transaction, and he and his wife had filed for personal bankruptcy because they had credit card debts of $59,500. Yet three years later, the man who went bankrupt because he could not pay off his credit cards controlled a company with a market capitalization of $6 billion! How could a penny stock in Calgary have become one of the most valuable mining companies in the world in such a short period of time? The answer reveals a lot about greed and people's desire to strike it rich.

The story begins with John Felderhof, a geologist who twenty-nine years ago helped discover one of the largest gold and copper deposits in the world, at Ok Tedi in the remote highlands of Papua New Guinea. Felderhof believed that substantial mineral deposits could be found in neighboring Indonesia at Busang Creek. Although the Australian company that had been backing him decided against developing the claim, Felderhof was undeterred. He convinced David Walsh to back him. Although Walsh had recently been bankrupt, he sold options in Bre-X, bought 90 percent of the Busang claim for $180,000, and hired another geologist named Michael de Guzman.

Walsh and the two geologists started to promote their opportunity. Even though no exploration had yet taken place, the price of Bre-X's stock shot up ten-fold. Others obviously wanted to believe that Busang might become another Ok Tedi.

In early 1994, de Guzman found gold near Busang Creek. The stock price increased more than forty-fold. With more tests, estimates of the find were raised again, to 30 million ounces. The stock price tripled again. In three years, it had gone up 150,000 percent; $1,000 invested in 1993 was now worth $1.5 million. Yet no outside observer had actually checked the claim. No one seemed to care. Investors had caught the gold bug.

In April 1996, Bre-X moved to the respected Toronto Stock Exchange. In May, the stock price reached a high of $25. In June, it hired J. P. Morgan, a true white-shoe firm, as its investment banker and increased its estimates of the find to more than 50 million ounces. This made Busang potentially the largest gold mine in the world.

The Indonesians began to maneuver for a stake of their own. Bre-X agreed to pay President Suharto's son $40 million to arrange the mining permits. A competing company, Barrick Gold, offered to buy Bre-X for $5 billion, and agreed to give Suharto's daughter 10 percent if she could force Bre-X to sell. Another company upped the offer to $5.5 billion. But Bre-X cut a deal of its own. To get capital, it sold a 15 percent stake to Freeport MacMoRan. To get the support of the Indonesian government, it gave a 10 percent stake to the government itself and sold 30 percent to a company controlled by President Suharto, his eldest son, and his closest advisor. With capital and with the government as a partner, Bre-X seemed like a can't-miss proposition. Estimates of the gold find were increased again to 200 million ounces, making it by far the largest mine ever.

Still, there were a number of very troubling signs that any investor should have noticed. During 1996, there was a large amount of insider selling in Bre-X. Walsh, his wife, Felderhof, the CFO, two other officers, and a director sold at least $50.5 million in stock. If the find was so valuable, why were the executives selling?

In January 1997, a fire destroyed all of Bre-X's gold-deposit test results. There were no duplicates. You would think investors would be concerned when all of a company's records disappear, but few took much notice. After all, Bre-X owned the biggest gold mine in the history of the world.

In March, Michael de Guzman, the geologist who was responsible for the test results, jumped from a helicopter and committed suicide. He wrote a note claiming that he had malaria and hepatitis. De Guzman had become hugely rich. He had four wives who undoubtedly loved him, and he was about to be lionized as the man who found the largest gold mine in history. Yet few investors seemed troubled that he jumped to his death. Greed and ignorance can be a powerful combination.

On March 26, Freeport issued a statement that its independent tests revealed that there was only a limited amount of gold in Busang and it might not be profitable to mine it. On March 27, the price of Bre-X's stock dropped 83 percent. Trading was stopped for three days. When trading opened again on April 1, the volume was so great that it actually broke the computer at the Toronto Stock Exchange. A mineral services firm was hired to do an independent analysis. Three weeks later, it came back and said that there was little gold in Busang and that what gold was there could not be profitably mined. On May 3, Bre-X filed for bankruptcy. In four months, $6 billion of market value evaporated.

Bre-X did not just sucker individuals. Some of the top analysts had been pushing the stock, and some of the most respected investment advisors owned large amounts. But many individuals did fall for Bre-X. They wanted to believe that the largest gold mine in the world lay buried in the jungles of Indonesia. They were convinced by all the action surrounding the stock, and they never asked why no one had verified the find, why there were no records, why the insiders were selling, and why the chief geologist committed suicide. Few understood anything about Indonesia or gold mines. They just wanted to believe that there was a pot (or, in this case, a mine) of gold at the end of the rainbow. What they found was that easy money is not always as easy as it seems. In investing in Bre-X, these individuals were as far from their home turf as possible, at least on earth.

— · —

An individual investor, like a guerrilla approaching a heavily armed modern army, should respect the strength of the enemy and avoid making a frontal assault in areas in which the enemy is well entrenched. For the most part, it means that the individual should avoid: predicting the market, trading aggressively, trading on earnings announcements, actively trading big-cap stocks, trying to hit home runs with options, playing mergers and acquisitions, buying into IPOs, investing in businesses that are too complex to understand, investing in emerging markets on their own, and chasing stories that are too good to be true. There are always exceptions, but by and large, most investors will do better if they err on the side of caution.

The professional obviously has huge advantages over the individual, just as the modern army has huge advantages over the guerrilla. But the individual can still defeat the professional, just as the guerrilla force can defeat the modern army. To do so, individuals must find their own strengths and the professionals' weaknesses, and look for ways of changing the field of battle to their advantage. If individuals take the opportunities that the market offers without trying to overpower the more well-trained opponent, victory not only is possible, it is likely. The key for the individual is to find those areas in which an advantage can be gained over a more-experienced enemy.

CHAPTER FOUR

Fight on Your Home Turf

Guerrilla warriors fight against stronger enemies. That's why it is critical for them to set the time and place for each battle in a manner that provides maximum advantage. Because the army has more planes and tanks, the battle should not be in the open. Instead, the guerrilla should seek to engage the enemy along mountain passes or in jungles, where the army cannot use its modern weapons. It should seek to fight house-to-house in cities, where it can blend in with the rest of the population and where the alleys are too narrow for the army's equipment. It should fight under the cover of darkness, when it can see the army but the army cannot see it. It should fight during monsoons, when the army's air cover is grounded and its tanks are mired in the muck. It should use every element of local knowledge to stage surprise attacks and then quickly disappear. In short, the guerrilla should seek to engage the enemy on the terrain in which it is most comfortable and in which its strengths can be used to the greatest advantage. **We call this terrain home turf.**

The principle of fighting on one's own home turf applies equally well to investing. Professional investors have more knowledge, capital, and time than amateurs. In direct, open combat, they will win. To offset these advantages, the guerrilla investor must set the terms of battle to maximize the advantages of home turf. This means investing in companies you have first-hand experience with. Like local knowledge for the guerrilla fighter, this first-hand experience can give the guerrilla investor a decided edge over the professional.

Every investor has home turf. People come into contact with public companies in their profession. They view industry trends, deal with suppliers and customers, and analyze their competitors. They also come into contact with public companies as consumers. They shop in stores, eat in restaurants, fly on airlines, select long-distance carriers, and surf the Net. Finally, they come in contact with public companies in their hometowns or through friends. Because of their knowledge of their own terrain, individuals are often able to gain insights that Wall Street misses. This home-turf information does not come neatly packaged, like an analyst's report. But that does not make it less valuable. The task for individuals is to figure out how to utilize what they see around them. The best edge that the individual investor has is to find information on home turf that the professional lacks.

HOME TURF IN YOUR PROFESSION

The most obvious home turf for an investor is the individual's own profession. The individual knows his or her own industry in a way that the analysts on Wall Street do not.

USE YOUR SPECIALIZED KNOWLEDGE OF TECHNOLOGY

You are a doctor. You read about a new treatment in your medical journal, attend a seminar on biotechnology, treat patients, and talk to other doctors about the success of various procedures. While you may not know a lot about specific stocks, your knowledge of medicine is superior to that of most analysts. It is probably easier for you to get a report on these stocks than it is for the analysts to gain your knowledge of medicine. If you use your professional knowledge, you may be able to out-compete Wall Street.

A company named Somatagen was a high flyer in the biotechnology field. The stock was loved by most analysts because the company had developed a new process for creating recombinant hemoglobin that it claimed could save lives. But a number of doctors did not agree. They thought that Somatagen's product was far too expensive for the benefits it delivered and that health plans would not pay for the treatment. Some of these doctors talked to Paul Kelly, then a young analyst at UBS Securities. After talking with the doctors, Kelly rated Somatagen a Sell. The Sell rating was especially daring because Kelly was a new analyst. But Kelly understood that the doctors knew something that other investors did not. Somatagen dropped from $19 to $5.

You work on the Help Desk for a manufacturer of personal computers. A software company has introduced a hot new title. In the first week after its release, you are inundated with calls from irate customers screaming that the software does not work on your computers. You check with a competitor. Its computers are having the same problem. The software obviously has a major glitch, and no one on Wall Street has yet picked up on this information. If the software is an important product, the chances are good that the company producing it will have problems. By the time the analysts figure out there is a problem, the stock could be down sharply.

PROFIT FROM THE RESTRUCTURING OF YOUR INDUSTRY

You are a banker. You see medium-sized banks in your market being bought up by the large super-regionals. A gigantic consolidation is occurring. You have an opinion as to which banks, including your own, would make attractive takeover targets. While people on Wall Street also evaluate potential mergers, you are in a better position to make investments because you are an insider and know the players.

You are an independent pharmacist. You see the chains buying the independents, merging with each other, and then making deals to handle all the prescription business of large companies. They are getting stronger while your profits are being squeezed. It may be difficult to buy stock in someone who is trying to put you out of business, but no one understands the economics better than you.

You work for a telephone company. For years, you have watched new companies enter the long distance, cellular, local access, and paging businesses because of deregulation. You have often thought to yourself that you could now be rich if you had put in your own application for a cellular phone license. But if you can think strategically, you can still spot ways of profiting from the deregulation of your industry.

CAPITALIZE ON INDUSTRY TRENDS

The issues you live with every day should enable you to find investment opportunities if you look at the broader implications.

You are in the oil business. You receive a call from an associate who tells you a rumor. Someone has made a strike in the North Sea which could rival that of the Mideast. If he is right, the companies involved will be big winners, while oil prices as a whole will decline.

You manage an HMO. The government is discussing a new bill that will increase cost containment. In the past several months, you have attended three seminars on this bill. You know far more about the potential impact than do the analysts on Wall Street. It may be their profession, but it is your life. While you may be primarily concerned about your own company, you will find a variety of investment opportunities if you stop and look at the big picture.

You import products from Asia. The decline in Asian currencies has enabled you to obtain great bargains. Most of your prices have dropped by 20 percent, while your competitors, who buy products in the United States, Europe, or Latin America, are not able to lower their prices. Your margins are expanding, and you are gaining market share. You know that other importers are in the same position. Look at the products that come from Asia. Identify those companies that will benefit and those domestic manufacturers that will be hurt. They do not have to be your direct competitors. They just have to be impacted by the same industry conditions. If you use your experience, you can act ahead of most investors.

You are a banker. You see credit card delinquencies increasing rapidly. Unless there is something unique about your local market, the chances are good that other banks are facing the same problems. You know which have the largest credit card exposure. You may not know much about the stock market, but you do know about credit card risk, and you do know that these stocks will not fare well if credit quality continues to deteriorate. Neither will the stocks of some major retailers that receive a large percentage of their earnings from credit cards. Manufacturers and retailers of durable goods—such as autos and furniture—and firms in basic industries—such as steel—that supply the manufacturers could also be hurt.

FIND INVESTMENT OPPORTUNITIES FROM COMPETITORS

You know your competitors better than the professionals on Wall Street do. You deal with their executives in industry meetings, and have the same customers, suppliers, and union. You have friends who work in each company. If you focus on what you know, you will find significant investment opportunities among competitors in your industry.

You are in the clothing business. When you walk through the stores, you see a new brand (not the one you sell) that appears to be getting more shelf space. You talk to the retailers. They tell you that this brand is the hottest line in the country. You look at the merchandise. You know a winner when you see it. The analysts must wait until the company tells them about the sell-throughs, but you can act now, because you know the goods are selling.

You own a restaurant. A popular theme restaurant, similar to Planet Hollywood, has opened down the street. You see the crowds flocking there. You go in to see what all the fuss is about. As you watch the customers, you ask yourself whether these new theme restaurants are the wave of the future or merely a short-term fad. You ask these questions not because you are an investor, but because they are threatening your livelihood and because you must find a competitive response. But the questions you ask are the same that investors ask, except that your perspective is probably better. If you use your eyes and talk to the people who work and eat in the theme restaurants, you can go with your instincts.

You work for a forest products company. The company has just sold a small piece of land in California to developers at a huge profit. You know that two competitors own much larger pieces of neighboring land. You do not know if these companies will sell the land, but if the price is high enough, they eventually will not be able to resist. If you buy the stocks now, you will be well ahead of most other investors.

BET ON THE PEOPLE YOU KNOW

Most people inside an industry have a better feel for the strengths and weaknesses of managers than do people on Wall Street. They see managers in the real world, rather than through spin control. They also see the changes that the managements are implementing faster than investors do. Betting on someone you actually know in an industry that you understand is probably the best way to invest.

You are a systems engineer. Your mentor has been hired away to become the president of a software firm that develops applications for electronic commerce. He wants to hire you. *"This is a chance of a lifetime,"* your mentor tells you. *"This company has unbelievable technology."* You know his track record and see the opportunity, but you cannot relocate. That still should not stop you from buying the stock. No one knows your mentor better than you. Just because you cannot relocate does not mean that you should not bet on him.

You read your trade press regularly. You see that a key executive has left one of your competitors. You call your stockbroker and ask how the stock has reacted. The broker tells you that there has been no announcement of the resignation. Because companies often delay reporting bad news, you have an edge on Wall Street. This is your equivalent of inside information. People in the industry know about the resignation, but professionals on Wall Street do not.

Trust your instincts about executives you know. Companies are run by people, and good people run companies much better than mediocre people. When good senior managers leave one company and join another, there is usually an investment opportunity.

BEAT THE STREET WITH KNOWLEDGE OF YOUR SUPPLIERS

You work for an automobile manufacturer. The company has decided to expand its outsourcing in order to cut costs. It should be relatively easy for you to identify those products that will be outsourced and those companies that will pick up the contracts.

You are a lawyer in a small office. Do you remember when your secretary first asked you to let her open an account at one of the office supply superstores, such as Staples? She told you that its prices and assortments were much better than those of the distributor with whom you had been dealing. You started to buy from the superstores. The distributor called and complained. You guessed that you were not the only account that he was losing. You talked to a few other lawyers. Their secretaries were also using the superstores. When you stopped writing checks to the distributor and started writing checks to Staples, you could have realized that these superstores represented an exciting new investment opportunity.

You are a data processing manager responsible for handling the Year 2000 changeover for your company. You interviewed twenty companies, but only found three that appear to have a solution to the problem. You recognize the magnitude of the Year 2000 issue and the opportunities for those few companies that are specializing in solving it. Buying stock in all of these companies will probably hold you in good stead.

PICK UP GOOD INVESTMENT IDEAS FROM YOUR CUSTOMERS

You make batteries. One of your largest customers starts delaying your orders. You visit the stores. All of the assortments are broken. There are no AA or D batteries in stock. You get a call from an associate in accounts receivable, who tells you that the retailer is ninety days late in payment. You feel a gnawing in the pit of your stomach. You have lived through this before. You guess that this retailer is going to go bankrupt. Analysts and investors do not have the same gnawing in their stomach.

You sell real estate. An aggressive Real Estate Investment Trust has begun to buy up many of the midsize real estate companies in your market at excellent prices, and is rapidly upgrading the properties. You have sold two pieces of property to the CEO of the REIT. He is the toughest negotiator that you have ever dealt with. Although dealing with him was no picnic, buying his stock will probably be a smart move.

You work for a travel agency. The new casinos in Las Vegas suddenly start offering incredible bargains. Rooms that had cost $200 are now going for $29.95. If this is a short-term price war, the stocks of the casino companies can continue to go up. If Las Vegas now has too much capacity, they will go down. On the other hand, airlines are offering no bargains. The fares are sky-high. Sky-high airfares should be good for airline profits.

TRUST YOUR INSTINCTS

A friend called me recently to complain about a stock that she had purchased named Mossimo. My friend was in the apparel business. *"Why did you buy the stock?"* I asked. *"The broker said that the analyst had a good record and the stock was likely to go up,"* my friend said. *"But when I looked, I saw that the stores were packed with goods, and that they were all marked down. I could kick myself. I knew the goods weren't selling, but I still bought the stock."* My friend could have saved herself a lot of money if she had trusted her instincts. She knew the business and had checked out the merchandise. The analysts may not have done the same. People in an industry often have excellent knowledge and should not be nervous about using it in making investment decisions.

HOME TURF AS A CONSUMER

People shop in stores, stay in hotels, fly on airplanes, buy cars, and select long-distance phone companies. They watch TV with their children and visit the mall. Changes that occur first on Main Street often take a long time to be recognized on Wall Street. If you can figure out what you know about your home turf as a consumer, you have a big advantage over the professional investor.

THE PROS DON'T SHOP AT WAL-MART

Just remember, many of the country's professional investors live in New York City. They do not shop at Wal-Mart. There is no Wal-Mart in New York City. Besides, even if there were, how many Wall Street professionals would outfit their kids there? **The professionals in New York do not see things that are happening in mainstream America.** They vacation in the South of France or in Vail, not in the Florida Panhandle or in the Ozarks. They may not even know where the Ozarks are. How many do you think have ever been to Branson, Missouri, or Pigeon Forge, Tennessee, two of the five most popular tourist destinations in the United States?

Wall Street professionals may invest in companies that manufacture RVs, but they do not travel in them. They do not stay at Motel 6 on business trips or buy time-share condos. They eat at Lutece and the Four Seasons, not at Denny's or Pizza Hut. They go to the theater, not to the multiplex at the mall. Many may have never owned an American car, except for four-wheel drives. They shop in boutiques, not at Sears or JC Penney. They buy food in gourmet stores, not in Safeway. While the professionals know a lot about the companies they follow, they know less about average life than most Americans.

Because individuals tend to know a lot more about life in mainstream America than do most professionals on Wall Street, they have an advantage in making investments in businesses that they patronize on a regular basis. Just as guerrillas can perceive small changes in local turf more easily than can the troops of the invading army, so individual investors can perceive small changes at stores as they shop, at restaurants where they eat, and in the services they purchase. These small changes are critical, because they often lead to the changes in sales and earnings on which Wall Street depends.

You are a housewife with three children. You buy clothes at T.J. Maxx. You are struck by the fact that the bargains are much better than they were at this time last year. You bought twice as much this year at T.J. Maxx. So did your friends. As a customer, you can recognize that T.J. Maxx must be receiving better bargains. This is good for T.J. Maxx and bad for the companies that produced the clothes. It will take weeks for TJX, the parent of T.J.

Maxx, and the apparel companies that supply it to report sales and earnings, but your eyes can tell you when the stores have good inventory and when they do not. You can see which of the apparel companies are giving the biggest discounts. (If apparel companies are selling large amounts of merchandise to stores at big discounts, they are in trouble.) Because you shop in T.J. Maxx often, there is an excellent chance that you are seeing a trend first. Just remember, most investors and analysts do not shop at T.J. Maxx.

THE "KIM INDICATOR"

A smart portfolio manager once told me that he had an almost perfect method for trading TJX. He called it the "Kim Indicator." I had never heard of the "Kim Indicator," so I asked him how it worked. He pushed his intercom and yelled, *"Kim."* A young woman, about twenty-three years old, came into the room. She had big, bleached-blonde hair and more than ample makeup. *"Did you go to T.J. Maxx this weekend?"* the portfolio manager asked.

"Of caws," Kim replied in a thick New Jersey accent. *"They had great rags on the new racks. I bought a dress from Jones and an outfit from Liz Claiborne. That makes three weeks in a row I've found stuff I like."*

The portfolio manager picked up the phone. *"Buy 25,000 shares of TJX."* Then he turned to me. *"Investing in this company is simple,"* he said. *"Kim is their customer. She shops there every week. If she buys something three weeks in a row, I know that the merchandise is hot and the sales will be good. So I buy the stock. If she buys nothing for three weeks in a row, I know that the merchandise is cold and the sales will be bad, so I sell the stock. Kim is my perfect indicator. She is never wrong."*

As hokey as this story may seem, it gave this portfolio manager a perfect tool for deciding when to buy and sell the stock. He understood that a retailer is only as good as its merchandise. He lived in a penthouse on Fifth Avenue, so he had no clue to the merchandise. But he knew that Kim was T.J. Maxx's ideal customer. In six years, the "Kim Indicator" was right far more than it was wrong, and it had a much better batting average than any of the high-priced analysts on Wall Street. Anyone who is a regular customer of a store can judge the merchandise as easily as the combination of the portfolio manager and Kim. The business is not complicated. If you are buying a lot more than you did last year, business is probably good and earnings should follow suit. If you are buying a lot less, the business is probably weak and earnings should be disappointing.

Every store has its equivalent of Kim. These are the target customers it depends on for the bulk of its business. If you are one of the target customers, you can easily judge the nature of the business. Two years ago, Ann Taylor decided to change its focus. It broadened its product line and reduced its emphasis on its traditional tailored clothing. Its core customers were the first to notice the change, and few liked it. When a retailer seeks to change its focus, it usually turns off its core customers well before it attracts new customers. In the short term, this almost always results in lower sales and earnings. If you are a core customer of a store and you no longer see what you like, don't wait around to see how long it will take the analysts to discover that the store is in trouble. Ann Taylor's stock dropped from over $40 to under $10.

Even if you are not a store's core customer, find your own "Kim Indicator." There is a portfolio manager at Chancellor Capital Management named Marion Schultheis. Marion previously had been the premier retail analyst at American Express. When I would talk to her about certain fashion stocks, Marion would say, *"I'll have to check with Lisa."* Lisa was not another analyst. Lisa was Marion's teenage daughter. Marion did not rely on Lisa to pick stocks, but she did rely on Lisa's opinion as a customer. One day, she told me that Lisa and her friends had stopped shopping in a particular chain because the merchandise had turned stodgy. Marion convinced American Express to sell its stock in the chain. Within six months, the price had dropped in half. Marion had inputs from every analyst on Wall Street, but she understood that it was more important to get the opinion of a customer.

STUDY ADS AND SALE PRICES

There is more to retailing than just merchandise. Look at pricing. If all of the stores seem to be having fewer sales, the chances are good that the margins and the earnings will be higher than last year. Customers can always tell how well a store is run. Look at the circulars you receive in the Sunday newspaper. If two competitors are advertising the same product and one has a lower price, it is the better-run company. It is better run not because it is offering a lower price, but because the other company is foolish for advertising an item in which it is not price-competitive.

GOOD SERVICE EQUALS GOOD INVESTMENTS: CONSIDER HOME DEPOT

Many years ago, I went into a Home Depot in Arizona. An associate came up to me immediately and asked if I needed help. I said I wanted to put in some outside lighting. The associate told me what to buy and how to install it. Home Depot was running an advertising campaign, "Friendship Not Membership," because its competitor, Home Club, was a membership club. Then I went to Home Club. It took about ten minutes to find someone to help me. The clerk told me that I had to become a member before I bought anything. I mentioned Home Depot's advertising and asked what Home Club had to offer. *"We offer membership, not friendship!"* the clerk replied condescendingly. Guess where I decided to shop? It did not take a professional analyst to realize which of these companies was going to win.

I have a friend named Howard Perksy who is the president of a very successful computer consulting company. Howard loves to putter. He can spend hours in Home Depot on Saturday discussing home-improvement projects with other putterers. His wife Wilma used to always grumble about the amount of time he spent there while she cooled her heels outside. But then suddenly she stopped complaining and actually seemed happy to wait for him. One day I asked her about the change of heart. *"I bought a lot of Home Depot stock,"* Wilma replied. *"I figured if it could keep Howard entertained for an entire day, it must be some fantastic store. Now the stock is worth ten times what I paid for it, so Home Depot is paying for my new kitchen, bathroom, and swimming pool."* Like Howard's wife, anyone who bought the stock the first time she, or her husband, spent the day hanging out in the store would now be rich. It is much easier for a customer who is actually seeking help to understand and appreciate the level of service in a store than it is for an analyst who is reading financial statements.

CHECK THE LABEL FOR INVESTMENT IDEAS

Individuals can find good investment ideas from the products they purchase. You are a female Baby Boomer. When you started working twenty years ago, all your clothes had the same label, Liz Claiborne. When you bought the clothes or read stories about the company's great success, you may have often thought to yourself, *"I should have bought the stock."* If you had, your profits could have paid for all of your clothes.

The same process can apply to things that you are buying now for yourself or for your children. Your teenage sons only want to wear Tommy Hilfiger and Nautica. You take them to school. Everyone is wearing Tommy and Nautica. Is this a fad or a trend? If it is a fad, you will know when it ends, because your boys will want to wear something else. If it is a trend, the sales and earnings of these two companies will continue to surge. If you are shelling out money for a particular brand, think about buying the stock. Your judgment is likely to be right.

I remember when Snapple was first introduced. People cut back on sodas and coffees and started drinking Snapple. If I had put my money where my mouth was, I would have made lots of money when Snapple was taken over by Quaker Oats. Then the copycats started. While the financial analysts were raising earnings estimates, anyone who stood in the checkout line could have seen that people were buying less Snapple. The Snapple business turned into a black hole. Quaker Oats lost hundreds of millions of dollars, and the price of its stock was driven down. Most consumers did not need an analyst's degree to realize what was happening. They only had to look at their own shopping carts.

While everybody eats, the supermarket may yield fewer opportunities than one would imagine. Because most of the consumer goods companies are multinational, it is often very difficult to correlate things that you see on the supermarket shelf with changes in earnings or stock prices. With

Coke and Pepsi, the critical battlefields are now Beijing, Bombay, and Buenos Aires, not Boston, Buffalo, and Baltimore. Nonetheless, you can still find clear investment opportunities at the supermarket. Two years ago, a price war broke out among producers of cereal. Profits and stock prices went down. In 1997 the price war ended, and profits and stock prices went up. Anyone who bought cereal knew what was happening.

FIND INVESTMENT OPPORTUNITIES WHEN YOU EAT OUT

A restaurant chain is no better or worse than the quality of food and the level of service in each of its units. Restaurant chains are often difficult for analysts to follow because quality can change rapidly, and because, with low barriers to entry, there are always a large number of publicly owned companies. Bloomberg lists over 110 public companies that are wholly or significantly in the restaurant business. Excluding those selling for $3 or less, these include:

PUBLICLY OWNED RESTAURANT CHAINS

APPLE SOUTH	CONSOLIDATED	GARDEN FRESH	PICADILLY	SIZZLER
APPLEBEE'S	PRODUCTS	GARDENBURGER	CAFETERIAS	INTERNATIONAL
INTERNATIONAL	(Steak & Shake)	GB FOODS	PIZZA INN	SKYLINE CHILI
ARK RESTAURANTS	COOKER	(Green Burrito)	PJ AMERICA	SONIC CORP.
ARTHUR TREACHER'S	RESTAURANTS	HOST MARRIOT	PLANET	SPAGHETTI
AU BON PAIN	CRACKER BARREL	IHOP	HOLLYWOOD	WAREHOUSE
BACK BAY	DARDEN (Red	IL FORNAIO	QUALITY DINING	STAR BUFFET
BENIHANA	Lobster, Olive	J. ALEXANDERS	QUIZNO'S	STARBUCKS
BERTUCCI'S	Garden, Bahama	LANDRY'S SEAFOOD	RAINFOREST CAFE	TACO CABANA
BIG BUCK BREWERY	Breeze)	LOGAN'S	RALLY'S	TCBY
BLIMPIE	DAVCO	ROADHOUSE	HAMBURGERS	TIMBER LODGE
INTERNATIONAL	DAVE & BUSTER'S	LONE STAR	RARE HOSPITALITY	TOTAL
BOB EVANS FARMS	EATERIES	STEAKHOUSE	ROADHOUSE GRILL	ENTERTAINMENT
BOSTON CHICKEN	EINSTEIN/NOAH	LUBY'S CAFETERIAS	ROCK BOTTOM	TRICON GLOBAL
BRINKER	BAGEL	MAX & ERMA'S	REST.	(Pizza Hut,
INTERNATIONAL	ELEPHANT & CASTLE	MCDONALD'S	RUBY TUESDAY	Taco Bell, KFC)
BUFFETS	ELMER'S	MORRISON	RYAN'S FAMILY	UNIQUE CASUAL
CASA OLE	RESTAURANTS	MORTON'S	STEAK	RESTAURANTS
CHART HOUSE	ELXSI	NATHAN'S FAMOUS	SBARRO	WALL STREET DELI
CHEESECAKE	FAMOUS DAVE'S	NPC INTERNATIONAL	SCHLOTZSKY'S	WENDY'S
FACTORY	FOODMAKER (Jack in	OUTBACK	SHELLS SEAFOOD	INTERNATIONAL
CKE (Carl's Jr.)	the Box)	STEAKHOUSE	SHONEY'S	WSMP
	FRIENDLY ICE CREAM	PAPA JOHN'S	SHOWBIZ PIZZA	
	FRISCH'S		TIME (Chuck E.	
			Cheese)	

You probably eat in a number of these restaurants. If you like one of them, ask the manager to have the company send you financial information. The last two times I asked a restaurant manager for financial information, he not only sent it to me, but he also enclosed coupons for free dinners. If you like what you see after you get the financial information, eat in a few other branches of the chain. You want to make sure that the restaurant you eat in regularly is the rule, not the exception. Because you eat in these restaurants, you will be able to judge whether the service levels stay strong or deteriorate, which will give you a great advantage over most of the analysts.

INVEST IN THE SERVICES YOU USE

When cellular telephone service first started in the early 1980s, many of my friends bought the phones. One friend who was a doctor thought the cellular phone was the greatest invention of all time because it allowed him to play golf and still deal with his patients. He was so infatuated with cellular that he bought shares of every major participant in the industry. As cellular thrived and many of these companies were bought out, my friend made huge gains.

Look around your home. How many telephone lines do you have? How many did you have three years ago? Did you count your cellular phone and beeper? Think about the companies that are making the equipment and providing the services. Their names are on the products or on the bills. Rates may have come down, but you are probably spending more for phone service than you did before.

Think about the long-distance business. How many sales calls have you received in the past three years asking you to change long-distance carriers? Did each salesperson offer you a bigger discount? Did you wonder how all these companies could increase their profits if they were engaged in a price war? Your experience as a consumer would have served you well if it kept you away from AT&T. Despite the raging bull market, the price of AT&T dropped by more than one-third from the middle of 1993 through the middle of 1997. You don't need an earnings model to understand that it is difficult to increase profits during a price war.

IF YOUR KIDS LOVE IT, SO SHOULD YOU

Your children can be an excellent source of investment ideas. If you watch the fads they jump on, you should be able to make a substantial amount of money. I know many parents who bought stock in Disney a decade ago because their homes were filled with Disney movies and toys and their children loved Disney World and Disneyland. These parents may not have known Disney's p/e ratio, but they knew their kids loved the Disney characters. Few investments have ever worked out as well.

When my son was three, he and his friends became addicted to the Teenage Mutant Ninja Turtles. Every parent knew that Ninja Turtles were hot, and that any company making Ninja Turtle merchandise would do well. Yet while Wall Street was still focusing on the Ninja Turtles, my son and his friends suddenly changed their allegiance to the Mighty Morphin Power Rangers, relegating the Turtles to the closet. They were six months ahead of the investors and analysts on Wall Street. As fast as analysts may be to jump on a new fad, they are no match for a four-year-old.

Parents can beat Wall Street professionals on both the upside and the downside by listening to their small children. When Discovery Zone play centers opened, every child had to have his birthday party there, and the stock of Discovery Zone soared. Parents had a big advantage over the professionals on Wall Street, because initially there were no Discovery Zones in New York. A year later, Discovery Zone started to fade. Any parent who took kids there realized that many of the centers were poorly run. In addition, competing fun centers started to open, and restaurants such as McDonald's opened play areas. Finally, Discovery Zone went bankrupt. Almost any parent should have seen it coming. Many professional investors did not.

As your children get older, the things they buy and use can often lead you to excellent investment ideas, especially if they are into technology and you are not. Ten years ago, your children may have been the ones who convinced you to buy an Apple computer (as well as Apple stock). Four years ago, they switched to Windows. (Of course, you sold your Apple stock and bought Microsoft and Intel.) Your children also convinced you to order a computer from Dell over the phone, something you never would have done on your own. (Of course, you bought Dell stock as well.) It was your children who brought educational software into the house and told you about the Internet. It was your children who made you sign up with AOL, and buy its stock, instead of Prodigy, and it was your children who filled up your hard disk and made you upgrade your computer or buy a zip drive from Iomega.

Listen to what your children have to say about technology, and see if there are investment implications. When they talked about search engines, did you think they were babbling about missing trains, or did you stop and look at the new technology? When they told you they needed a new high-speed modem to get on the hot websites, did you buy it for them? You probably did. But did you ask if the maker of the modems was a public company and if you could profit from the upgrading of everyone's computer? You probably did not. Your children can often be your technology analysts.

Children are on the cutting edge of most trends. Think about sports. You ski, but they snowboard. You jog, but they blade. They want a fat-tire mountain bike so that they can ride off-road. Most of the time when there is a new trend, there is a company that profits from it. Watch how your children spend your money and look for investment implications. Your kids can often enable you to be well ahead of most professional investors.

IF YOU NEED IT, SO DOES YOUR PORTFOLIO

Individuals can find good investment ideas as they reach middle age and start to plan for their retirement. You are fifty. Your kids are in college. Your primary concerns are to build equity for your retirement and to secure enough insurance so that you do not have to worry about catastrophic problems. Every Baby Boomer you know is in the same position. If you believe Baby Boomers are going to keep saving for retirement, then buy stock in the mutual fund companies that are managing your money and in the brokerage firms that handle your accounts. And if you believe that Baby Boomers are going to keep buying insurance, then buy stock in the insurance company you use. Because you are older, you look at life differently than a young analyst does, but because many people are getting older, your view of what's hot may turn out to be correct.

IF RETIREES WANT IT, INVEST IN IT

In many ways, retirees are more on the cutting edge of future trends than younger people. The population is aging. No segment is growing as fast as retired people. The trend will only accelerate. Within fifteen years, masses of Baby Boomers will retire. You can use the experiences of people who are retiring now to discover some of the best investment opportunities for the next several decades.

Your parents have just retired. They no longer buy work clothes or commute every day. They have more leisure time. Your father takes up golf. He buys Big Bertha woods, special irons, and new golf clothes. Your mother takes up gardening, crafts, and reading. Companies produce and sell these products. Your parents spend their winters in Florida or Arizona. You think about what these markets will be like when tens of millions of Baby Boomers begin to retire. Local home builders, land developers, real estate investment trusts, banks, hospitals, service providers, and other companies in these markets will benefit from the influx of retirees.

You watch health issues begin to crop up for your parents and their friends. They are taking more drugs, perhaps including some of the new biotech medicines. While analysts know a lot about a company, no one should know more about an experimental drug than patients or their immediate families. The analysts are earning a living, but for the family it may be a question of life or death. If a new drug begins to work, look at the stock of the company that produces it. You can see the success of the product firsthand.

Older people also visit the hospital and the doctor more often. You might be impressed with the hospital, HMO, or nursing home they use.

You might find one with a strategy you believe is unique. Further, if you are dealing with it on a daily basis, you will have a reasonably good perspective on the quality of its management. Many companies in these industries are public, and many are growing rapidly. Some, however, are having problems with reimbursing patients and doctors. If your HMO is not paying you on time, it is in trouble.

Illness can lead to other investment opportunities. When my father became ill, he had to be confined to a wheelchair. I investigated the market and found that one company, Invacare, made the best products. I had remembered wheelchairs as old, clunky products, but new state-of-the-art materials had made them much lighter and more mobile. As I watched Invacare making moves to dominate the market, I decided to buy the stock. I was sure that wheelchairs would be a growth industry for an aging population.

Individuals should use their experience as consumers to find investment ideas, but they should make sure that the information is significant to the company's fortunes. You should not sell stock in an oil company just because the attendant in your service station did not wash your windows. Nor should you sell stock in Intel and Microsoft just because your computer crashes, or in the Tribune Corp. because the Chicago Cubs missed the playoffs. (By that logic, no one would ever own stock in the Tribune Corp.) Nonetheless, the type of information the consumer obtains is critical to understanding the quality of the company and the potential of its product.

HOME TURF FROM YOUR COMMUNITY

A person's community often yields tidbits of information that give the individual a significant edge in investing against Wall Street professionals. A community is the town in which someone lives, but it's also the collection of social circles in which the individual interacts. Clubs, churches, schools, and friends are all part of an individual's community. As people read the local newspaper, attend parties, or chat with former schoolmates, they constantly come in contact with information about public companies.

Most of the time, people ignore this information as being of little value. This is a mistake.

The most obvious source of information in your community can come from a direct personal relationship with a senior executive of a public company. CEOs, CFOs, and other senior executives belong to clubs and civic organizations, participate in sports, have children, and are often extremely visible in a community. If you are friendly with a senior executive of a company, you have an advantage that most analysts would kill for. Don't be shy about utilizing it. The analysts would utilize it if they had the contact.

You are in a bridge game with the president of the local chain of funeral homes. Two weeks in a row, he misses the game. You call his office to see if he is all right. His secretary tells you that he is away on business in a particular city. You know that the largest national funeral home operator is in that city and that it has been buying up regional chains. Is an acquisition of your friend's company in the works? Perhaps. When he comes back, you ask him, but he tells you that he cannot comment on it. This is your friend. You have played bridge with him for ten years. If nothing was going on, he would have told you. You think that his chain could be an acquisition target. You will never get perfect inside information. That would be illegal. But you can make a guess. If your guess is that there will be a deal, take a chance and buy the stock. In the same position, virtually every professional on Wall Street would. The only difference is that most professionals do not play bridge with your friend.

Many people live in small cities which are home to a few prominent public companies. The "feel" that individuals have for local public companies often gives them an edge over the professionals on Wall Street, especially if the company is in a small or medium-sized city that is somewhat distant from the major financial centers. In fact, the farther your city is from the major financial centers, the greater the likelihood that you can find an edge in picking good local companies.

People in these communities tend to see emerging companies first. They often know the management, either directly or by reputation. They learn about the strategy of the company from stories in the local media, and they hear the "buzz" about the company from friends who work there. Most analysts and investors, without direct contact, want to wait until the sales and earnings come through, but people with local knowledge can often make a bet based on their direct perspective of the company and its management.

Arkansas. The people in Arkansas discovered Wal-Mart well before analysts on Wall Street, not just because they shopped in the stores, but also because they knew people who worked at the company. These people knew that Sam Walton was a genius, and that should have been enough for any investor.

Seattle. The people in Seattle discovered Nordstrom well before anyone else. Nordstrom's service was legendary. Anyone who shopped there had stories about the quality of the service. The people in Seattle also discovered Microsoft before the rest of the country. A decade ago, everyone I knew from Seattle talked with reverence about Bill Gates and his company. They all owned stock in Microsoft, too.

Omaha. The same may be said for the people of Omaha regarding Warren Buffett. Before Buffett became a major international investment seer, he was just another local businessman. But the people in Omaha knew he was something special, and they invested in Berkshire Hathaway.

Oregon. The entire state of Oregon is a paradise for runners. Fifteen years ago, my nephew, Sam Helphand, who was then a little boy, told me that he wanted to buy stock in Nike. To me, Nike was just another sneaker, but to my nephew, it was a local religion. Sam may have been just a kid, but, living in Oregon, he knew a great company when he saw one.

Silicon Valley. I have a good friend from the Bay area. He is a professor of economics and one of the least computer-literate people I know. Yet in the past decade, he has built a great investment record in technology stocks. His philosophy is simple. When he socializes with people in technology, he listens closely to all of the gossip. When someone starts to talk about a new startup, he always asks, *"How smart is the management?"* Whenever his techie friends tell him that the management is the smartest in its particular niche, he buys the stock. Sometimes he will call me and ask what the company does. I look in my database and read him the company's mission statement and some excerpts from analysts' reports. Most of the time, his interest level fades quickly. He never really wants to know what the company does or what it is expected to earn. He is not trying to analyze the technology himself. Instead, he is betting on the advice of his colleagues, who do know technology.

The professor is lucky to live in Silicon Valley, because this area has been the spawning ground for many of the most successful technology companies in the world. But every region of the country has been the spawning ground for some type of industry. There are clusters of technology companies around Seattle, Salt Lake City, Boston, Austin, and the Research Triangle of North Carolina. There are entertainment companies in Los Angeles, furniture companies in North Carolina, automobile companies in Michigan, petroleum companies in Texas and Oklahoma, agricultural companies in the farm belt, and government contractors near Washington, D.C. Many people who live in these areas have some knowledge of these industries, and most have friends who know about specific companies. People in these regions often learn about the companies before most professional investors. The trick for individuals is to recognize the value of the information they receive from their local communities.

THE INTERNET COMPLETES THE HOME-TURF ADVANTAGE

Many individuals think that the information they obtain on their home turf is not as valuable as that obtained by professional investors. Professionals obtain hard inputs, such as earnings announcements and annual and quarterly reports from the company; research reports, earnings estimates, and First Call notes from analysts; and charts from technicians. Individual investors receive soft inputs, such as gossip at an industry trade show or the experience of eating in a restaurant. Of the two, the hard inputs would appear to be the more valuable and difficult to duplicate. But this may not be the case.

With the emergence of the Internet, business television, and other forms of communication, individual investors can receive much of the hard data available to the professionals on a relatively timely basis. On the other hand, the professionals cannot receive the firsthand experience of the individual, unless they actually live it. The Internet can provide the individual with the earnings statement from Wal-Mart, but no equivalent tool can provide the professional with the experience of actually shopping in the stores. **The Internet gives the individual the hard data on which the professional has depended, but it doesn't give the professional the soft data which the individual has available.** The task for the individual is to combine the soft inputs from home turf with the hard data available on the Internet to gain a more complete financial picture of the company in question.

CHAT ROOMS AND MESSAGE BOARDS

One of the major advantages professionals have is their community of other investors. They spend much of their day trading thoughts with each other. If professionals know each other well and have the same investing style, they will often give each other advice. But primarily, they use other professionals as sounding boards to test out new ideas. Some even try to find an investor with a different style who can be a devil's advocate. Few professionals are secure enough in their own knowledge to go it completely alone.

With the exception of investment clubs, individuals have never had these opportunities. Now, chat rooms and message boards put them in a community of other investors with whom they can exchange ideas. A chat room is a live venue in which investors can exchange ideas. A message board is a location at which investors can post comments on particular stocks. If you use the Internet regularly, you've probably seen both chat rooms and message boards. If you are brand-new at the on-line investing game, start with the message boards. They are simpler to use because they are organized by stock. If you do not have a favorite financial website, start with the message board at your search engine. For example, if you click on a stock quote on Yahoo, you will see a list of choices, including charts, profile, news, and messages. Click on messages. It will lead you to a list of all the messages posted on a particular stock.

The number of messages per stock will vary dramatically. The table below shows the number of messages posted on Yahoo from November 26, 1997, through January 15, 1998, on a selected number of stocks. It is quickly apparent that people who chat want to talk about fast-growing tech stocks, like Compaq, Intel, and Microsoft, or about recent disasters, like Oxford Health Plans and Rainforest Café, rather than about more stodgy stocks. Many of the largest and most actively traded stocks received very few postings. While a site with too few postings has no information, a site with too many often becomes cluttered with garbage.

MESSAGES ON YAHOO

STOCK	MESSAGES	STOCK	MESSAGES	STOCK	MESSAGES
Compaq	4509	Rainforest Café	541	Mobil Oil	69
Intel	2890	IBM	237	General Motors	57
Microsoft	1553	Merck	231	Bristol Myers	53
Iomega	1440	Coca-Cola	189	Chrysler	45
Dell	962	General Electric	169	J.P. Morgan	22
Netscape	905	Wal-Mart	152	Allstate	16
Yahoo	835	Pepsico	142	TJX	8
Oxford Health	614	McDonald's	133	Cigna	4
Micron	572	Hewlett Packard	87	May	3

Look through the list. Check out a few of the postings. See if they are of any interest to you. Post a question of your own. See if you get a helpful reply. If you find the message boards interesting, look at the boards when you go to other financial sites, such as Motley Fool.

As you are navigating around the Web, you will probably bump into a live chat room. Go in and take a look at the conversation. You can register with most of these sites and participate for no cost. While message boards are best for obtaining information on particular stocks, chat rooms are best for trading stock ideas, especially with people who have a similar investing style. Chat rooms take up a lot of time, and you may not find one in which you are comfortable. Don't worry if you do not find them useful. Chat rooms may be fun, but they are not essential for success in the stock market.

In early January 1998, I decided to go to the message board at Yahoo and see what people were saying about Rainforest Café. It is a theme restaurant that had reported weaker-than-expected sales and earnings. The stock, which had gone from $18 to $38, had dropped back to $17.

Most of the Rainforest postings were about how each investor thought the stock would perform. Before the stock dropped, one investor ventured that Rainforest would go to $100, while another guaranteed that it would not drop below $30. (Boy, were they wrong!) When the stock broke down, everyone had an opinion. Some thought it would go to $10. Others thought it would bounce back up. Some chatters told people to buy. Others told people to sell short.

Taking financial advice from someone in a chat room is dangerous. You do not know who they are. (I suspect that the George Soros on the Yahoo message board might not be the real George Soros.) You do not know if they have a financial ax to grind. For all you know, the person saying bad things about Rainforest Café may have just gotten fired from the company or may work for Planet Hollywood. Further, you do not know their investment style. It is foolhardy to ask someone what the price of a stock is going to do. If they knew, they would not be in a chat room.

As the Rainforest stock kept dropping, the messages got nastier. About one-third of the messages were chat-room participants attacking each other, some even using four-letter words as they took out their frustrations on the bulls or the bears. Engaging in or reading these types of discussions is a waste of your time. If investors are so mad that they are swearing at each other, it is unlikely they will be rational enough to communicate good information. (One enterprising investor, however, was trying to make time with another.)

Nonetheless, some of the information on the message board was useful. Investors compared notes about eating in the Rainforest restaurants. They informed each other about newspaper articles and about appearances of the management on CNBC. They clarified confusion about a coming stock split and about earnings-related issues. They discussed the pending lawsuits against the company, and they also presented excellent details on insider selling and management changes.

Your objective in entering one of the many chat rooms or message boards for investors should not be to find some new, exotic stock idea in which you can invest, nor should it be to ask for investment advice from some anonymous "expert," even if he calls himself George Soros. Instead, your objective should be to better understand some company in which you already have a home-turf advantage. If you are interested in a bank, ask if anyone knows how banks value other banks in takeovers. If you are confused about a subject, such as a stock split or the difference between primary and fully diluted earnings, ask about it.

The Internet can thus fill in many of the blanks for an individual with some home-turf knowledge. Through the Web, the individual can obtain earnings estimates, reports, financial statements, and other types of hard data that the professionals utilize. Through the chat rooms, the individual can test ideas with other investors, much as the professionals do. If guerrilla investors combine the hard data and chat from the Web with information from their home turf, they have an excellent chance of defeating the professionals.

CHAPTER FIVE

Attack the Enemy's Weaknesses

Any enemy, no matter how strong, has a weakness. In fact, size itself can be a disadvantage. Like a modern army, Wall Street professionals can bring a huge amount of weapons to bear against an individual. If power is matched directly against power, the individual has no chance. But the very size of the professionals can be a liability; their hugeness makes it more difficult for them to change directions quickly or disguise their actions. Just as the guerrilla warrier can capitalize on the lack of mobility of a mechanized army by attacking quickly and then retreating into the jungle, so the guerrilla investor can capitalize on the lack of mobility of the professional by finding those areas in which the professionals' size and strength actually work against them. There are five strategies for taking advantage of the enemy's size that the individual investor should consider:

- Buy smaller capitalization and under-followed stocks.
- Buy and hold.
- Act before the professionals can change direction.
- Capitalize on the professionals' need for short-term performance.
- Allow the professionals to overextend themselves, then counter-attack.

BUY SMALLER CAPITALIZATION AND UNDER-FOLLOWED STOCKS

If the mechanized army has an advantage on the open plain, the guerrilla has an advantage in more narrow terrain. The same applies in investing. If institutions are at a big advantage in buying and trading bigger stocks, they are often at a corresponding disadvantage in buying and trading smaller stocks. This disadvantage works to the benefit of the individual.

Too Small for the Big Guys

Despite the excellent potential of many small stocks, most institutions cannot be bothered with them. A money manager can only buy 4.9 percent of a company's stock before having to file documents with the Securities and Exchange Commission. If the holdings go over 10 percent, the SEC restricts the manager's ability to buy and sell. So, as a rule, managers very rarely buy more than 10 percent of a company. Look at the list of the top-rated stocks on page 127. One of the companies rated 1.0 in 1996 was Sirena Apparel, a maker of bathing suits. Sirena is currently selling for $3 and has about 4.6 million shares outstanding. In other words, its total market capitalization is $13.8 million. If a money manager bought 5 percent of Sirena, the investment would be only $690,000. While this might seem like a lot of money to you, it is nothing to a professional.

Investment advisors own varying numbers of stocks, but an advisor managing a $5 billion fund (less than one-tenth the size of Fidelity Magellan) would rarely own more than 200 different stocks. With 200 stocks in a fund of $5 billion, the average position would be $25 million. If that advisor bought 5 percent of Sirena, the $690,000 would represent about one-hundredth of 1 percent of the portfolio. **The advisor would have to own 7,246 stocks of similar size to fill a portfolio of $5 billion.**

It is almost impossible for any portfolio manager to keep track of that many stocks. As a result, many of the larger funds avoid smaller stocks.

Some have minimum cap sizes as high as $2 billion. Others have minimums of $1 billion. By the time you get down to a company with a market capitalization of $200 million, the number of institutions that can invest in it is far more limited. At $200 million, a 5 percent position is only $10 million. For the Magellan Fund, this represents 1/5,000 of the portfolio. Even for someone managing $5 billion, it only represents 1/500 of the portfolio.

If a stock with a $200-million market capitalization is too small for most money managers, how do you think they will react when an analyst calls about a stock with a $13.8-million market cap? They may laugh, hang up, or yell at the analyst for wasting their time with a stock that is too small to own. Despite the high ratings, most managers can never consider buying a stock this small. (Unless it was a really great idea. Then they might buy it for their own personal portfolio.)

Even if a portfolio manager could invest in smaller stocks, it is extremely difficult to trade them. Just as a mechanized army cannot move en masse through a jungle, so a professional cannot quickly move large sums in or out of a small, illiquid stock. Smaller companies tend to be less well followed, so institutions lose some of their advantages in terms of information. The stock of smaller companies is also more difficult to trade in institutional quantities, making size a detriment.

Two final factors also benefit the individual investor in small-cap stocks. If the company does not have listed options, professional investors cannot utilize some of the sophisticated options games that give them an advantage over the individual. In addition, if the stock is not in a major index, many investors cannot buy it. Some institutions have a charter that requires them to buy only stocks that are in a particular index, such as the Dow Jones or the S&P 100. If institutions are blocked from buying a stock, either by choice or by charter, the competition for that stock is much less, and the opportunities for the individual investor are much greater.

THIS REQUIRES PATIENCE

While individual investors should trade smaller capitalization stocks, these stocks do have one significant problem. Because they are small, they often do not move as quickly as many investors would like. If the market is being driven by major institutions buying large-cap stocks, these smaller stocks may be temporarily left in the dust. But trends in the market do not continue forever. If sales and earnings are strong, investors will eventually turn to smaller stocks that offer more upside and less downside. All the investor needs is a little patience.

Investors may not like being patient, but it is a small price to pay for being able to gain an advantage over the professionals. In many of these small companies, the individual can gain a home-turf advantage by having direct experience with the company, while the normal advantages of the professional are nullified. With these small stocks, the power balance swings from the professional to the individual. Given the disadvantages that the individual faces in buying larger stocks, these smaller stocks present a huge opportunity for discovering bargains in small-cap companies and outperforming the market.

WHY THE PROS IGNORE BURLINGTON COAT

Burlington Coat Factory (BCF), an operator of off-price stores, is not a small company. In fiscal 1996, BCF had sales of over $1.6 billion and a net worth of $413 million. It also has almost fifty million shares outstanding. But at the end of 1996, there were no major analysts following Burlington. When no analysts follow a company, there are no earnings estimates or guidelines that investors can use to judge whether the company is doing better or worse than expected. There is also no one promoting the stock. Institutional investors are extremely busy keeping abreast of the stocks they own and listening to analysts and salespersons. If no one is posting First Call notes on a company, many institutional investors forget that it exists. In fact, when Burlington reported shockingly good sales for its Christmas 1996 quarter, the stock barely moved because no one cared. In the next six months, it doubled, and still no one cared.

Why does a company like Burlington Coat Factory have no analyst coverage? There are four reasons:

Burlington does not have investment banking business.

The company has very strong cash flow, so it does not need to do offerings to raise cash. Nor does it need investment bankers for acquisitions. Without the possibility of investment banking revenues, brokerage firms have no major incentive for following it.

Burlington has low trading volume. Burlington is very closely held, with 56 percent of the shares owned by officers and directors. As a result, it does not trade very much. For all of 1995, Burlington Coat traded 23.4 million shares for a total of $192 million. In one year, Burlington Coat had a dollar trading volume equal to what General Electric did in an average day. At these levels, the brokerage commissions are not sufficient to support the cost of analyst coverage.

Burlington had disappointed investors in the previous two years. Analysts hate to follow small companies that have disappointed them, so several dropped coverage.

Burlington has never done a good job communicating with investors and analysts. It rarely had conference calls, did not report monthly sales, and did not provide analysts with a wealth of data. Analysts like to be spoon-fed and do not like companies in which getting information is like pulling teeth.

Low trading volume not only discourages analysts from covering the company, it also makes it much more difficult for the institutions to trade the stock. With Burlington's small float, it could take a major institution months to establish a two-million-share position, and when that position was finally acquired, it would still represent only $18 million, based on the price at the end of 1996. Many institutions need to put five to ten times that much money to work in each stock they buy.

As difficult as it is to build such a position, liquidating it can be even harder. Suppose you owned two million shares of Burlington Coat and decided to sell. If the stock only traded 95,000 shares a day, it would take you a month to liquidate the position, and during that month, the constant selling would probably push down the price. In such a situation, the best hope for the manager is to find another institution that wants to build a position in Burlington Coat, but without analyst sponsorship, it is difficult to interest another institution in buying.

If the company reported unexpected bad news, your only choices would be to dump the stock for an extremely low price and thank God that you only own a few illiquid stocks or to sit tight and hope that business eventually gets better. Because of size, the institutional investor is often locked in while the individual investor is not. An individual can almost always find another individual to buy 1,000 shares of stock, but the institution may have to wait months for another institution to step up and buy. In a stock with a limited float, the small trading volume almost always benefits the small investor at the expense of the large institution.

The small float and lack of analyst coverage combined to put Burlington Coat below the radar screen for institutional investors, but they should not have been negatives for individual investors.

Here's a summary of company characteristics that are positives for individual investors:

- While brokerage firms like companies that want to raise money, individuals should like companies with low levels of debt and high free cash flow.
- High levels of insider ownership should be a strong positive for individual investors. If insiders own 56 percent of the shares, you can be certain that they are keenly interested in maximizing shareholder value. Their ownership perspective may be much more long term than that of most professionals, but this should be a positive, not a negative, for the individual investor.
- The small float, which discourages institutions, creates opportunities for individuals, who now actually gain an advantage in trading.
- When analysts walk away from stocks, individuals are much better off because they can study these companies

without being concerned about analysts suddenly changing their estimates.

- When companies do a poor job of communicating, it is the professionals, not the individuals, who are disadvantaged. Individuals do not usually keep track of monthly sales or get on conference calls anyway. Individuals continue to obtain home-turf inputs while the institutions are shut out. **Never confuse the analyst's frustrated desire for information with the health of the company, especially if management continues to buy stock.**

OTHER STOCKS PROFESSIONALS IGNORE

You should never jump on a stock merely because no analyst covers it. However, just as individuals have a clear advantage in smaller stocks, they also have an advantage in larger companies that are under-followed, as we saw with Burlington Coat. The fewer the analysts who follow a company, the lower the flow of information to the institutions. Some companies may not be well followed merely because they do not fit into neat industry groups.

Most analysts cover specific industries. Retail analysts cover retailers. Oil analysts cover oil companies. Analysts are rated against their peers in an industry. Substantial dollars are involved for those elected to the All-American Team. So analysts want to focus all their energy on one narrow segment. Few want to waste their time following a company that is outside their industry. To do so would hurt their compensation. As a result, most companies in well-followed industries have ample analyst coverage. (Burlington Coat Factory, for the reasons cited above, is an exception.) But many companies that are not in major industries fall through the cracks.

Harman International is a world-class maker of loudspeakers and sound systems (JBL, Infinity, and Harman Kardon, among others). Because there are no other major publicly owned consumer electronics companies in the United States, Harman had almost no coverage for many years. The same situation applies to Oneida, the largest publicly held maker of silverware.

Larger companies can have limited coverage if they bridge industries in a manner that makes it difficult for analysts to follow them. HSN Inc. (formerly Home Shopping Network) is a billion-dollar company, but it has been covered by very few analysts. Its problem is that it is part retailer and part broadcaster. Retail analysts do not want to cover it because it is a broadcaster, and media analysts do not want to cover it because it is a retailer.

Valmont Industries is one of the two world leaders in the irrigation business and one of the top manufacturers of street lamps and towers used for wireless communications. Both irrigation and wireless communications would appear to be great businesses for the future, and Valmont has an excellent record. Yet Valmont also has almost no analyst coverage. In fact, during a six-month period in 1997, there was not even a First Call note on Valmont.

Much the same happens with conglomerates. When Sears owned Allstate, Dean Witter, Discover Card, Prodigy, and Homart, it was under covered, even though it was a Dow component. In order to follow Sears, an analyst had to understand the retailing, insurance, stock brokerage, credit card, real estate, and on-line industries. Now that these businesses have all been sold or spun off, Sears is more well covered, and so are Allstate and Dean Witter (now Morgan Stanley Dean Witter).

No matter what the reason, companies that are poorly followed often offer good opportunities for individual investors. With a lack of analyst coverage, the professional no longer has substantial advantages in terms of information, and sometimes may even walk away from these stocks. If the professional doesn't compete in these stocks, the individual has a much better chance of winning.

There are many ways to find out how many analysts cover a company. Most of the financial sites on the Web will give you a list of the number of analysts following a particular stock and the analysts' current ratings. Some, such as Zacks.com, will allow you to screen for various categories of stocks, such as stocks with high or low analyst following. But you should not be on a treasure hunt for the world's most hidden companies. Instead, you should focus on companies that you find on your home turf. If one of these companies has limited analyst coverage, this will be an advantage for you.

BUY AND HOLD

If a mechanized army has an advantage in maneuvering on the battle-field, the guerrilla may have an advantage biding his time and allowing the enemy to make a mistake. The same situation applies in investing. **If the professionals have an advantage over the individual in trading, the individual may actually have an advantage over the professional in *not* trading.** This does not mean that all individuals should hold stocks forever, but it does mean that individuals should resist the temptation to over-trade.

THE PRESSURE TO TRADE

Professionals feel tremendous pressure to trade stocks. Salespersons and analysts are paid to make trades, not to hold hands. They do not get paid more if the stocks go up and less if they go down. Their only interest is to make the customer take some action. How often has a broker called to say, "*I love your portfolio. Don't do anything!*"

Institutional investors are bombarded with calls from analysts and sales-people. Salespeople are usually pretty good at persuading people. That is why they are salespeople. Companies also give impressive presentations. It is hard to have lunch with the CEO of a multibillion-dollar corporation and not be tempted to buy the stock. The individual faces little of this. His or her broker may push trades, but if the investor does not respond, the broker will stop calling, and on-line brokers do not call. Since the individual has no great advantage in terms of trading, this may be a hidden benefit. While standing pat is not as much fun as making trades, it can be more profitable.

TRADING STOCKS CAN HURT PERFORMANCE

The pressure to trade stocks does not necessarily improve performance. Think for a minute about the process of trading. Every time a stock is traded, there is a buyer and a seller. Only one will be right. But most trades involve institutional investors. When a 100,000-share block hits the tape, both the buyer and the seller are probably large institutions. Both are staffed by highly paid and respected professionals, and one of them will be wrong. However, once the cost of trading the stocks is taken into account, the net impact for every trade is that the two institutions will, in sum, end up behind. It is difficult to tell a portfolio manager who is struggling to overtake a competitor that trading will reduce his overall return.

Sometimes, institutions buy and sell stocks because their view of the market changes. One fund buys technology and sells drugs, while the other fund buys drugs and sells technology. (Given the recent performance of technology stocks, the portfolio manager who bought them would probably also have to buy drugs—tranquilizers, for instance.) Sometimes professionals buy and sell stocks because they think that one will give them a better return than the other. One buys General Motors and sells Ford, while another buys Ford and sells General Motors. (Although they both probably drive Mercedes.) One may be right and the other wrong, but the market as a whole will not change.

If both stocks move by the same amount, both managers will have been wrong. The only one that will have profited is the brokerage firm that handled the trade. There is a cost to trading. For the institution, it may not be significant. Institutions pay only about $.05 per share in commissions when they trade. If they bought and sold Ford and General Motors every year for ten years, the total cost for both stocks would be $1.00 per share. At an average stock price of $40 per share, this is only 2 ½ percent. While this is not enough to discourage a manager from making a trade, it still could end up being the difference between outperforming or underperforming the market.

For the individual, the economics of buying and holding can be more compelling. If the individual trades on the Internet, the costs are similar to or even lower than those of the professional. Given the current pricing offered by some Internet brokers, individuals may actually pay less than $.01 per share. But if the individual trades through a traditional brokerage firm, as most currently do, the commissions will be much higher. At $.25 per share, the cost of trading Ford and General Motors each year for ten years will be 12 $^1/_2$ percent of the stock price. Individuals must also pay capital gains taxes if they have a profit. Had they not made the trade, they would have had no transaction costs or tax liabilities, and everyone, except the government, would have been ahead of the game.

WHAT'S YOUR TRADING RECORD?

Make a list of the last thirty trades you have made. In a bull market, most of the stocks you bought probably went up, but what about the stocks you sold? Compare the returns of the stocks you bought with those you sold. Did the stocks you bought do better? In many cases, the answer for the individual, as for the professional, is no.

Now assume that you had not made any trades and as a result, had not paid any taxes. Is your current investment position better than it would have been if you had avoided trading? Don't be distressed if the answer is, again, no. **With taxes and trading costs, more than half of all investors would have been better off not making trades.** This is not to say that you should buy stocks and hold them forever, but it is to say that most investors hurt themselves by over-trading. If you would have been better off making no trades, think carefully before swapping one stock for another in the future.

Thus, the individual can compete on a level playing field against the professional by buying good companies at attractive prices and then holding them. While it is difficult to sit there and watch stocks go up and down without doing anything, you should remember that as the stocks trade, half of the professionals are wrong. Because you do not face the same short-term performance pressure as the professional, buy and hold is a strategy that can and will work.

ACT BEFORE THE PROFESSIONALS CAN CHANGE DIRECTION

At many times, the guerrilla needs patience to outwait a more powerful enemy. At other times, he needs to be able to act quickly when the enemy begins to change direction. A large, mechanized army cannot change directions quickly. Because of its size, an army gives off unmistakable signals when it is moving. If the guerrilla watches the signals, he can use his smaller size to act before the army has completed its move.

Professional investors give off the same types of signals when they are getting ready to change directions. While the individual investor should tend toward a buy and hold strategy, that investor must also be ready to act when professionals telegraph major changes in direction. While this may seem like a contradiction, it is not. For the most part, individuals are better off buying and holding. But if they watch the actions of the pros, they can often spot major moves before they occur, and in so doing, find better times to buy and sell.

If a stock has been moving up with heavy volume, it will usually continue to move up. The buying might get weaker or stronger, but the direction will not change. Major institutions do not instantly go from aggressive buyers to aggressive sellers, unless there is a sudden event that entraps everyone. But when a stock is getting ready to change directions, there are very often signs of the coming change. These signs occur because institutions cannot quickly change directions.

Many people think that stocks change directions when major events are announced, but most major changes are foreshadowed in the action of the stocks. Look at stocks that get clobbered on a particular day. Most had already been heading down. In the three months before it announced its disaster, Oxford Health Plans had already declined from $89 to $68\,3/4, while in the weeks before its plunge, Rainforest Café had dropped from $38 to $29. In both cases, the market had foreshadowed that something bad was going to happen. Look at stocks that suddenly jump up. Most had already been moving to new highs. Once again, the market had foreshadowed the move. The reason that the market foreshadows the future direction of individual stocks is that the very size of the professionals makes it difficult for them to change directions quickly. Because the professionals have to move cautiously, tops and bottoms of markets and stocks are usually well defined.

Institutions have to act carefully when they move in or out of a stock.

Think about the portfolio managers who own more than ten million shares of General Electric. Even though G.E. has great liquidity, it is difficult to sell this large a block without disrupting the market. The portfolio manager has two choices: dump the stock at a discount or parcel it out carefully so as not to disrupt the market. Most portfolio managers will choose the latter alternative so they won't incur a big loss.

When a portfolio manager starts to parcel out a major block of stock that has been going up, most investors can easily spot the trading. Volume will increase as the stock plateaus and begins to drop. If the institution owns more than 5 percent of the stock in a company, it will have to file a record of its sale. This filing may trigger other selling, since most investors will believe that the institution will further reduce its holdings. The institution, however, must sell carefully because it doesn't want to trigger widespread selling of the stock. The institution hopes to maintain an orderly market by selling small parcels at a time. If individual investors see selling pressure accelerate, they can often move faster than institutions in selling their stocks.

WHEN BUFFETT MOVES . . .

The problem for the professional, and the opportunity for the individual, grows if the institution owns a huge stake and is a famous investor. At the time of the last filing, Warren Buffett owned 200 million shares of Coca-Cola. When investors saw Buffett building a position, they bid up the price of Coke, under the assumption that Buffett was usually right. But if Buffett's buying caused the price of Coke to go up, his selling would clearly cause the price of the stock to go down. You cannot move 200 million shares without attracting some notice.

This is exactly what happened on August 21, 1997, with another of Buffett's holdings, Wells Fargo. On that day, the price of the bank closed down $7.50 on fears that Buffett had reduced his holdings. In fact, Buffett had not reduced his holdings. Instead, he had received permission to have "partial" confidentiality, which meant that he could keep some holdings from public view for up to fifteen months. When investors looked at his filings and saw no mention of Wells Fargo, they panicked and shaved $1.3 billion from its market value within one hour. It was a billion-dollar misunderstanding. Imagine how the market would have reacted if Buffett really had sold his stake.

ANALYSTS TELEGRAPH THEIR ACTIONS

Like portfolio managers, analysts also have to move carefully. Even if analysts discover new information that radically alters their view of the company, they usually cannot change from a Buy recommendation to a Sell overnight, primarily because of concern about the reactions of their customers. How would a money manager feel if he had bought one million shares of a stock on Monday at $31 based on an analyst's Buy recommendation, then received a call on Tuesday from the same analyst saying that business was "softer than plan" and he should sell the stock at $28? The money manager would probably slam down the phone, curse, and perhaps even instruct his trading desk to stop doing business with the analyst's firm. Because analysts do not like to lose major accounts, they usually carefully telegraph their actions so that their clients do not get blindsided. For instance, they may spoon-feed clients by maintaining their Buy recommendation but slightly lowering their earnings estimate on a company. When this occurs, the small investor who is paying attention can use his or her advantage of speed.

The actions of the institutions in building or liquidating positions are delineated in the charts of stocks. If investors utilize the charts, they will be able to see when major institutions are preparing to change direction. In Chapter 7, we'll be looking closely at how to use the stock charts you can find on the Internet to anticipate the actions of the professionals.

The individual can thus exploit the professionals' size by capitalizing on their inability to change directions quickly. Watch the charts for clear signs of a bottom before buying. The professional may need to move early in order to buy a meaningful position, but the individual can wait until the stock has bottomed out (stopped going down and built a solid base). Also watch for clear signs of a top. In most cases, stocks that have been rallying do not suddenly drop. They top out (stop going up and strain to maintain price on higher volume). When you see a top, sell. The professional cannot unload a major position all at once, but when professionals start to lighten up on a stock, the increase in the volume of selling is unmistakably clear on the Internet charts. Because the individual has much less capital to move around, it is extremely easy to spot these changes and act.

CAPITALIZE ON THE PROFESSIONAL'S NEED FOR SHORT-TERM PERFORMANCE

At the time of elections in their home country, the generals of an invading army are often under pressure to produce results so political leaders can proclaim that "victory is at hand." Just as generals feel intense pressure to win battles just before elections, so investment advisors feel intense pressure to show good performance before the end of the quarters, when ratings are totaled. The difference between 15 percent and 17 percent might not seem like much to you. On a base of $10,000, it is only $200. But to a portfolio manager whose direct competitors are all at 16 percent, it is the difference between winning and losing.

In the money management business, finishing with a winning record is not enough. As in professional sports, those who finish first can make tens of millions of dollars, while journeymen who finish in the middle of the pack are often cut from the team. Think about publicity that you have seen. How often do you see a company spending its advertising dollars trumpeting, *"The Sixth Best Small-Cap Growth Fund"*? How often have you seen Lou Rukeyser introduce a guest on *Wall Street Week* by saying, *"Our guest's fund is in the middle of the pack"*? And how often have you seen *Barron's* start an interview with a money manager by saying, *"Joe has had a few bad quarters, but we still have faith in him"*? Wall Street has little patience for poor results. In big-time money management, as in sports, no one cheers for the average player.

The pressure to be a superstar impacts the trading decisions of most portfolio managers. If the manager is in second or third place, only a percent behind the leading competitor, it is very tough to stand pat and feel confident that your particular stocks will suddenly rally and boost you into the lead. Similarly, if the portfolio manager is in first place, it is difficult to sit back and relax, because in the stock market, unlike in sports, you cannot clinch the pennant before the season ends.

There is nothing more frightening to a money manager than to approach the end of a quarter significantly behind the market or behind his peers. As the situation becomes desperate, managers often erupt into a trading frenzy. I have often received calls from frantic money managers *"Find me a great stock,"* they beg. *"I need to make the quarter."* A money manager about to get fired cannot sit quietly and hope that the portfolio will suddenly improve. Instead, such a money manager will often trade like a wild man in order to salvage his career.

Assume that you are a manager in a large mutual fund company. You have had a good career, but many younger managers are moving up quickly. As the year draws to an end, you are 3 percent behind your peers and 2 percent behind other managers in your firm. If you can suddenly raise your performance above your peers, you will receive a large bonus and your fund will be widely promoted. If you cannot, you will become a journeyman, as other fund managers eclipse you. In this situation, what would you do?

BIDDING UP STOCKS

On the last day of the quarter, there are a number of tricks that fund managers can play to improve their performance. I will explain these end-of-the-quarter trading games, then briefly discuss how individual investors can capitalize on them. By far the most common trick is to aggressively bid up highly volatile stocks that the fund already owns. Let us say that your fund owns one million shares of Marshad Technologies, an Internet commerce company. Marshad, which is thinly capitalized and highly volatile, is selling at $30. You decide to buy another 100,000 shares. Normally, when a fund buys a stock, it tries to pay as little as possible. If the stock is volatile, the fund will usually give the order to one broker, with a purchase limit and instructions to work carefully so as not to disrupt the market.

But on the last day of the quarter, the game may change. To show better performance, you want to drive the price of the stock up. If you can get Marshad Technologies to close up $6, this will add at least $6 million to the fund's performance. If the fund has assets of $600 million, this is a 1 percent improvement. With three such stocks, you can draw even to your peers in one day.

How do you get the price of the stock from $30 to $36? You do it by breaking most normal investing rules. Instead of giving the buy order to one brokerage firm, you split it among four firms, making it look like there are multiple buyers for the stock. Instead of giving it to quality brokers who will carefully work the order without disrupting the market, you give it to aggressive brokers who will disrupt the market. Instead of putting price limits on the stock, you tell the brokers to buy it at any price.

When other investors see four aggressive firms all stampeding to buy Marshad Technologies, they pull back their sell orders. The trading action makes it appear as if something fundamental is happening with the company. Besides, it has broken through its previous resistance barrier and looks like it is heading straight up. The stock jumps up $6 on December 31. You paid an average of $33 for the last 100,000 shares. You probably could have bought the same 100,000 shares over the next several days for $31. By driving the stock up, you may have overpaid, and two days later, the stock may retreat back. But at the time of the last trade on the last day of the year, the day on which your performance is measured, the stock closed at $36, and your performance was enhanced by $6.3 million.

Was driving up the price of Marshad Technologies the right thing to do? Not if you are a long-term investor. Was it in the fiduciary interest of your shareholders? Probably not. Was it smart investing? Certainly not. If you were the fund manager and your job depended on it, would you do it? Perhaps and perhaps not. Not all fund managers play these games. Many reject them as against the interests of their shareholders. Many are unwilling to sacrifice long-term performance for short-term gain. Many run funds that are too large or own stocks that are not volatile enough. But for all of the managers who reject these games, there are a substantial number who do play.

DUMPING POOR PERFORMERS

Another game that many managers play does not improve their performance, but it does improve their image. Before the end of the quarter, they dump stocks that have performed poorly or have been tainted with scandal. They do this because the fund company does not want to publish a prospectus showing the tainted stocks, and the fund manager does not want to go on interviews and explain why he owns the "bomb of the year." Even when performance isn't an issue, investors often react very negatively when they see a stock in a fund's portfolio that has been a bomb. Their first thought often is, *"This manager must be an idiot for getting suckered into this stock."* You would be surprised how often potential investors are turned off by one particular investment more than by the performance of the entire portfolio. To avoid this type of reaction, money managers routinely dump their losers at the end of a quarter so that they do not have to show up on the fund's record.

Individuals can capitalize on the end-of-quarter trading games by turning the professionals' need to perform against them: buying the stocks they are selling and selling the stocks they are buying. If the professionals are driving up the price of some stocks, such as Marshad Technologies, in order to improve their performance, individuals can sell into the spikes and often receive much higher prices than they would have thought possible. The best time for these trades is right before the closing bell on the last day of each quarter. The stocks that are the best candidates are those that are the most volatile. While it may only happen infrequently, these patterns offer an opportunity for the individual.

Individual investors may also be able to buy stocks that others have dumped. This is not an encouragement to buy junk, but the fact remains that at the end of most quarters, decent companies that have disappointed investors often get thrown out by portfolio managers who do not want to answer incessant questions. While they may not be great companies, the prices at which they are dumped usually do not fully reflect their fundamentals. This is especially true at the end of the calendar year, when there is heavy tax-loss selling. In many cases, the stocks that perform the worst in December often perform the best in January. If the individual watches for stocks that the institutions are throwing out, they can often find highly attractive entrance points.

At the end of the quarter, the professionals are operating with one eye on their day-to-day performance and one eye on their long-term image. Their trading may actually be against their long-term interests, but the short-term pressure to perform is powerful.

ALLOW THE PROFESSIONALS TO OVEREXTEND THEMSELVES, THEN COUNTERATTACK

Professional investors, like professional armies, have a tendency to overextend themselves. The individual can almost always win by choosing a course counter to their actions. A truism in investing is that the professionals as a group are always wrong. If everyone thinks that the stock market can only go up, it must go down. If everyone thinks that the stock market can only go down, it must go up. **Whenever a majority of the professionals agree on something, they will always be wrong.** This at first might seem like a highly contradictory theory. But it is almost infallible. If the amateur can understand and act on it, this rule offers substantial opportunities to defeat the professional.

Let us say that your broker calls and says his firm believes that the market will go up by 1,000 points in the next six months. Then you turn on *Wall Street Week*, and see that everyone is predicting the same 1,000-point increase. Finally you read *Forbes, Fortune,* and *BusinessWeek*. Once again, there is unanimity of opinion; every seer says that the market is going to go up by 1,000 points in the next six months. You rush to place an order. But wait! Have you noticed that you always seem to get these bullish calls just as the market has reached an all-time high, and, in retrospect, just before it started a decline? It is not an accident that the market seems to behave in a way contrary to what virtually every expert says.

Think about what the professionals were saying three years ago, before the current leg rallied the bull market to historic proportions. Most were extremely cautious. Most held large amounts of cash, and most talked about a major correction. You probably received few calls from brokers telling you to buy. Most of the calls probably told you to sell. Then, of course, the market did the opposite of what most people thought: it staged one of the greatest rallies in history. This is not happenstance.

The reality is that no one actually knows how the stock market is going to perform. The market strategists, portfolio managers, and brokers at the various investment firms all have ideas, but they do not actually know. If they did know, they would not waste their time writing market letters or calling you to share their opinions. They would be playing the option market and living on a yacht in the South Pacific. Your broker might be a very nice person, but if he had perfect insight into the market, he would probably lose your phone number in an instant. Still, in those instances in which the professionals do agree on the direction of the market, they will invariably be wrong.

Why does the market always behave contrary to what most experts believe? The reason is simple and logical and relates to changes in expectations. If everyone believed that the market was going to go up by 1,000 points in the next six months, everyone would already be extremely bullish. If everyone was already bullish, there would be no one left to turn bullish. Those who have been bullish can remain bullish, but that will not push the market higher. For the market to go higher, expectations must change in a positive direction, but with everyone already bullish, expectations cannot get much more positive. Unless a new class of investors, such as newly rich Latin Americans, suddenly enters the market, there would be no one left to push it up any higher. On the other hand, with sentiment so bullish, there would be many people who could turn more bearish. If people turn bearish without other people turning bullish, the market will go down. So when everyone says that the market is heading up, it will head down.

The exact same pattern exists at the other end of the spectrum. Whenever a large number of investors and strategists start talking about a crash, the market is usually much closer to its low than to its high. If most investment advisors are bearish, they will have already sold stocks and be sitting with a large cash position. For professionals, this can be difficult. When they are sitting on cash, they are not investing. Further, many fund managers have limits to the amount of cash that they can hold. (Many believe that Jeff Vinik left Fidelity because he wanted to hold more cash in the Magellan portfolio.) With lots of cash, they are not in a position to sell. If business gets worse, fund managers won't sell, because their cash position is already large, but if business gets better, they will increase their expectations and buy. Hence the following progression occurs:

1. If every expert believes that the stock market can only go up, every expert will be fully invested.
2. If every expert is fully invested, there is no more cash to buy any stocks.
3. Without buying, the stock market cannot go up.
4. If everyone is bullish, expectations can only get more bearish, even if only a few investors change.
5. A negative direction of change will create selling.
6. Since there is no more money to buy, selling will push down the price of the market.
7. Thus, even if most experts are still bullish, the market will go down because the direction of expectations is changing for the negative.

It is obvious there will never be a complete consensus. You can never get thousands of experts all to agree. But you do not need absolutely every expert to get this system to work. All you need is the consensus of a strong majority of professionals.

The Sentiment Indicator

The cumulative opinion of all the professional investors is called the "Sentiment Indicator." The indicator, which is listed every day in *Investors Business Daily*, is one of the most watched market signals on Wall Street. It works on the same principle of reversals I just described. According to *Investors Business Daily*, a bearish, or negative, signal is indicated when more than 55 percent of the investment advisors are bullish or fewer than 20 percent are bearish, while a bullish, or positive, signal is indicated when fewer than 35 percent are bullish or more than 50 percent are bearish.

On July 11, 1994, with the Dow at 3,700, the level of bullishness reached a low of 23.3 percent. Because there had not been a corresponding increase in bearishness, the Dow continued to trade within a narrow range. However, on December 12, 1994, the level of bearishness reached a high of 59.1 percent. On that day, the Dow was at 3,682. With few people bullish and most people bearish, cash positions were high, expectations were low, and the Dow was obviously poised for a sharp increase. Over the next seven months, the Dow jumped to 4,752, an increase of 29 percent. Over the thirty months following December 12, 1994, the Dow Jones Industrial Average jumped a staggering 122 percent.

On the other hand, during the past five years, there was only one time in which there was a high degree of bullishness and a low degree of bearishness at the same time. This bearish signal occurred on January 21, 1992. In the twelve months prior to January 21, the Dow had increased by more than 25 percent. But from the time of the bearish signal, the increase stopped. Over the next seven months, the Dow declined.

This Sentiment Indicator is rarely wrong over an extended period of time. Institutional investors almost always go to extremes of bullishness and bearishness. When these extremes occur, the individual investor often has a great opportunity to act contrary to the consensus. Before you invest, take a look at what the professionals are doing. You will rarely lose by betting against them if there is a high degree of consensus.

There is, however, one caveat for this Indicator. The market will tend to keep going in the same direction until either the level of bullishness or the level of bearishness gets out of line. If the market is going up and the level of bullishness increases, the market will probably continue to go up until the level of bullishness exceeds 55 percent and remains there for a few weeks. Similarly, if the level of bearishness decreases, the market will probably continue to go up unless the level of bearishness drops under 20 percent. During the recent run up, there have been weeks of moderate bullishness and limited bearishness, but the percentages have never reached the levels of excess needed for a turn. While it is always good to bet against the experts, it is not good to anticipate the direction of sentiment. Wait until the Sentiment Indicator shows a change in direction and then act.

The Fate of the Universally Loved (or Hated) Stock

Much the same advice applies to specific industries and stocks. When an analyst comes out with a Buy recommendation, the salespeople for the analyst's firm call their customers and push the story. If the story is a good one, the salespeople will find buyers, and the stock will go up. The stock may continue to go up if a second, third, or fourth analyst recommends. But what happens when there are twenty analysts following the stock and all have Aggressive Buys? Most people would guess that any stock that was loved by all of the analysts would outperform the market and be hitting new highs every day. Most people would be wrong.

When many analysts are recommending a stock, their salespeople have already all made their phone calls. Every portfolio manager, broker, and casual investor has heard the story. Anyone who liked the story has already bought the stock. Further, if every analyst rated the stock an Aggressive Buy, there would be no more analysts left to raise the ratings. Now the only action that an analyst could take would be to lower the rating. When an analyst lowers the rating on a stock which had previously only had Aggressive Buys, the downgrade often sets off selling. Of course, a company could always surprise by reporting better than expected earnings. But when analysts have Aggressive Buys on a stock, they also often have aggressive earnings estimates, so it is difficult for a company with a bullish following to continually surprise the Street on the upside. This is not to say that people should avoid strong industries or popular stocks. It is to say that when everybody is convinced that the market or a particular stock can only go up, it will almost surely go down. **As with the market as a whole, too much bullishness can be bad for the price of a stock.**

To test this theory, I took a random sample of stocks that had been rated 1.0 or 1.1 on First Call by the analysts in early 1996. A 1.0 is a perfect rating. It means that every analyst who follows the stock has given it the highest rating possible. A 1.1 is an almost perfect rating. It means that at least seven analysts follow the stock and six have given it the highest rating and one has given it the second highest rating. From the viewpoint of the analysts, the 1.0 and the 1.1 rated stocks are the *crème de la crème*. At any one time, of the thousands of stocks that are followed by analysts, only about twenty merit a 1.0 or 1.1 rating.

How did the stocks in my sample perform?* From the time of the upgrade until August 20, 1996, the stocks rated 1.0 advanced an average of only 9.2 percent, below the average of the market. Further, over the next seventeen months, more than half of these stocks declined below their price at the time of the upgrade. During a market that increased by more than 30 percent, more than half of the highest-rated stocks showed declines.

Not surprisingly, these stocks had increased in price a startling 59 percent during the previous year. But during the previous year, most of these stocks had not yet received the analysts' highest ratings. They only received the highest rating *after* having performed the best. Thus, stocks tend to receive universal acclaim from the analysts after they have performed spectacularly, but once these stocks were upgraded to the highest rating, most of them (there are some exceptions) did not perform as well as the market.

The performance of the stocks that were rated 1.1 should also have been outstanding, but it was horrible. During one of the greatest bull markets in history, the stocks rated 1.1 showed an average decline of 14.6 percent. Of the fifteen stocks, only five showed increases, and only one outperformed the market by any measurable amount. More significant were the disasters. Daka International and Intervoice both lost about half of their value in less

---

* To eliminate distractions caused by investment banking and allow for a sufficient timeframe after an upgrade, I excluded from the sample companies that had been upgraded after June 22 and companies that were new issues.

than five months. Quicksilver lost almost half of its value in four months. U.S. Robotics lost more than one-third of its value in four months. EIS International lost more than one-quarter of its value in two months. Inphynet Medical lost more than one-quarter of its value in less than five months, while American Oncology lost 60 percent of its value in slightly more than two months. During the next seventeen months, most of these stocks continued to underperform the market.

Thus, the highest-rated stocks—those with 1.0 and 1.1 ratings—declined during the period in which they had these ratings. Despite the fact that the stock market was constantly making new highs, these stocks as a group not

STOCKS RATED 1.0

NAME	DATE OF UPGRADE	PRICE 8/20/96	PRICE AT UPGRADE	PRICE 1 YR. BEFORE UPGRADE	PERCENT CHANGE FROM UPGRADE	PERCENT CHANGE FROM PRIOR YR.
Pediatric Service	2/22/96	$21	$23	$16.5	-8.7	39.4
National Health	3/7/96	$33.125	$33	$25	0.4	32.0
Performance Food	6/20/95	$15.375	$13.625	$14.2	12.8	4.0
Consolidated Pro	1/24/96	$15.25	$15	$9.5	1.7	57.9
Micro Warehouse	2/12/96	$25.375	$42.375	$31	-40.1	-36.7
Sirena Apparel	3/13/96	$2.625	$6	$6.875	-56.3	-12.7
Rational Software	1/20/96	$52.75	$22	$9.375	139.8	134.7
Atmel	1/19/96	$26.125	$26.875	$16.875	-2.8	59.3
GT Interactive	2/20/96	$21.75	$14.25	N/A	52.6	N/A
Papa John's	1/5/96	$40.5	$27	$18.375	50.0	46.9
Dave & Buster's	7/6/95	$21.5	$18.125	N/A	18.6	N/A
Natural Micro	4/17/96	$38.125	$32.125	$14.5	18.7	121.6
Tommy Hilfiger	3/20/96	$51.875	$45.75	$21.25	13.4	115.3
Allied Group	6/22/96	$37.125	$38	N/A	-2.3	N/A
SmartFlex	9/1/95	$10.875	$18.375	N/A	-40.8	N/A
J.P. Foodservice	2/21/96	$22.5	$21	$12.375	7.1	69.7
International Rectifier	4/12/96	$19.375	$21.375	$12.5	-7.6	71.0
AVERAGE					**9.2**	**59.0**

only underperformed, they actually lost money for investors. Some were disasters. The explanation is simple: by the time these stocks achieved their lofty ratings, there were huge expectations built into them. Every analyst was bullish. Every portfolio manager had heard the bullish story many times. The good news was in the price of the stocks. Once reality set in, many of the stocks underperformed and many others dropped precipitously.

This is not to suggest that investors should short every stock that the analysts love. But if a stock has only strong Buy recommendations, the individual should watch for a sign of a top. When stocks that are universally loved top out, the next move is often sharply down. **Never underestimate the ability of the consensus to be wrong.**

The same is true with stocks on the downside. When stocks disappoint or make the pros look stupid, the analysts often walk away muttering, *"I don't care how cheap the stock is; I hate the company."* Analysts can

STOCKS RATED 1.1

NAME	DATE OF UPGRADE	PRICE 8/20/96	PRICE AT UPGRADE	PERCENT CHANGE FROM UPGRADE
O'Charley's	3/6/96	$11.25	$14	-19.6
Daka International	4/3/96	$12.5	$24.5	-49.0
Healthsouth	4/1/96	$34.125	$36.625	-6.8
Swift Energy	3/11/96	$22	$12	83.3
Sanmina Corp.	11/14/95	$31.375	$27.75	13.1
Hummingbird Comm.	1/18/96	$27.75	$33.5	-17.2
Intervoice	3/25/96	$12.625	$26.5	-52.4
Bay Apartment	3/14/96	$27.25	$24.125	13.0
Quicksilver	4/29/96	$19.375	$37	-47.6
U.S. Robotics	4/28/96	$46.875	$76	-38.3
Inphynet Medical	4/4/96	$13.375	$18.5	-27.7
Newpark Resources	4/25/96	$34	$30.5	11.5
SGS/Thompson	4/9/96	$38	$36.25	4.8
EIS International	5/17/96	$19.375	$26	-25.5
American Oncology	6/4/96	$9.125	$23	-60.3
AVERAGE				**-14.6**

develop blind spots more easily than can individuals. This is not to say that individuals should buy shares in bad companies. Nor should they rush in right after a company has disappointed investors. Investors have long memories, and stocks do not usually rebound quickly. But many decent companies that have been hated by professionals because of previous disappointments often offer the individual excellent opportunities. When investors see stocks that are universally hated form a base and begin to move up, they usually have a good buying opportunity.

Analyst ratings are covered on many sites throughout the Internet. Zacks.com has its own website with ratings; Briefing.com provides constant updates on ratings; and most of the Internet services that provide quotes have links to one or more sites with analyst ratings. Investors should check the ratings of analysts on the stocks that they own or are interested in owning. Watch especially for extremes of bullishness or bearishness, and then look at the charts available on-line. Tops and bottoms are usually very easy to spot, and most investors will do well if they act when they see these formations. Watch especially for extremely bullish ratings on weak charts, which could portend a disaster, or extremely bearish ratings on strong charts, which could portend a great buying opportunity. Thus, while betting against individual professionals can be risky for the individual investor, betting against the strong consensus of professionals usually guarantees victory. **If individuals can remember that the consensus is almost always wrong and have the fortitude to bet against it, they have an excellent chance of winning.**

REMEMBER SUN TZU

The key to investing is simple. Individuals compete against better-trained and better-equipped professionals who have a huge advantage. Individuals must avoid attacking the professionals' strength. Instead, they must turn their strength against them. Like a well-trained guerrilla force against a mechanized army, the individual can defeat the professional so long as he or she remembers the dictum: "Know yourself. Know your enemy. In one hundred battles, there will be one hundred victories."

PART 2

The Weapons of Warfare

CHAPTER SIX

Fundamental Weapons

Although guerrilla warriors may be able to avoid the enemys' strengths, identify their weaknesses, and find advantages on home turf, they still need weapons to fight the enemies. The enemies may have airplanes, submarines, and missiles, but these will be of little use to the guerrillas. The weapons of the guerrillas must be simple and suited to the terrain on which the war will be fought. The same types of conditions apply on Wall Street. The professionals have huge weapons systems. They have unlimited research, direct inputs from companies, and sophisticated trading systems. The individual cannot match the professional in terms of resources. But individuals can still find weapons systems of their own.

In the stock market, there are two principal types of weapons: fundamental information and technical analysis. Fundamental information concerns the underlying business of a company—its sales and earnings, the quality of its management, its new products, its competition, etc. With good fundamental information, the investor can analyze the components of a business and make a judgment about its current and future earnings potential. Technical analysis concerns the trading patterns of stocks. These patterns can enable the investor to observe the movements of the market and have an early warning system when professionals change direction. To win consistently, the individual must use both of these tools. This chapter and the following one will explain these two important weapons of warfare.

LET THE ANALYSTS DO THE WORK

Fundamental analysis is critical to understanding a company. To win, individuals must understand the company's business and its earnings potential, as well as where the professionals are likely to be wrong and where they can gain an edge. Analyzing a company is a complex undertaking. Analysts are trained in financial analysis and accounting and spend years learning about companies. They meet with management, study financial statements, build an earnings model, and make earnings estimates. It is very difficult for individuals to duplicate their work.

Analysts have an additional advantage because most specialize in one industry. Analysts can spend a lifetime looking at no more than twenty companies. They know these companies intimately. They talk to them every week and also talk to competitors, customers, and suppliers. They read trade publications, attend conferences, and study the specific financial systems and terminology that are unique to each industry. Oil analysts study all of the factors that impact world oil prices. Biotechnology analysts study medical journals and monitor trials of new drugs. Real estate analysts study the special accounting rules for real estate, and analyze the occupancy and rental rates by market. Semiconductor analysts study new technological developments and factors impacting worldwide demand. The differences between industries are so extreme that experienced analysts almost never switch coverage areas.

With their in-depth industry knowledge, the analysts are experts at figuring out the valuations of their companies. They know when to use earnings per share and when to use cash flow. They understand which companies are growth stocks and which are value stocks, and they know how to analyze balance sheets and income statements. This is not to say that they are always right. They are not. But they are operating with a level of knowledge that the individual can never match.

If the analysts have such a huge advantage, how can the individual ever hope to compete? The answer is easy. **Individuals do not have to do the work, because the analysts do it for them.** The analysts work closely with the companies and write reports that accurately tell the company's story. These reports serve as a reference point around which a good deal of the information flow on Wall Street is based. If individuals use the work of the analysts as a base, they do not need to build models or figure out valuation techniques. They only have to decide when the analysts are too optimistic or too pessimistic.

Get ten reports on any well-followed company, especially one that has just done an offering and paid a lot of firms on Wall Street. You will notice that most of the analysts present the story in the same way and have similar models, valuation techniques, and ratings. A few reports will differ from the norm, but these will be the exceptions. This is not to say that the analysts are correct. In fact, they are often wrong and certainly have a bullish bias. The virtue of their work lies not in their being right or wrong but in their ability to present a unified picture that investors can use as a guideline.

FIND THE CONSENSUS

If eight of ten analysts say that a company is going to grow by 18 percent a year, that percentage becomes the consensus around which the company's results are judged. If eight of ten analysts say that the growth will come from two core divisions, those divisions become the focal point of investors' interest. If eight of ten analysts say that the stock will earn $2, those are the earnings investors will expect. If the company earns $2.20, those earnings will be an upside surprise, even if two analysts had thought it would earn $2.25.

While absolute results are important, it is the consensus and the reaction to earnings results that most influence the stock price. How often have you seen a stock surge on what looked like mediocre earnings because it beat "consensus"? And how often have you seen a stock plunge on what looked like great earnings because it missed "consensus"? It seems fine for a company to earn $1.00 compared to $.50 in the previous year, but if investors had been expecting earnings of $1.50, the stock will almost certainly plunge. Because the consensus is so important, companies work hard to ensure that analysts have the "right" numbers and spin control on the business. In fact, some companies try to ensure that the analysts are always a little conservative in their estimates, so that they can "surprise" the Street on the upside.

Here is a neat trick once pulled by a company I know. Five analysts were covering the company. Two had estimates of $.20 and three had estimates of $.21. The average was $.206, which rounded up to $.21. The company knew it was going to report $.20, but it still wanted to find a way of beating consensus. Management knew that stocks that beat consensus usually went up, while those that missed consensus usually went down. The CFO found a young analyst who was looking to hustle investment banking business and who had a very small following on Wall Street. He convinced the analyst to begin covering the company and to use $.13 as an earnings estimate. No one took much notice of the estimate, but when the new analyst's $.13 was added to the others, the average dropped from $.21 to $.19. This made the company's $.20 an upside rather than a downside surprise. When the company reported $.20, the analysts indicated that the earnings beat consensus and the stock jumped $2.

These games notwithstanding, the existence of a consensus makes life much easier for an investor. Stocks will only move when people change their buying and selling behavior. If everyone agrees with the consensus, the stock is unlikely to move very much. But if investors believe that the consensus is too conservative, they will buy and push the stock up, while if investors feel the consensus is too aggressive, they will sell and push the price of the stock down. **Thus, the consensus forms the yardstick around which investors make their bets.**

To win, the investor has only to pick correctly whether the consensus is too high or too low and move before others can. While this sounds difficult, it is not. Because the consensus has outlined the key aspects in the field of battle, the investor merely has to draw on home-turf advantages to find a few companies in which the consensus is wrong. The first step, however, is to understand the consensus.

Find the name and phone number of the director of investor relations. If you cannot find the name in the annual report, look at the company's profile on any of the financial websites. When you call investor relations, ask for a complete investor's package including an annual report, a 10K, the most recent 10Qs, and some analysts' reports. (These reports are available on the Web at Edgar.com, but it is still worthwhile to call the company.) Some investor relations departments may ask if you are an individual or a professional money manager. I know some people who answer that they are a "small institution" in the belief that it will get them better service from the company. They give a name and address that makes them sound like a money management firm. They say, *"Send it to John Doe at Doe & Buffett Capital Management in Omaha, Nebraska."* No one knows the name of every small institution, and no one will ask if Buffett is Warren or Jimmy. So making up a name probably won't hurt.

Some investor relations departments are not friendly to individual shareholders, and instead focus on the larger money managers that own the bulk of their stock. There is nothing you can do about this. If the company will not answer your questions, you might be better off finding another company. Besides, if a company does not want you, why should you want it?

Some companies will send you analysts' reports as a matter of course. They are proud that someone is writing about them. Others will send analysts' reports only if you ask. Some will not send them at all and will instead refer you to the brokerage houses. In most cases, if you beg politely, the company will send you some reports, especially if the reports say nice things about the company. Do not expect the company to send you reports with Sell or even Hold ratings, unless the stock has already soared and the writers of the reports look like complete idiots. Not having these reports is not as much of a drawback as it might appear. Relatively few reports have negative ratings, and also the primary reason for getting the reports is to understand the consensus. In most cases, negative reports will fall outside of the consensus.

FIGURE OUT THE INVESTMENT THESIS

When you get the reports, the next step is to figure out the investment thesis. The investment thesis is the sentence at the top of most reports that tells you the analyst's opinion, which is not critical, and the core issues surrounding the stock, which are. While some analysts will go their own way, most will coalesce around a particular thesis that will form the basis of the stock's valuation. Some investment theses will be straightforward and relate to earnings growth. This is especially common for complex companies that have multiple drivers to earnings. The following thesis for IBM is a straightforward one:

"We believe that IBM can grow its earnings by 16 percent per year. Selling at 13x projected earnings, the stock is undervalued relative to its growth rate."

A thesis like this is saying that the key items on which to focus are the earnings growth (the rate at which earnings per share will grow over time) and the p/e ratio (the stock price divided by the earnings per share). In this case, the p/e ratio is inexpensive relative to the estimated growth rate.

Some investment theses will be more complex, spelling out the specifics of the earnings argument. A smart analyst wrote about Tiffany:

"We are forecasting 20 to 25 percent average annual EPS growth over the next several years, assuming 10 percent to 12 percent unit growth budgeted by the company, 8 to 9 percent same-store sales growth in both the U.S. and Japan, and continued margin expansion from improving operating efficiencies. At 19.7x our fiscal 1998 EPS, TIF is selling at a 21 percent discount to its long-term growth."

A thesis like the one above makes it easy for any investor to understand how the world looks at a company. If earnings growth (20 to 25 percent) remains higher than the p/e multiple (19.7), the stock will probably go up. As a potential investor, you should focus on the two key issues for earnings growth: Can the company find good sites for its new stores? Will same-store sales remain strong both in the United States and in Japan? Given this investment thesis, how do you think the stock of Tiffany fared when the Japanese stock market dropped in October 1997? As you might expect, Tiffany declined by 25 percent as many investors bet that the economic problems in Japan would hurt the sale of luxury goods.

Some investment theses are relative, looking at the valuation of a particular company compared to other companies. An analyst wrote about PETCO Animal Supplies:

"Our simple investment thesis is that PETCO is about as strong a performer as the larger player, PETsMart, but PETCO trades at a substantial discount to PETsMart, and trades in line with other growth retailers."

Because this analyst is focusing on relative values, the investor needs to look at the fundamentals of both PETCO and PETsMart, the p/e multiples of both stocks, and the p/e multiples of other growth retailers. During the first nine months of 1997, PETCO had superb results. Its earnings ranked in the 95th percentile of all stocks, but its stock performance was slightly below average. The reason was simple. PETsMart's earnings fell apart and its stock dropped from $29 to $7. If the thesis was that PETCO's valuation was tied to that of PETsMart, then once PETsMart blew up, it was difficult for PETCO to advance. Any investor who ignored what happened to PETsMart lost.

Some investment theses deal with issues other than earnings, such as takeover value:

"Cullen Frost has a dominant position in the San Antonio banking market and could become a likely takeover target. While the stock is currently selling for $32, we believe that its takeover value is $55."

In this thesis, the analyst is projecting the takeover of the company at $55. There is little discussion of earnings growth. Instead, the value of the company is in its franchise. If the thesis is that a takeover is likely, then the investor should focus on other takeover action in the industry in general and in the Southwest niche in particular.

The investment thesis may or may not be correct. Just because an analyst indicates that a company will grow by 22 percent does not mean that the results will follow suit. In fact, it is almost certain that the results will in some way be different. When Rational Software Corp. was selling for $38, an analyst wrote:

"Rational [is] . . . the market leader in an industry segment which we expect to see a 55 percent CAGR through the year 2000. Rational clearly values revenue predictability. The company has established conservative accounting practices and . . . does an excellent job of managing its quarter-to-quarter business."

Nine months later, the price of Rational's stock had dropped from $38 to $10. The revenues had significantly fallen short of plan. But that did not make the investment thesis less valuable. In fact, it enabled investors to focus on the key issues. When the *revenue predictability* failed to materialize, they trashed the stock. (You may remember Rational Software. It was one of the top-rated stocks, listed in Chapter 5.)

For better or worse, the issues on which analysts focus are normally the issues on which investors focus. If the fate of these issues vary substantially from the analysts' stated opinion, the company will likely perform much better or worse than expected. An analyst wrote the following on Just For Feet:

"Given the unique superstore format and a differentiated merchandising strategy, FEET is well-positioned to gain market share."

When Just For Feet made an acquisition of a chain of stores with a smaller format, investors sold, and the stock plunged from a high of $33 to a low of $11 in just nine months. The reason was simple. Just For Feet did not have a p/e ratio of 40 because it had the best earnings record. It had this lofty multiple because investors believed that its large stores made it unique. When Just For Feet bought smaller stores, it was saying to investors that it did not think its large stores were so special after all, and investors, as a result, decided there was no reason to give it a 40x multiple.

The investment thesis gives investors a road map for looking at a company. It details the issues that should drive earnings and valuation. The first step is to decide if you can understand the thesis. If you cannot, drop the stock. There are many other companies. If you can understand the thesis, you have four choices. You can decide that the thesis is right and go along with the masses. You can decide that it is too optimistic, in which case you should be selling. You can decide that it is too pessimistic, in which case you should be buying. Or you can decide that it is the wrong thesis, in which case there should be a great opportunity on either the short or the long side.

THE STREAM OF EARNINGS

If you look at the investment theses cited above, you will notice that most of the valuations are based on some assessment of the long-term earnings growth rate of the company. This is because when investors buy stock, they are purchasing a share of that company's stream of earnings. A share of stock does not entitle investors to assets or even products. Compaq does not send its shareholders a computer at the end of each quarter. A share of stock does not guarantee investors a dividend. Nor does it offer investors any return of capital, unless the company is sold or liquidated. All that a share of stock offers an investor is a participation in the earnings stream of that company.

Therefore, the price that the investor is willing to pay will be determined by the amount and the timing of that earnings stream. If you think the stream will increase, you will be willing to pay more. If you think it will decrease, you will want to pay less.

Most sophisticated investors take a company's projected earnings for the next fifteen to twenty years and then discount them back to find the *present value* of the earnings stream. That tells them how much the stock is worth. The reason for discounting is that future earnings should be worth less than current earnings because of inflation, risk, and the opportunity cost of owning the stock. By discounting future earnings, the investor should arrive at a fair present value for the earnings stream.

While earnings in the first year are more valuable than earnings in later years, the companies with the highest valuations are those with the highest projected growth rates. This is because of the power of compounding. In the stock market, investors pay more for growth than they do for current earnings. Which would you rather have—$5 now or a stream of payments that would start with $1 now and grow by 20 percent a year for the next ten years? The $5 is worth $5, but the stream that starts with $1 and is compounded by 20 percent is worth $26. Even if you discounted the future payments back to the present at a 10 percent rate, it would still be worth $14.50.

The power of compounding is the reason analysts are so concerned with a company's long-term growth rate. Take a hypothetical company that everyone agrees will earn $1 per share in 1998. The value of the company depends on the estimate of its growth. If earnings decline by 10 percent per year, the company will earn $5.04 during the next fifteen years. If earnings are flat at $1 per year, the company will earn $7.94 in the next fifteen years. If earnings increase by 10 percent, the company will earn $13.99. At 20 percent, the company will earn $27.15, and at 30 percent, it will earn $56.11.

15-YEAR EARNINGS GROWTH*

Annual Earnings Change	-10 percent	0 percent	10 percent	20 percent	30 percent
Year 1	$1	$1	$1	$1	$1
Year 10	$0.15	$0.39	$0.91	$2	$4.11
Year 15	$0.05	$0.23	$0.87	$2.94	$9.01
15-Year Total	$5.04	$7.94	$13.99	$27.15	$56.11
P/E Ratio	5.0x	7.9x	14x	27.2x	56.1x

* These growth rates are assuming that you are discounting future earnings by 10 percent per year.

What would you pay for this discounted stream of earnings? In each case, you would probably pay an amount equal to the present value of the earnings. This would mean that you would pay $5.04 per share if you thought that the earnings would decline by 10 percent per year, $7.94 per share if you thought that earnings would be flat, and a huge $56.11 if you thought that earnings would grow by 30 percent per year. The impact of the discounted earnings stream shows clearly why investors will pay $56 per share for a company they believe will grow its earnings by 30 percent per year but only $5 per share for another company they believe will show an annual earnings decline of 10 percent per year.

Of course, a change in the discount rate can have a significant impact on the valuations. Think of the discount rate like the interest on your mortgage. It reflects both the cost of money and the risk that something will go wrong. When mortgage rates are high, you cannot afford to pay as much for a house. When they are low, you can pay more. The same is true of discount rates and stocks. The higher the discount rate, the lower the value of the earnings stream, while the lower the discount rate, the higher the value of the same stream. If the discount rate is 10 percent, the company with a 10 percent annual growth in earnings would be worth $13.99. If discount rate dropped to 5 percent, the company with the same earnings would now be worth $20.78. If the discount rate jumped to 15 percent, the company would be worth only $9.77. Since the discount rate is determined by the level of interest rates, it is clear why interest rate changes can have such a major impact on stock prices.

THE CHALLENGE OF THE UNKNOWN

If the long-term earnings growth of a company were guaranteed, it would be easy to figure out the appropriate price of the stock. The investor would simply calculate the present value of the earnings stream. But the long-term future is never guaranteed. Competition, changing market conditions, new technologies, and other factors can significantly alter expectations. Investors must assess the likelihood that the company will do better or worse than plan and incorporate some factor for risk.

In practice, this means that companies with long-term earnings visibility will usually sell with higher price/earnings ratios than companies whose future is much less certain. Companies like Coca-Cola, Wal-Mart, Microsoft, and others that have proven they can grow consistently and have dominant market positions which should ensure continued growth normally maintain higher multiples than companies with more uncertain futures. If you decided that Coca-Cola or Wal-Mart could grow earnings by 17 percent per year, you would probably be comfortable taking these earnings out ten or even fifteen years.

Yet even here, the distant future can be difficult to project, especially as companies begin to saturate their markets. It is easy to look back at the history of Microsoft, Intel, Wal-Mart, or other great companies and see the power of compounding, but for every company that has sustained fantastic growth, there are hundreds of wannabes that stubbed their toes. At one point in time, Wang, Polaroid, and Kmart were growth stocks whose prospects looked as exciting to investors then as those of Microsoft, Intel, and Wal-Mart do today. Yet these companies ran into trouble as competition changed and management slipped.

If assessing long-term growth is a difficult task with strong and consistent companies, it is much harder with small, rapidly growing companies. Netscape is one of today's great growth companies, but what will this company look like in ten years? The bull case says that Netscape will dominate the Internet. The bear case says that Microsoft will dominate the browser market as it has dominated other businesses, and Netscape will become the Visicalc of the browser market, a long-forgotten footnote in the evolution of technology. The difference between the bull and the bear cases represents a huge differential in price. The same may be said of a company like Iomega (maker of Zip drives). Iomega is currently growing extremely rapidly, but what will the company look like in ten years? Will earnings grow by 40 percent per year as everyone buys a Zip drive, or will someone invent a new drive that makes all of Iomega's products obsolete? To arrive at a valuation for Netscape and Iomega, the investor must look at the possible alternatives, assess the likelihood of each occurrence, and then calculate the present value of their future earnings stream.

The same techniques apply to cyclical stocks. Cyclical companies by definition have cyclical earnings. During boom periods, earnings can be very high, while during bust periods, the company may even lose money. But there is no difference in the analysis. The investor is still buying a long-term stream of earnings. It is just that the growth rate is not consistent over time. The multiple that an investor is willing to pay is based on the sum of the earnings, discounted back to the present by some reasonable amount.

IT'S ALWAYS EARNINGS

There are cases in which analysts focus on measures other than earnings, but even in these cases, the investor is purchasing an earnings stream. Analysts may base their valuations on price-to-book or breakup value. These types of valuations usually occur with companies that currently have weak earnings. But the analyst's justification for the valuation is that, in the future, the company or whoever buys it will be able to generate a higher earnings stream from these assets.

If the price of the stock equates to the stream of earnings projected by the analysts, it should be relatively easy for investors to pick the winners and losers. Because analysts clearly spell out their assumptions, the individual investor merely has to study the assumptions of the analysts and decide whether they are too bullish or too bearish. If the analysts have not fully taken into account the risks, the stock will eventually go down. If they have not fully factored in the opportunities, the stock will eventually go up.

So the trick for investors is to find some piece of information that will let them decide if the growth rate selected by analysts is too high or too low. Just because an analyst says that a company will continue to grow at 25 percent a year does not make it happen. Many companies exceed analysts' targets, while others fall short. **If the investor can gain some insight into the company's ability to surprise analysts on the upside or the downside, that investor can move before the professionals have time to react.**

You should, however, be cautious when short-term results play havoc with long-term valuations. Analysts use short-term earnings to make long-term projections. If a company growing at 15 percent has a strong quarter, with sales and earnings up 30 percent, analysts will reflect this improvement by raising their long-term growth rate. You may not think that a few good months should dramatically change the long-term growth rate of the company. You may be right over the long term, but because many investors focus on short-term momentum, stocks often respond dramatically to these changes in valuation. If analysts are raising growth rates and the stock price begins to rise, do not rush to sell. On the other hand, when companies report a weak quarter, analysts will suddenly revise their growth estimates downward. Even if you think the change is inappropriate, don't immediately rush to buy the stock. You can be overwhelmed by momentum. Let the short-term players make their move first, then reassess the growth rate.

WHEN THE MARKET AND THE ANALYSTS DISAGREE

Sometimes there will be a vast gap between the analysts' valuation and the market price. The analysts may all say that the stock should sell for $50, but the market price will remain stuck at $30. When this occurs, either the market or the analysts are wrong.

If the company is small and covered by only one or two analysts, the chances are reasonably good that the stock should be worth $50 and is selling at $30 because it has fallen below the radar screen of most professionals. This can often be an excellent buying opportunity.

If the company is large and well covered by many analysts, the chances are reasonably good that the stock should be worth $30 and the analysts are wearing rose-colored glasses and have missed a critical risk factor. If you see a group of analysts all contending that *"the stock is highly undervalued relative to its growth rate,"* what the analysts are really saying is, *"No one believes our projections."* If the market professionals do not accept the analysts' projections on a well-followed stock, neither should you.

— · —

Thus, the task for the individual investor is easier than it seems. At any point in time, the price of a stock reflects the collective wisdom of all buyers and sellers. If the stock is reasonably well followed, it should efficiently reflect the current consensus. The stock will move up when the consensus changes for the positive. It will move down when the consensus changes for the negative. The analysts' earnings projections and valuation parameters usually form the basis of the consensus. To win, the individual investor does not have to build an earnings model, analyze the balance sheet, or study valuation techniques. **The individual merely has to find a hole in the projections and/or the valuations and act upon it. It is far easier to allow the analysts to do the work and then react off them than it is to duplicate their work from scratch.**

DO A REALITY CHECK

Before you begin looking for specific financial holes in the analysts' projections, do a reality check. Decide if the company's strategy makes sense. For instance, a company announces that it plans to launch satellites to mine minerals on asteroids. The analyst thinks that the asteroids have unlimited resources and the company can strike it rich. **Does the mar-**

ket exist? Perhaps, but there is no way of knowing if it is feasible. You are taking a shot in the dark, unless you are an astronomer or a physicist. If you cannot evaluate the consensus, you should not play the stock. Another company announces that it intends to launch a fleet of satellites that will allow people around the world to talk seamlessly on cellular phones. Does the market exist? You believe it does. **Can the company capture it?** That depends on the costs and the competition. You may have an opinion, but you have no real edge.

Cott, a maker of private-label sodas, was once a high-flyer. The analysts said that Cott could undercut Coke and Pepsi and take 20 percent of the market. Does this concept make sense to you? It did to many investors. But betting that companies like Coke and Pepsi will willingly give up major chunks of their markets is not usually a good way to win. At the beginning of 1994, Cott was selling for $30. Two years later, it was selling for $5. Then, another hot private-label company, USA Detergents, hit Wall Street. The analysts said that it could capture 20 percent of the detergent market from Procter & Gamble and other major manufacturers. Investors jumped at the stock, giving it a huge multiple. But again, the reality was different from the hype. At the beginning of 1997, USA Detergents was selling for $46. By the end of the year, it was selling for $8. Companies like Procter & Gamble don't get where they are by allowing small competitors to take 20 percent of their markets. This is the type of reality check that you should easily be able to make.

Reality checks are not difficult. Listen to the concept and see if it makes sense. At times, a company makes a claim so outlandish that no one should believe it, yet both professionals and individuals often do. One of my favorites was made by Value Merchants, a retailer that operated dollar stores. In 1991, management announced that it intended to corner the market on dollar stores. It talked about cornering the market on $1 items the way that someone would talk about cornering the market on gold or silver. The concept seemed truly bizarre, but investors loved it. The stock surged from $256 to $1,358 and sported a 26x multiple.

Value Merchants opened stores everywhere, even in the Galleria in Dallas. The idea must have been that after shopping in Neiman Marcus for a designer original, women would buy their kids a present for $1. Meanwhile, the company was burning cash, laying out tens of millions of dollars to corner the market on junk. The junk did not sell as well as expected. Value Merchants started to lose money. The price of the stock plunged from $1,358 to $.50 (cheap enough to be sold in the company's dollar stores). The lesson of Value Merchants was simple. The concept of cornering the market on dollar stores was idiotic. It is impossible to corner the market on junk. But because investors often like to buy into exciting-sounding concepts, few did a reality check until it was too late. Remember, junk is not a growth industry.

PRICE OF VALUE MERCHANTS' STOCK

DATE	PRICE
October 1990	$275.00
October 1991	$1,358.00
October 1992	$460.00
October 1993	$95.00
October 1994	$28.50
October 1995	$.50

Wall Street is littered with companies that should never have passed anyone's reality check. Do you remember Silk Greenhouse, the company that ran artificial flower superstores? It was a ridiculous concept, but it also was a high-flying stock. Many professionals, who were inundated with pitches from analysts, salespersons, and the company itself, never did a reality check until Silk Greenhouse self-destructed. They could not see the forest for the (artificial) trees. Here the individual may actually have an advantage. Anyone who walked into one of these cavernous stores would have realized that this was a concept which could never work.

In doing a reality check, you must go beyond the basic concept and look at the valuations. Many concepts are great, but they may not be worth the multiple at which the stock is selling. After coming public, Netscape rallied to over $80 and had a market cap of almost $8 billion. Netscape's browser revolutionized communications, but the valuation did not take into account the economics of the Internet or the potential competition from Microsoft and others. It had a great product, but its valuation should not have passed your reality check.

In doing a reality check, it is often far more important to look at the risks before the opportunities. Analysts and companies want to tell the positive side of the story. Few companies will come out and say that Wal-Mart has taken over their share of the market, and few analysts will issue reports contending that the management has no clue to controlling costs. Instead, most accentuate the positives. Thus, in doing a reality check, investors should spend more time looking at the potential negatives than they do looking at the potential positives.

REALITY CHECKS BEGIN AT HOME

When doing your reality check, draw on your direct experience. Review the process outlined in Chapter 4 and see if you have any home-turf advantage. Do you have any specialized knowledge about the basic business? Do you use the company's products? Do you know anyone who works for the company, or for its competitors, customers, or suppliers? You see things every day that you can use in making investment decisions. You just have to be able to appreciate the value of those things and dig for information. If you have no home-turf advantage, look for another company.

If you read a report about a fast-growing retailer catering to teenagers, visit the stores. Are they crowded or empty? Does the merchandise look new or old? Is everything at full price, or is it on sale? Are the customers buying one item or many? Talk to the teenagers. Ask how they like the store and where else they shop. If they tell you that they would never shop anywhere else, you may have a winner. If they tell you that they are getting bored with the store, you may have a loser.

Watch the people who work in the stores. Are they helping the customers or sitting in the back chatting? A store with helpful sales personnel is often a well-managed company. When the store has quieted down, go talk to the employees. Tell them that you own the stock. Ask how they like the company and how business is. Don't be shy about talking to employees. Most people like to talk and will tell you interesting things about their company. You are not looking for inside information. You are only looking for a flavor of how the business is running.

Little things may tell you a lot. Have you ever wondered why the greeter in front of the Wal-Mart store always seems to smile, while the greeter in front of the Kmart store does not? One day I asked. The Kmart greeter growled:

"The Wal-Mart greeter has worked there for twenty years. He has so many stock options that he bought a second home. I live in a trailer. On weekends, I mow his lawn while he goes to the beach. When Kmart's stock is at $60 and Wal-Mart's stock is at $10, I'll smile for you."

For information about a manufacturer of a consumer product, follow the same pattern. If you are interested in a bicycle manufacturer, hang out in a bike shop. If you are-interested in a maker of computer peripherals, go to a CompUSA store. If you are interested in Mattel and Hasbro, go to Toys 'R' Us. Talk to the customers. Ask the salespeople if the products are selling, if there are delivery problems, and if the quality is up to par. If everyone tells you that a business is hot, it probably is.

The same process applies to other businesses, like restaurants. Look at what the analysts are saying is the key to success and see if you can see it for yourself. Are the parking lots full? Does the restaurant turn its tables? Ask to speak to the manager. Tell the manager that you are an investor in the company and ask about the key issues in running the business. Managers will spend time with you if they are not too busy. They may even buy you a drink. After all, they do not know whether you own 100 or 100,000 shares.

If you are interested in a company that you buy from professionally, ask your sales representatives for information. See if you can get them to explain how the company works. If the analysts are focusing on a particular point of competitive advantage, ask about it. Most of the salespeople will have an opinion and most will give you a straight answer. After all, they want to keep your business. If you buy the stock and it goes down, you will lose money, and they could lose the account.

If you work for a company that is a supplier of products and you are interested in one of your customers, talk to the person whose job it is to actually buy your company's products. When you visit the customer, look at the facilities and talk to the people. If you have been in a business for a while, you will usually be able to tell the good companies from the bad. If analysts are talking about new growth plans for your customer, ask your customer about them. Most customers will be pleased to see that you are taking an interest in their business and will get you the answers.

If the company you are interested in is in your hometown, look at stories in the local newspaper. Talk to your friends who work there. Tell them what the analysts have to say and ask their opinion. Ask if they are buying the stock of the company. You only need a small edge to win.

Try to zero in on the key issues. If you work for an advertising agency and are placing on-line ads with one of the search-engine companies, ask the company about the economics of the business. Perhaps the search-engine company will say, *"We are planning to move beyond advertising and start taking a fee for every product sold on our search engine."* Go back to the analyst reports. No one has calculated any direct product sales in their models, but as you think about the business of electronic commerce, you realize that a huge amount of business will be done on-line. You now have a piece of information that will put you ahead of the analysts.

When you talk to someone who works for a company, try to gain insights that other people do not have, especially if they can affect a key issue for the company. Most people relate to their own work experience. Ask a person about his or her own job, the company's management, and its corporate culture. Ask the type of questions that you would want to know if you were going to work for a company. Employees usually have a good feel for the people who run the business. If the company has a key executive who has gotten a lot of press, ask for an opinion on that person.

Your objective in this process is very simple. You need to uncover some piece of information that will lead you to a different view of the company than other investors have. Don't waste your time asking questions that the person cannot answer. Don't ask a salesperson about earnings estimates. Salespeople usually do not know, and you can easily find the answers on-line. Ask about the things that will give you a special insight.

TALK TO INVESTOR RELATIONS

Once you have found a key issue you can use to differentiate yourself from the consensus, your next step should be to talk to the company. Call back investor relations. (The first time you called, you simply asked for an information package.) The key in talking to investor relations is to get a handle on some facet of the business that will enable you to decide if the consensus is wrong.

Don't be afraid to ask questions. The professionals aren't. Don't worry if your questions are not perfect. This is not an exam. It is a learning process. The worst that can happen is that investor relations can hang up on you. **Don't worry about asking stupid questions. If this were a crime, half of Wall Street would now be in jail.** I remember going to a lunch with the chairman of an athletic shoe company. During the presentation, he passed around his company's most high-tech basketball shoe. *"This shoe,"* the chairman said, *"is state of the art for only $105."* A portfolio manager who ran a $400 million fund looked up. *"Each?"* she asked. *"We sell them by the pair,"* the chairman said, trying to avoid a smirk.

It is unlikely that you can ask a more foolish question than if sneakers are priced by the shoe. Investor relations departments are accustomed to foolish questions from even the largest investors, so don't feel self-conscious if you do not understand everything. But do your homework in advance. Companies will spend more time with you if they think you know what you are talking about.

WHAT TO ASK

- **Ask about specific things you do not understand.** This is especially true if the business has a complex technology. Don't be embarrassed if you do not know what an EEPROM is. Many professionals don't either. Explaining these issues is the job of investor relations. If after the explanation, you still don't understand, drop the company. You will never win if you cannot understand its business.

- **Ask about the economics of the business.** You are not expected to know the intricacies of each industry, but you should be able to understand the issues that drive the valuation. It is perfectly acceptable to ask, *"How do I understand the economics of your company?"* If the investor relations person talks about cash flow, go to the cash-flow page in the annual report and have them walk you through the numbers.

- **Ask about anything in an analyst's report that seems controversial or at odds with the company's stated objectives.** Companies will go to great lengths to explain why they think an analyst has gotten a story wrong. If an analyst says that the breakup value of a company is twice the stock price, ask investor relations why the company does not break itself up. The answer may be very interesting.

- **Ask about your direct experience with key issues.** An auto company talks about its cost-cutting measures. You have received four recall notices for your own car in six months. Ask whether the lower costs have resulted in quality problems. A discount store chain talks about its rapid new store-opening programs. You could not find bicycles or gas grills in three of the branches at the start of the spring selling season. Ask whether the growth plans have exceeded the logistics capabilities of the company. An on-line service touts its growth, but you can never get connected. Ask whether the company has capacity constraints and how it intends to resolve them. Direct experience can lead you into an interesting dialogue with a company, but make sure your questions are corporate ones and not minor customer service issues that apply primarily to you. Do not tell investor relations that you could not find the car color you wanted or you had to wait in a long line, unless you believe that these are companywide problems. If you can get in a dialogue with the investor relations person, you can often get a solid piece of information that can help you make your investment decision.

WHAT NOT TO ASK

- **Don't ask what the company is going to earn.** Companies do not usually give projections. Check on the Web for the analysts' estimates. Then ask if the company is comfortable with the range. If the company is comfortable at the low end of the range, analysts may lower estimates, and the stock may come under pressure. If it is comfortable at the high end, analysts may raise estimates, and the stock may go up.
- **Don't ask if the stock is going to go up or down.** These people don't know, and if they did, they would not tell you. Ask about the price action of the stock only when there are major increases in volume and volatility and you have first checked the news, analysts' ratings, and earnings estimates.
- **Don't ask if an analyst has just upgraded or downgraded the stock.** Check on the Web for analysts' upgrades and downgrades before calling. If an analyst has recently changed the ratings or the estimates, ask why. The company may merely say, *"That is one analyst's opinion,"* but it is a question worth asking.
- **Don't ask if you should buy or sell.** That is your decision, not theirs. This question will always give you away as an amateur. Your focus should not be on getting investment advice, but rather on finding out when the consensus is right or wrong.

You can also call the investor relations departments of the company's customers, suppliers, and competitors. Some of the best information comes from firms that deal directly with the company in which you are interested. No one has a better feel for how a company is doing than its customers and suppliers. These people know which products are selling well, but they must be careful in commenting on the companies they deal with. If you want to get information from them, you have to be a little cagey. Instead of asking point blank how a supplier is doing, start asking questions about the customer's own business, and then segue into questions about the companies in which you are interested. For example, if you want to know about branded men's clothing, call investor relations of a department store chain. When investor relations talks about men's clothing, you might comment, *"I heard that Polo and Tommy were doing well, but that Mossimo was doing lousy."* You may get no reaction, but sometimes the customer will give inputs that can be invaluable.

Talking to competitors can also be very valuable. Competitors obviously have an ax to grind. They are, after all, competitors. But competitors will always give you a different point of view. They will usually tell you why they are better than the company in which you are interested. Comparing one view with the other may be extremely useful. But in talking to competitors, you should have done your homework. You cannot call up Compaq just to ask about Dell. If you call Compaq, you should first ask about its business, then ask how it compares with Dell. Further, be sure that the two companies really are competitors. Coke and Pepsi are clearly competitors, but Coke and Budweiser are not. Unless the competition is direct or intense, one company will probably not give you good feedback on the other. A small, regional discount store may consider Wal-Mart to be its competitor, but the reverse may not be true. Still, it is usually worth asking the questions. Some investor relations departments have people who know a lot about their industry and are willing to share information.

LOOK FOR HOLES IN THE NUMBERS

Once you have a basic view of the company, the next step in fundamental analysis is to look for holes in the numbers. All you are trying to do is identify if the consensus is too optimistic or too pessimistic. You do not need to figure out what numbers are the most important. As we've seen, most reports will highlight the critical issues. Nor do you need to build an earnings or valuation model or calculate the ratios. The analysts have already done this. Your job is to look at the numbers and spot the holes.

Don't bury yourself in details. Find the page in the annual report that gives you the five- or ten-year summary. The summary page often combines numbers from the income statement, balance sheet, and cash-flow statement, as well as other numbers that the company considers to be critical to its business. A retailer might show the number of stores and the sales per square foot. A real estate company might show square footage and rents. A cable television company might show the number of households in its market, the percentage with cable, and the average revenue per household. The biggest advantage to the summary page is that it has only the most important numbers and presents them with a long-term, historic view. While you may miss out on some of the details by looking at the summary page, the advantage of having a good overview more than compensates. When talking to companies for the first time, I have often pulled out the summary page and reviewed it line by line. The company puts its most important information on this page, so using it will put you on the right track.

When you look at the summary page, see if you can spot any patterns. What does sales growth look like historically? Has it been consistent or erratic? Have margins been getting better or worse? How have expenses compared to sales? What has been the trend in earnings per share? How has return on equity (ROE) varied over time? How has the debt-to-equity ratio changed? What are the industry-specific issues on which the company has chosen to focus? We will be looking at each of these issues. You don't need to be able to do detailed analysis, but understanding these issues will help you spot changes and patterns.

Unless there have been many acquisitions or divestitures, most companies will show clear patterns. Make a mental picture of the patterns. Then look at the analysts' projections. Are any of their numbers inconsistent with the historical trends? If so, these numbers may be the key to the story. Don't worry about the numbers that are consistent. Try first to focus on the areas in which you see significant changes. This will usually lead you to the issues that are at the heart of the company's future success or failure.

This is not to say that change cannot occur. It can. But change is less common than constancy. Think about people. People can change. Overweight people can lose forty pounds, and middle-aged couch potatoes can run a marathon. But most of the time, overweight people will stay overweight, and couch potatoes will choose to watch the marathon. It is the same with companies. Most will continue to follow the same patterns they have followed for years. **So if someone is suggesting that the company is about to be transformed from a middle-aged couch potato into a marathon runner, the investor needs to focus on whether that's possible and why.**

WATCH THE CHANGES IN SALES AND MARGINS

After looking at the summary page, the individual investor should look at the income statement in the annual report. The company's income statement has the historical income numbers, while the analysts' models include their projections. In looking at the income statement, the critical task is once again to look for changes. If sales, margins, expenses, and earnings per share have historically grown 10 percent every year, and analysts are projecting a 10 percent growth rate, there is not much to the story. If analysts say a company that has been growing by 10 percent is now going to grow by 20 percent, you have a key issue on which to focus.

The first thing on the income statement you should focus on is sales. For many companies, sales are the most important item. Look at the long-term historical record. Some companies grow consistently, while some have records that are much more cyclical. Look at the more recent record. Is growth accelerating or declining? See what the analysts expect. You could win or lose right here. This may be a good time for another reality check. You can usually form your own opinion about sales growth. Let's say a company has grown from controlling 5 percent to 35 percent of a market by buying up small competitors. The analysts say that they believe it can capture 55 percent, but as you look at the competition you believe that growth may become more difficult. Ask investor relations where the company thinks it can gain market share. Ask the competitors the same question, or go back to your home turf and see if you can find any inputs on your own.

QUESTIONS TO ASK FOR SALES-GROWTH REALITY CHECK

- Ask about the overall growth of the market. Think about whether it is sustainable. People in a company are often more optimistic than people outside of it.

- Ask about industry-specific issues that could impact sales. Is technology changing? What are the competitors doing? Some companies have a narrow view of their environment and can get blindsided.

- Ask about any projection by the analysts that you have difficulty accepting. If an analyst says that same-store gains, which have been averaging 2 percent, will jump to 10 percent, ask why. When the company explains the answer, see if you really believe it. This could be the heart of your investment decision.

- Ask what external factors most worry the company. Don't settle for pie-in-the-sky answers, like, *"The stock market could crash."* These types of comments are useless. Keep asking until you get specific answers, such as, *"We are terrified that Microsoft will turn out a product that competes directly with ours."*

- If you see a product line that you believe is starting to sell very well, ask about it versus the analysts' expectations. Venture a concrete opinion and force investor relations to give you an answer. *"I think that your new products are selling better than the analysts think and that sales will surprise on the upside."* If you are right, investor relations may confirm your view or at least say that the company is optimistic. Concrete questions often bring concrete answers.

As you look at the income statements, next focus on the gross margins as a percent of sales. Gross margins are the profits that a company makes on its sales. Margins should show a relatively consistent historical pattern. They may be flat, or they may be going up or down slightly, but there is often a discernible trend. Once again, the key is not the trend itself, but rather the changes in it. If margins start dropping sharply, it could mean that competition is getting more difficult. If margins start increasing sharply, it could mean that the competition is being less aggressive, which is good, or that the company is getting greedy, which is bad. If margins jump to record levels, it could mean that the company has conquered its competition—or is playing games with the numbers. If there are significant changes in the actual or the projected margins, the investor must find out the cause.

This is not as difficult as it sounds. Factors impacting margins should make common sense. Higher competition should lead to lower margins as competitors squeeze each other on price. Lower competition should lead to higher margins as competitive pressures abate. Look at the competitive landscape. Does the change in margins reflect a change in competition? Look at the closest competitors. Are their margins moving in the same direction? If your company has higher margins while the closest competitors have much lower margins, something could be wrong. Do another reality check. If a bicycle manufacturer tells you that there is less competition from imports, walk into Wal-Mart or Target and look for yourself.

COMPANIES CAN HIDE EARNINGS IN INVENTORIES AND RECEIVABLES

After looking at the income statement, turn to the balance sheet. Many investors are scared of working with balance sheets, but they are very simple. Remember, don't worry about industry standards or ratios; just look at the changes from period to period. Look first at the inventories on the balance sheet. Inventories should grow at about the same rate as sales. If they grow faster, the company is either making too much product or not selling enough.

The importance of inventories in most companies cannot be overstated. **Unlike fine wines, inventory does not improve with age.** A company that has too much inventory can be seriously overstating its earnings. Suppose that a computer manufacturer ended 1996 with sales of $100 million, up from $90 million in 1995, and gross profits of $50 million, up from $40 million. At first glance, it would appear that the company had a good

1996. But assume that inventories grew from $10 million to $40 million. What do you think last year's computers will be worth next year? Not much! The inventory may be sitting on the books for $40 million, but there is no way that anyone would ever pay that amount for the old computers. If you see that inventory jumped from $10 million to $40 million while sales increased by only $10 million, you know the company has a major problem.

If the company had sold the extra inventory for a $20 million loss, profits would have plunged to $30 million. What looked like a good year was really a disaster. By keeping the extra inventory, the manufacturer was able to report much better profits, but it was only jeopardizing its future.

Companies frequently put spin control on the level of their inventories. One of the most common sayings is, *"Inventory is on plan."* Don't try to ask what *"the plan"* is. You will never get a straight answer. Companies also say they are *"bringing in new merchandise early"* or *"building inventories for better sales in the future."* While there are times when these statements are appropriate, in most cases, higher inventory is a bad sign. The rule with inventories is simple: If inventory is growing faster than sales, current earnings may be overstated and future earnings could be at risk. If inventory is growing slower than sales, the current earnings could be understated and future earnings could be better than planned.

The next item on the balance sheet to look at is receivables. This is the money that the company is owed by customers. Receivables should be growing at the same rate as sales. If they are growing much faster, it could be a sign of trouble. It means that the company is not getting paid and that it is giving special terms to customers to generate business. This practice can artificially inflate its sales and margins.

Consider the computer manufacturer. Instead of selling the computers at a big loss, the manufacturer might "sell" them for $50 million and make another $20 million profit. It would now appear to have record sales, record earnings, and no inventory problem. Analysts would be falling all over each other to raise estimates and pronounce the manufacturer a "growth company." However, in order to get the retailers to take the lousy merchandise, the manufacturer might have to promise that the retailer would not have to pay for two years, and that any computers not sold could be returned for full credit. This, of course, is a sham. If the retailers do not have to pay and if they can return what they do not sell, then the sales are bogus and the earnings are way overstated. Unless you looked at the receivables, you would never see that there was a problem. But if you did look at them, you would recognize that something was seriously wrong. It is fine for a company to say that it sold goods and made a nice profit, but if it never gets paid, what is the point?

These types of practices occur much more frequently than most investors believe. For years, at the end of many quarters, the major manufacturers of personal computers, such as Compaq and IBM, have offered special deals so that the computer resellers would "buy" extra computers. (In the industry, this technique is known as "stuffing the channel.") Because the resellers could return what they did not sell, many of the sales were not "real." But it was a convenient way for the manufacturers to get extra merchandise off their books and make their sales gain look better than it really was. In a world in which small changes in sales can impact the company's price-earnings ratio, these "deals" have had a major impact on the prices of the stocks. Of course, if the computers are sitting in warehouses waiting to be returned, the manufacturers are just postponing their day of reckoning. The moral is simple: If receivables are growing much faster than sales, some serious games may be going on. If companies are offering special deals to move merchandise, the deals will usually come back to haunt them.

Analysts often do not pay enough attention to inventories and receivables or get suckered in to a company's spin control. As a result, inventories and receivables often offer a good opportunity for individual investors to spot opportunities that the analysts miss.

MAKE SURE EXPENSES ARE IN LINE

Turn back to the income statement and look at the relationship of expenses to sales. These lines show how the company is managing the cost side of its business. If expenses are declining very slightly as a percent of sales, it is usually a sign that management is doing a good job of running its business. If expenses are going up faster than sales, it could be a sign that the management is losing control. If the expenses are declining much faster than sales, it is usually a sign that management has taken draconian measures with regard to costs. Often this is very positive, but sometimes cost-cutting can backfire.

If there is more than one category for expenses, note where the numbers are getting better or worse. When you have more detail, you can better judge whether the company is building for the future or just trying to report the best possible numbers in the present. If a company is spending more money for marketing and advertising, these expenses may hurt its current year but make it stronger in the long term. If, on the other hand, the company is cutting back dramatically on these expenses, it may make more money this year, but lose in the long term. There is a fine line between saving money now and building for the future. Every type of industry has critical issues. Research and development is a critical expense for technology and drug companies. Maintenance expenses are critical for real estate companies. Drilling exploratory wells is critical for an oil company. When you look at a company, make sure that it is not cutting back on a critical category to meet its earnings estimates. If it is, the current year may be fine, but the long-term growth rate may be at risk.

Extraordinary Gobbledygook Can Make You Money— If You Understand It

Before you go any further, see if there are any special items that impact the earnings. Companies have learned how to turn a simple income statement into gobbledygook by making acquisitions and divestitures, writing off goodwill, and taking reserves for extraordinary items. If the company has made a major acquisition or divestiture, ask if the analysts have correctly understood its financial implications. If they have not, there is a problem, because the company has done a bad job of explaining the deal and the consensus is working with wrong information. If the company's explanation is too confusing, find another stock.

If you can understand the gobbledygook, the company may be worth looking at. Through the wonders of accounting, many companies have learned how to use gobbledygook to allow them to report better-than-expected earnings in the future. When a company makes an acquisition or a divestiture, it often takes reserves for closing facilities and discontinuing product lines. Without these reserves, these costs would impact future earnings, but now they are buried in a one-time charge that most investors ignore. If the reserves are sufficiently high, the company could be almost guaranteed of beating or at least meeting earnings estimates in the upcoming years. If you see that a company has made a simple acquisition or divestiture, ask investor relations about the amount and composition of its reserves. If you can understand how these reserves will impact future earnings, it could be worth the trouble to push through the gobbledygook.

WATCH FOR CHANGES IN INCOME

Look next at the income statement for the level of pretax income as a percent of sales. Is it consistent with the company's historical pattern? Some companies have very simple patterns. For the past ten years, pretax income might have been 8 percent of sales or it might have grown from 7 percent to 9 percent. In either case, the pattern will be very easy to see. If the projections show a sharp divergence from the historical pattern, ask what has changed in the company or the environment that could lead to this divergence.

Some companies, such as those in the steel, auto, and oil industries, have much more cyclical patterns. They can go from making a lot of money to losing money. With these companies, looking at a pattern becomes more difficult. Some companies, such as cable television or real estate investment trusts, may have low or no income because of high depreciation and amortization. Others, such as biotechs, may have high research and development expenditures that reduce income to zero. In these cases, there are obviously no pretax income patterns that can be of use. If pretax income as a percent of sales is not a good measure, ask investor relations what is.

If there is a reasonably stable pattern of pretax earnings as a percent of sales, look at the annual earnings progression. Many companies will have a consistent historical pattern. Growth companies, such as Intel and

Microsoft, will show 20 percent-plus improvement in pretax income. More mature growth companies, like Wal-Mart or Coke, should show 15 percent growth. Well-managed industry leaders, such as May Department Stores, will grow 10 to 15 percent each year.

Some companies are very good at managing their earnings. Stable companies often take extra reserves if business is a little better than normal and fewer reserves if business is a little worse than normal so that they can show a consistent pattern. If you see a company that has reported twenty straight years of improving earnings, with each year in a relatively narrow band, you can be reasonably sure that not only is this a good business, but also management is expert at managing its earnings. Investors, especially professionals, almost always pay more for earnings consistency, because it is easier for them to sleep at night with companies they know will not disappoint them. This is not to say that you should buy stock only in companies with consistent records. These companies are usually well followed and have high p/e ratios. But consistent companies, for better or worse, present fewer challenges for the investor and that is why these stocks always look more expensive than comparable companies.

If the profit level changes significantly from historical levels, you should ask why. If a company has been growing by 15 percent a year and suddenly shows a year of 25 percent growth, you must ask, *"Was the increase a flash in the pan or is it sustainable?"* If the increase is sustainable, the company will gain a new p/e multiple, and the stock will soar. If the increase is not sustainable, the price of the stock may come down.

The reverse happens when companies have years that are below par. If a company that has been growing by 15 percent per year has a year of 5 percent growth, investors may rethink their views. If the 5 percent growth continues, the stock may be dead money or worse, but if the 15 percent growth rate returns, the stock could be very attractive.

CASH FLOW: SHOW ME THE MONEY!

After you've looked at the income statement, turn to the cash-flow statement. Cash flow reflects all moneys flowing into and out of a company.

Because cash flow focuses on money rather than on reported earnings or balance sheet items, it can often give a very different view of the company. Because cash flow is not as simple a measure as earnings, some analysts give it less attention than it deserves. **Reading this statement often gives investors an opportunity that analysts miss.**

The first part of the cash-flow statement is the *Sources of Funds from Operations*. These are the moneys generated by the company's business. The first source of funds is profits. (Losses are a use of cash.) The next sources are depreciation and amortization. While these are charges against earnings, they have no impact on cash and so are added back in to the sources side of the cash-flow statement. Finally, there are changes in inventories, receivables, and other working capital items. The total of the earnings, depreciation, amortization, and changes in working capital comprise the sources of cash available to the company.

The next section of the cash-flow statement is the *Uses of Funds in Operations*. It includes capital expenditures and acquisitions. The difference between the sources of funds and the uses of funds is the free cash flow.

Compare the levels of capital expenditures and depreciation. Capital expenditures are the funds that the company is spending to build new facilities. Depreciation is used to write down the value of older assets. Theoretically, if the company is not growing, depreciation and capital expenditures should be in balance. If the company is growing, capital expenditures should be higher than depreciation.

Be cautious if capital expenditures look too low. Some companies, especially those that are highly leveraged, often spend less than they should. If an airline has capital expenditures that are half of depreciation, it is probably not replacing its old planes fast enough. Its fleet may be aging, and it might soon start to face higher breakdowns or worse. If you see a company reduce its capital expenditures, ask what is happening. The company may be jeopardizing its future.

Amortization is similar to depreciation except that it is usually used with intangible assets. Items that are amortized, such as goodwill, come when a company makes an acquisition. Goodwill represents the difference between what a company paid for a business and the business's real assets.

Under the assumption that the value of the business will decline over time, the goodwill must be written off, or amortized.

In most cases, depreciation and amortization provide a fair view of the value of older assets, but sometimes the value of an asset declines faster or slower in the real world than it does on the books of the company. If the assets are declining in value faster than they are being depreciated, the earnings of the company will be overstated. This often happens with technology companies. If the assets are declining in value slower than they are being depreciated, the earnings will be understated. This often happens in real estate and media.

In real estate, for example, companies have to depreciate their buildings, but the value of the buildings may not be declining. It may actually be increasing. Yet each year, the company must take a charge against its earnings and reduce its book value by depreciating the property. This charge clearly understates the company's financial position. Properties that are written down to almost nothing on the books can be worth millions. For that reason, cash flow is a better measure than earnings and book value in looking at real estate companies. Cash flow is also a better measure for media companies which have to depreciate and amortize the costs of their stations, even though the stations usually increase in value.

THE IMPORTANCE OF POSITIVE CASH FLOW

Once you know the sources and uses of funds, look at free cash flow. If cash flow is positive, a company can use it to make acquisitions, buy back stock, or otherwise enhance earnings. If it is negative, the company will have to raise capital to keep growing. Everything else being equal, positive cash flow is very important.

Rapidly growing companies can be cash-flow negative because they need capital to fund their growth. There is nothing wrong with being cash-flow negative as long as the company has cash on hand and has access to capital. If, however, something goes wrong, these companies could face a liquidity crisis. More than one fast-growing company has been forced into bankruptcy because it had too high a negative free cash flow and could not raise new capital. Thus, if a company is running a large negative cash flow, you should always check to see how much cash or lines of credit it has on hand. **Analysts are sometimes so caught up in the company's promise that they do not look closely enough at this issue.** If the company does not have enough credit to weather a storm, you may want to think about putting your money somewhere else.

Just because a company is growing does not mean that it has to burn cash. Many of the greatest companies in the country, such as Microsoft and Wal-Mart, have been cash-flow positive or neutral during many of their fastest-growing years. With the exception of a few industries that are extremely capital intensive, most great companies should be able to control their capital expenditures and their working capital in order to be cash-flow positive. If you look at two companies in the same industry with the same growth rate, the better company will usually have the higher free cash flow. Cash flow is a critical measure of a company's health and a good barometer of management's ability to run its business.

Investors who ignore the impact of cash flow can live to regret their oversight. The following table reflects the results of four sporting goods retailers from 1991 to 1993. During this period, Sports Authority added $366 million in sales, while generating $10 million of free cash flow, by closely controlling its capital expenditures and inventories. Its three competitors combined totaled only $301 million in sales and had a combined negative cash flow of $186 million. Because these companies did a poor job of controlling their capital expenditures and inventories, they burned money. Sports Authority became the leader in the industry, while SportsTown liquidated, and Sportsmart and Jumbo Sports fell on extremely hard times. Anyone who looked at the cash flow would have realized that Sports Authority would be the winner and the other companies would be losers. Interestingly, many of the analysts, who focused only on earnings growth, did not.

SPORTING GOODS RETAILERS—1991 TO 1993

Company	Sources of Funds (millions)	Uses of Funds (millions)	Free Cash Flow (millions)	Sales Gain (millions)
Sports Authority	$56	$46	$10	$366
Sports & Recreation	($32)	$61	($93)	$100
Sportsmart	($9)	$41	($50)	$122
SportsTown	($22)	$21	($43)	$78

Cash flow is thus a critical measure that investors should look at before valuing a company:

- For most companies, it is a valuable barometer for the ability of the management.
- Except during periods of maximum growth, most good companies should generate strong sources of cash. If they plow this cash into inventories and receivables or into capital investments that do not produce strong cash flow, they are heading for trouble.
- In real estate, media, and some other industries, it is a better guide than earnings.
- Because analysts focus primarily on earnings growth, they often miss the importance of cash flow, which provides an advantage to the individual investor.

The cash-flow statement ties into the level of debt and equity on the balance sheet. Equity is the same as net worth—the difference between assets and liabilities. If the company is generating positive cash flow, the ratio of debt to equity will usually decline. If cash flow is negative, the ratio will usually increase. While most analysts pay only lip service to this ratio, it often offers investors the opportunity to find companies that will surprise on the upside or the downside.

Look at the debt/equity ratio over time. Most companies try to keep this ratio within a narrow range. If the ratio is going up quickly, some of the company's recent earnings improvement may have come from higher leverage and the company may have problems financing future growth, especially if the stock market drops. On the other hand, if the debt/equity ratio has declined below its historical norms, the company may be able to leverage poor earnings by buying back stock or making acquisitions. **Analysts often ignore the opportunities to be found in companies with low debt/equity ratios because they are difficult to quantify.** Unless a company announces a buyback, most analysts will not incorporate the debt/equity ratio into their models. But companies with low debt/equity ratios very often releverage themselves, and in so doing provide upside surprises in earnings.

Return on Equity Is a Useful Measure

Take a quick look at the company's return on equity (ROE). Almost all annual reports show this ratio. Return on equity is a critical number. It shows the profits that a company has been able to generate with a particular level of equity. ROE often corresponds directly to the earnings growth rate. Generally, the higher the ROE, the better the company.

Analysts often underrate good companies with high returns on equity, if those companies lack glamour or upside earnings surprises. They may look at a company with a 20 percent return on equity and only a 10 percent gain in sales and assume that the company no longer has growth opportunities. But companies with high returns on equity can usually show strong earnings growth by making acquisitions or by buying back their stock. **Long-term investors can often well outperform the market by buying companies with a p/e ratio well below their ROE.**

The reverse also occurs. Analysts can fall in love with companies with mediocre returns on equity if they are in a hot industry or if they suddenly produce upside surprises in earnings. But no matter how much the analysts may love a stock and no matter how much it may outperform in the short term, few companies will be able to support a lofty stock price if their ROE is much lower than their p/e ratio. Except in high-growth start-ups or in businesses in which "equity" may not be a fair gauge, such as real estate, it is always useful for investors to compare the p/e ratio with the return on equity.

LET'S MAKE A DEAL: TAKEOVER TARGETS

The final thing you may want to look at is how much the company would be worth if it were taken over. That's called a stock's takeover value. Vast sums have been made in takeovers. In the early 1980s, the media companies were takeover targets. Then the action shifted to department store chains, the drug companies, and now to the financial services and brokerage companies. Almost every industry has seen a large number of takeovers, and most have been at a substantial premium to the original market price.

While you should not try to compete with the risk arbitrageurs (the professionals I warned you about in Chapter 3) on companies that are already "in play," it is a perfectly acceptable strategy to buy companies that you believe could become takeover targets and then hold them in the hope that lightning will strike. But if you intend to look at a stock as a potential takeover target, you must follow a few basic steps. See if other takeovers are occurring in the industry. If one of the stocks you regularly monitor (one you keep on your monitor list) is being taken over, take a look at its closest competitors. If you see a number of takeovers in an industry, go to a website such as Morningstar.net and screen the names of all the public companies in the industry. Takeovers follow patterns. When one company in an industry makes an acquisition, others commonly follow. Look at the last several acquisitions made in the industry or at the analysts' comments on them. Is there a pattern to the valuations? Cable television and cellular phone companies have recently been taken over for what was called price-per-pop (dollars per household). While the price-per-pop varied slightly by market, it was relatively easy to use the available figures to make a valuation for each business. Many banks have been acquired on the basis of price-to-book value. While faster-growing markets may justify a higher number, this valuation technique is relatively predictable. If there is serious merger activity in an industry, most analysts will have some type of takeover valuation you can use to figure out the stock's takeover value.

Also look at the stock's takeover premium. This is the difference between the current price and the price that the stock would probably have if there were no talk of takeovers. Now you have a very simple risk/reward analysis. Compare the takeover value to the current price. That gives you your upside. The takeover premium gives you your downside. Look at the level of deals in an industry, and make your best guess. You are interested in a large regional bank. You believe that it would be worth $60 in a takeover and would normally sell for $30 based on its earnings. If the stock is at $35, the takeover premium is only $5, and it is probably a good investment. But if it is selling at $55, with a $25 takeover premium it may already be too expensive. If the takeover premium is low and merger activity in the industry is high, the stock could be worth a look. If the takeover premium is high, it may not be worth your trouble.

Playing takeovers requires patience. If you are not sufficiently patient, you can often give up on a stock just before the takeover comes. If you play takeovers, understand why you are buying a particular stock. Watch the action in the industry. As long as the potential acquirers still appear to have an appetite, be patient. Your day will come.

DIVIDENDS: MUCH ADO ABOUT NOTHING

In most cases, dividends should be irrelevant or perhaps even a negative for the individual investor. Companies must pay taxes on their earnings, even if they pay them out as dividends. Individuals with taxable accounts must also pay taxes on their dividends at ordinary income rates. This means that dividends are taxed twice, both times at high rates. (For this reason, companies with high dividends are usually more appropriate for tax-free accounts, such as IRAs.) Generally, individuals will be better off if the company uses its profits to spur growth or to buy back stock instead of paying it out in dividends.

Investors often see companies with high dividends and think that they are getting a bargain. In some cases, they may be. But if the company is not earning its dividend, there is a risk that the dividend could be cut. Some stocks, such as real estate investment trusts (REITs), are considered to be "dividend plays." In these stocks, investors often equate dividends with earnings. The problem is that if the fundamentals are not strong, the dividends will be slashed. Over the past few years, utility investors have learned to their dismay that dividend plays can spell disaster.

Notwithstanding, companies with higher dividends tend to have less volatile stock prices. This is especially relevant when the market drops and investors seek some current yield. Some companies also use dividends as a way of signaling projected earnings. These are usually larger companies with a solid history of raising the dividend each year. If, for example, a company has raised its dividend between 10 percent and 15 percent every year for twenty years, and it announces that this year its dividend will increase by another 15 percent, it is reasonably safe to assume that the company believes its earnings will be better than average. In companies with this pattern, investors should look at dividends if the current earnings are disappointing. If the company continues to increase its dividend, it is sending a signal to investors that it is confident about its future.

VALUING A STOCK SUMMARIZED

Do not spend too much time with a calculator. You are not trying to become a Certified Financial Analyst. You are merely trying to spot some valuation areas in which the analysts are either too optimistic or too pessimistic by using the tools that have been discussed in this section.

Simple analysis is thus much less complicated than it would appear. All you really have to do is look at the consensus and decide when it is right and when it is wrong. Remember these steps:

- Listen to the strategy of the company. Does the concept make sense to you? Are the products good? Do you like the management? Draw from your own experience.
- Look at the expectations surrounding the company and its competitors.
- Look at the earnings. Are they clean?
- Look at the balance sheet. Are there items that appear to be growing too fast?
- Pay special attention to the inventory.

- Look at the cash-flow statement. Is the company generating positive cash flow?
- Look at the return on equity.
- Could the company be a takeover play?
- Look at the price/earnings ratio. Is it in line with the growth rate?

Look back at your analysis. See if you have an edge over the analysts. There are thousands of stocks to buy. It is best to find those in which you have an edge.

You've taken an important step for the guerrilla investor—gathering quality information on specific companies. You should now be in a good position to start making some investment decisions based on your fundamental analysis. However, before you do, it would be extremely useful to stop and look at the technical pattern of the stock. Very often technical patterns can show the guerrilla investor critical issues that analysts and institutional investors miss.

CHAPTER SEVEN

Technical
Weapons

In war, the guerrillas must develop better sources of intelligence if they are to defeat a more well-equipped enemy. At first, this may seem like an impossible task. The modern army has the best intelligence that money can buy, while the guerrillas normally have limited resources. But the guerrillas have one ironic advantage: Because the army is so large, its movements are easy to trace. Because it is so strong, its power reduces its need for subterfuge. The guerrillas can see where the army has come from and where it is going. On the other hand, the guerrillas are all but invisible to the army. While the army has military superiority, the guerrillas can often use their lack of size to avoid direct assaults and to counterattack.

Much the same situation applies in investing. The professional obtains the best intelligence money can buy by hiring analysts to predict earnings, technicians to chart stocks, and strategists to predict the market. Individuals do not have the time or resources to match the professionals. The task for the individual may sound daunting, but it is actually much easier than it would appear, because professionals on Wall Street, like armies, move en masse. Their investments often form clear patterns that individual investors can easily see and track. If an investor can gain a good overview of the professionals' movements, that individual can take measures to avoid the professionals' strengths and counterattack to expose their weaknesses. **Charts are the technical weapons that the individual can use to follow the actions of the professionals and anticipate critical changes in direction.**

CHARTS: THE EARLY WARNING SYSTEM

Charts in investing are the equivalent of satellite photographs in war. They present a picture of all the trading in a particular stock, index, or market. The chart shows how stock prices and trading volumes are moving, just as a series of satellite photographs will show how an army is moving. While the charts show the entire picture of a stock or a market, they are especially effective in showing the actions of professionals. The professionals make up most of the trading, so their actions make up the preponderance of the information on the charts. By studying the charts, the individual investor can see major changes in stock prices and trading volume. By waiting for these changes before acting, the individual will allow the professional to set the future direction of stock prices, but by moving quickly once these changes appear, the individual will be able to take action before the professional has been able to accumulate or sell a full position and before critical news events dramatically change the pattern of the stock. This early warning system can neutralize many of the advantages of the professionals.

The Internet has dramatically transformed the use of charts for individual investors. Prior to the Internet, most investors could not get charts, especially for specific stocks, unless they subscribed to an expensive technical service, and even then, the charts were often out of date. Now the charts on numerous sites are free and have up-to-the-minute information. They are also extremely easy to work with. Simple clicks can take you from one timeframe or chart system to the other. With the Internet, individuals now have technical resources that are as good as the professionals'. And since individuals can use the charts to track the professionals, the amateur investor can actually gain the upper hand.

A chart shows a historical picture of how a stock has performed, but many charts also seem to be able to actually predict the future action of a stock. A chart often shows when a stock is about to break out and begin a long run on the upside as well as when it is about to break down and begin a long move on the downside. Later in this chapter, we will be looking at some examples of charts and studying exactly how to follow patterns on various types of charts.

Most fundamental investors (those who rely on fundamental rather than technical weapons) reject the notion that chart patterns can foreshadow the future. They look at the analysis that technical investors depend on as akin to voodoo. While many portfolio managers use charts religiously, few institutional salespersons and even fewer analysts use them. When I was an analyst, I worked with a very smart salesman named Leigh Curry. Every time an analyst talked about a new idea, Leigh checked the technical pattern of the stock. In most cases, the analysts would have done well to listen to what Leigh had to say, because he often saw signs on the charts that the analysts had missed. The reality is that technical analysis is much more predictive than most fundamental investors would admit.

There are three major reasons why charts are often able to predict the future price behavior of stocks:

1. Because professionals cannot change directions quickly, their future actions are often foreshadowed on the charts. It is not that charts actually predict the future, but they give off signs of a move before that move has become apparent to most investors. Imagine that you had aerial photographs of an army on the battlefield. If you watched its moves, you might not be able to spot minor maneuvers, but you would be able to see when it was slowing its advance, stopping, then turning. The same is the case with charts and professional investors. You may not be able to see small blips up or down, but it is often easy to spot when a major trend is about to change.

2. Technical patterns influence technical investors. As trading patterns of stocks change, these patterns often become self-fulfilling prophecies, because many investors use technical patterns as their primary investment technique. Stocks that develop strong trading patterns will usually keep moving up because technical investors are buying, while stocks that develop weak trading patterns will usually keep moving down because technical investors are selling. In fact, stocks with strong or weak trading patterns can react in dramatically different ways to the same event. How often have you watched a stock that has been "acting strong" shrug off what appears to be bad news and continue moving up? Or how often have you seen a stock that has been "acting weak" get pummeled by a seemingly inconsequential piece of information? Thus, the actions of the technical investors combined with the actions of the mass of professionals will emphasize the direction of the stock, making it even easier for the individual to spot the future trends.

3. The trading pattern revealed by a stock chart very often foretells fundamental changes in a company. Individuals watching a stock chart may see a stock begin to break out and wonder what is happening. They may even call the company or the analysts and be told that there has been no change in the company's fundamentals. Then, several months later, when the company reports earnings that were much better than expected, it becomes clear that the trading action shown by the stock chart did mean something. Someone, company insiders or industry experts, knew that business was going to be better than planned and had aggressively bought the stock. They created the new trading pattern while the market as a whole was still ignorant.

How often have you seen a stock drop sharply on little or no news? Your broker tells you that an analyst reduced estimates by $.02, the market completely overreacted, and this is a great buying opportunity. You buy the stock. Then, three weeks later, the company announces that earnings will be disappointing. The stock plunges. *"I knew something was wrong,"* you mutter as you dump your stock. In retrospect, it was clear that someone had a different view of the company's fundamentals than your broker, and that they had been right. When stocks get crushed on a particular day because of a disappointing announcement from the company, look at the trading pattern in the previous weeks. In most cases, the stock will have already traded down substantially from its high, usually on strong volume. While the horrible news may have been a surprise to you, many investors had been expecting problems and had already been selling.

The most common error investors make is to ignore strong opposing signs on the charts. Investing long term is a good idea, but it's not good to become wed to a company. When a minor event occurs, all the analysts, who are similarly wed to the stock, rush to issue reports saying, *"The market has overreacted."* The investors read the reports and feel comforted. They want to believe that the analysts are right. But very often this "overreaction" turns out to be anything but that. When the direction of a stock changes, the smart investor should always study the trading pattern and try to figure out what others see. If investors watch the trading patterns, they can often spot changes in a company's fundamentals before they are recognized by the market as a whole. If you own a stock in which the trading pattern suddenly changes, you should assume that someone knows something you do not and the stock may be in for a major ride. Fighting or ignoring the tape can be a sure-fire way for investors to lose money.

As an early warning system for the actions of the professionals, charts are especially critical for individuals. The chart reflects the professionals' initial momentum, their reaction to current news, insiders' views of future events, and technicians' views of the future of the company. Because professionals tend to move en masse, the charts can allow the individual to see both where the professionals have been and where they are moving. With this knowledge, the individual's chances of defeating the professional are enhanced.

Because the technical patterns in the charts reflect the collective wisdom of all investors, the easiest way to spot future trends is to watch for significant changes in the patterns. Even if you are a fundamental investor, you should watch the chart of a stock and look for clues to its future direction. Sometimes the tape will not tell you much, but sometimes it will form a pattern so dramatic that even a novice can see bullish or bearish signals. If you see these signals, use them either to confirm an existing position or rethink a particular strategy. More often than not, it will enable you to significantly improve your performance.

THE TREND IS YOUR FRIEND

The first thing to understand about technical patterns is that once stocks start to go up, they go up much further than most people think, and once they start to go down, they drop much lower than most people think. Remember Newton's First Law of Physics: A body in motion stays in motion until stopped by a greater force. On Wall Street, traders refer to this as the "trend." A common saying is, *"The trend is your friend."* What it means is simple: Stick with what is working. Avoid what is not working.

This is a critical lesson for all investors, but it is especially critical for amateurs. You would not think of standing on a railroad track as a freight train came speeding toward you. Nor would you think of blocking the exit as hundreds of screaming people came rushing out of a burning theater. These would be acts of total stupidity. But would you think of buying a stock that was plunging to new lows on huge volume as professional investors rushed to the exit? Few investors know enough about a particular company to successfully buy when the masses of investors are selling or sell when the masses of investors are buying.

This is often a difficult issue for most investors, professionals as well as individuals, because most people do not like to admit when they are wrong. You see a stock you like, do your homework, find home-turf advantage, and buy it. Then something happens. Investors rush to sell as the stock plunges. You review your analysis and decide that you are right and the rest of the Street is wrong. You double your holdings. After all, you have studied the company and have home-turf advantages. But what about all the other people? What are they thinking? What do they know? This much is certain: Even if you did your homework, if everyone else is panicked, there will be no rationality in the price or the trading action of the stock. Admitting a mistake may be tough, but trying to stop panicked investors is tougher.

Stocks are much more volatile than most investors think. Look at Oxford Health Plan, which went from $15 to $90 and back to $15 in four years; or Rainforest Café, which doubled and halved in one year; or Just for Feet, which went from $12 to $36 and back to $12 in just over two years; or Rational Software, which went from $11 to $48 and back to $11 in little more than one year. Was it merely changes in fundamentals that accounted for these remarkable moves? The answer is no. These stocks had huge moves up and down because of the power of momentum.

A stock you watch may act like a dog, trading around the same price for months while the market rallies. Then, what seems like a small event occurs. Perhaps the growth rate is slightly higher than the analysts had expected. The event breaks the balance between buyers and sellers. The buyers nudge the stock up. It breaks through a resistance level and starts to run. As it does, analysts raise their estimates, technicians say the stock has broken out, and momentum investors pile in. The stock doubles or even quadruples. You look at the price of the stock and think that the market is irrational. From your point of view, it may be. But you should never make the mistake of betting against it. Momentum can take a stock much further up than anyone would ever expect.

Momentum works on the downside as well, as the owners of Oxford Health Plan, Rainforest Café, Just For Feet, and Rational Software can testify. The stock struggles to maintain its price, usually on higher volume. Then another seemingly small event occurs. Perhaps earnings were slightly lower than investors had expected. The stock breaks through a support level and starts to drop. As it does, analysts lower their estimates, technicians say the stock has broken down, and momentum investors flee. The stock plunges. In fact, momentum on the downside is usually faster and stronger than momentum on the upside. Some investors buy, believing the stock is now "cheap," but this is usually a mistake. When a momentum stock plunges, it will usually keep plunging. The first major decline is rarely the last.

You may look quizzically at stocks that surge and then fall back, wondering how the bulls can love them and then the bears hate them so much. There may be no completely logical answer as to why small changes in sales and earnings can transform a company from a dog to a growth company and back to a dog, but those who look for logic and fight the tape lose money.

It is often tempting for an investor to sell a stock that is going up strongly or buy a stock that has started to "correct." But most of the time, these decisions will be wrong. Holding your position against a powerful tape is like holding your position against a powerful army. You will be annihilated. In the long run, your judgment may be vindicated, but by then, you will have already been wiped out. If a stock has strong momentum, the wise investor should avoid fighting the tape and wait for signs of a top or a bottom before acting.

Investors often confuse betting against the trend with betting against the consensus. These are not the same. The consensus shows the views of all professionals, while the trend shows the direction of a stock or of the market as a whole. Typically, the consensus reaches extremes after the market has already had a major move. High levels of bullishness do not emerge when stocks or markets first break out and begin a trend to the upside. Instead, they emerge when stocks or markets reach peaks. Similarly, high levels of bearishness do not emerge when stocks start to break down. Instead, they emerge when stocks have bottomed out and the selling is over. In fact, the best times to act are when the consensus and the trend are at odds with each other. You should buy when the trend is up but the consensus is still strongly bearish, and you should sell when the trend is turning down but the consensus is still strongly bullish.

THE BREAKOUT

To be able to anticipate the moves of the professionals, every investor should understand a few simple chart patterns. The first is the "breakout." Every time a stock begins a major move, there is an instant in which the direction of the move becomes clear. The instant does not occur *after* the stock has begun the major run up or down. Rather, it occurs when the power balance between buyers and sellers is modified and the change in direction begins to emerge. It is typically defined not by a surge in price, but by a combination of a minor change in price and a major change in volume. **Whereas price is the factor that most investors watch, volume may be equally if not more important in determining future price movements.**

A stock may have formed a solid base by trading around the same price for six months, with buyers and sellers roughly in balance. The first sign that a change is about to occur is reflected in higher volume. If volume suddenly surges, it is a sign that a large number of people are making new bets. In most cases, when the volume surges, the bets are being made by professionals, and most of these professionals are reacting to some perceived change in the company. If volume surges while the stock inches up, it is a sign that more people are making bets on the upside. If you look at the chart of a stock, you can always see when these changes are occurring.

Identifying the breakout offers a great opportunity to make money. Since the breakout occurs before the stock has had much of a move, the individual is not allowing the professionals to make most of the early profits. Because it takes the professionals a long time to complete most moves and because technical investors do not jump on a stock until its direction becomes clear, the individual often can spot the breakout at the moment it occurs and move without much risk, since the professionals will drive the stock higher. If individuals can respond to the breakout by moving quickly, they can capitalize on the professionals' new behavior and still beat the move up.

THE TUG OF WAR

Think of the stock pattern as a tug of war between buyers and sellers. In a tug of war, there will be two teams pulling on a rope with a flag in the middle. The two teams may be fighting to a standstill, using moderate amounts of energy. But then one team begins to pull with greater power. This is the instant at which the tide has turned. The flag is still in the center. Both teams are still straining for an advantage, but you can look at the two teams and sense that the momentum has swung. The first team seems to pull with ease. The other team digs in. You can see the strain on the faces of its members. They are pulling as hard as they can. But they are not pulling to win. They are pulling to avoid losing. Both sides are now exerting more energy.

Then the first team exerts a strong, coordinated pull. The flag moves a few feet. The members of the second team scramble to regain their balance. Perhaps they even pull the flag back a foot. But then the first team exerts another coordinated pull, and the flag moves another two feet. The flag is still near the middle, but you know who is going to win. These are the "breakout" pulls that permanently set the direction of the tug of war. This is when you want to make your move. Some of the pullers on the second team begin to lose their footing. You can see the energy level draining from their faces. Their will is broken. They are no longer pulling with much force. The rout is on, as the first team now relentlessly drags the second team over the finish line.

This tug-of-war pattern is very common in the trading of stocks. The buyers and sellers may be fighting to a standstill with both sides even. Then some event occurs that gives one side an advantage. There will be a small change in the price of the stock and a big increase in the trading volume. The volume is the equivalent of the energy level in the tug of war. It is often a change in the volume, rather than a change in the price, that best reflects the change in momentum. The volume reflects the commitment of the professionals to changing the price of the stock.

When the momentum swings to the side of the buyers, the stock price inches up on very high trading volume. But the sellers do not immediately capitulate. They dig in, keeping the stock in the range. The tug of war is on. The buyers move the stock price up on very high volume, while the sellers bring it down on much lower volume. The price may still not have changed much, but you can see the differences in the power of the buyers and the sellers.

The tide permanently swings when there is a record increase in volume accompanied by a small increase in price that is often above the range in which the stock has been trading. This is known as the breakout. It is the instant at which the buyers have exerted their will over the sellers and the direction of the price of the stock has been set.

After the breakout, the volume declines from its peak, not because the buyers have lost their zest but because the sellers have capitulated. As the volume settles down, the stock moves up faster. In the tug-of-war analogy, this is the time when the sellers are slipping on the ground. As the stock continues its advance, most of the sellers finally capitulate. Volume often drops again as the price moves up. Finally, the sellers are routed.

The key is to understand the timing of the struggle between the two forces. **In watching the tug of war, the time to bet is when the momentum has turned, not when the losing team is lying on the ground.** In picking stocks, the time to buy or sell is when the direction becomes clear, not after the stocks have already moved. The easiest way to do this is to watch the trading patterns and understand the signals that they convey.

Nothing demonstrates the tug of war between buyers and sellers better than the Price and Volume Charts, such as the one on page 187. These charts show both the price and the volume at various points in time. The price is shown as a line across the top of the chart. (Prices are on the left-hand axis.) The volume is shown in columns at the bottom of the chart. (Volume is on the right-hand axis.) When reading the chart, investors should look at both price and volume together. Investors should seek to find the point when changes in volume are about to result in changes in price. If investors can identify this point, they can move before the market does.

The biggest opportunity to make a large profit comes in stocks that break out. As already discussed, these stocks tend to gain momentum and move up much further than one would ever imagine. In most cases, the pattern is easy to see. To summarize:

1. The stock builds a strong base at a price for an extended period of time.

2. During this time, it trades up on heavy volume and down on light volume, and refuses to break below the base.

3. Then, huge volume is traded on the upside as the stock price breaks out of the range.

4. The volume drops below the breakout level as the stock continues to move up.

5. The stock maintains its move as long as upside volume is higher than downside volume.

A CASE STUDY: ROSS STORES

Ross Stores, an off-price retailer, demonstrated this breakout pattern in 1995 and 1996. The chart on the following page shows the two major components of trading—price and volume. The price is depicted by the line in the upper section of the chart, while the volume is depicted by the columns in the lower section of the chart.

The first pattern investors should look for is a long solid base followed by strong breakout volume. In early 1995, Ross Stores formed a strong base at the $5 to $6 level. During the week of May 19, Ross traded five times its normal volume. This spike in volume was the first sign of a breakout and an unmistakable Buy signal. With this breakout volume, the price moved up to $6. While the volume had broken out, the stock price was still in the trading range. In August, the volume accelerated again. This was the second Buy signal. Ross broke above the critical $6 level and moved to $8, firmly breaking out of its trading range. Acting on either of these Buy signals would have enabled the investor to purchase Ross Stores at the beginning of its move.

Ross remained in the $8 range for eleven weeks, another good sign. When a stock moves up, it must form a new base, otherwise it is susceptible to sharp downdrafts. Think of the move up as flights of stairs. There must be landings where stocks can rest and catch their breath. Otherwise,

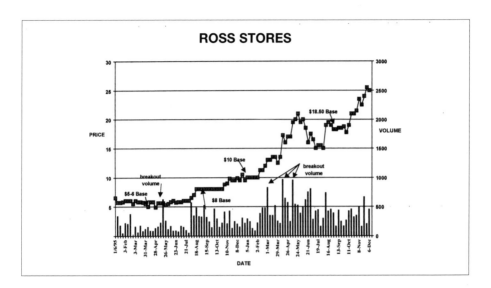

ROSS STORES

if they start to fall, they will drop back to where they started. A base is a place where a stock can consolidate its gains and stabilize itself. However, if the stock is to form a solid base, the volume must be moderate, indicating that many of the original investors are comfortable with their position. Moderate volume at a base is a sign of stability. Huge volume at a base is a sign of future instability.

Once a new base is formed, the stock should be able to break out again. A second-stage breakout should have volume that is substantially higher than the previous base ($8 for Ross) but lower than the original breakout. In early November, Ross began its second-stage breakout. As Ross continued its upward move, it followed this pattern of forming a base on moderate volume and then breaking out on higher volume.

After trading up to $10, it formed a new base for eleven weeks. Then, in February, it broke out again, trading very heavy volume as the stock went from $10 to $13. This move was especially critical for two reasons. First, the volume was higher than that of the original breakout. Because there were long and stable bases at $8 and $10, the strong upside volume was a very bullish sign, indicating that the breakout on higher volume could be sustained. Second, $13 was an all-time high for the stock. Whenever a stock reaches an all-time high, it is usually critical that it breaks through that high on very strong volume. If it does not, it will usually drop back.

In the previous ten years, Ross had moved above $10 on three occasions, but each time it had been unable to penetrate $12. Look at Ross's long-term chart. You will see that the stock kept bounding off $3 at the bottom and $12 at the top. While the stock moved back and forth, it was never able to break out of this range until the volume started to build in 1996. The more times a stock tries to break through a price and fails, the stronger will be the resistance at that price. There are always investors who will say, *"This stock can never get above $12,"* and sell when the stock reaches that price. Thus, if the stock is to continue its move upward, it must break through the all-time high with sufficient volume to maintain the momentum. Given the decade-long duration of this top, the strength of Ross's breakout was especially significant and indicated that the stock would keep moving up.

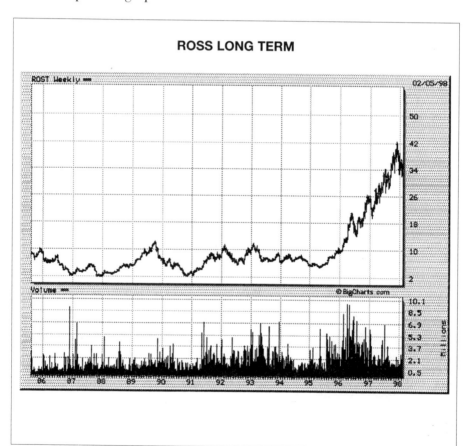

ROSS LONG TERM

Having broken through its last resistance, Ross no longer had a top to penetrate. It surged upward again. In seven weeks, it reached $21, trading 44.4 million shares.

No stock goes straight up forever. In the next ten weeks, Ross dropped to $15. This could have been the sign of a top, but the down volume was lower and of less duration than the up volume. Stocks do not collapse on light volume. As per Newton's Law, they need a greater force to change their direction. In the next four weeks, Ross moved back up on high volume. As it had done at $6, $8, $10, and $13, Ross now formed another base at $18.50. After forming its new base, Ross surged upward again and reached $25.

During 1997, with no top to hold it back and strong fundamentals, Ross Stores continued its run, reaching $40 by November. Most investors would have been pleased to participate in any major segment of the move in Ross from $5 to $40. However, anyone who took a close look at the chart could have bought Ross at the $6 level and held on to it for most of the run up. The tape was telling investors that the stock was going up. Any guerrilla investor who did not listen lost out on most of the move.

THE ROUND TRIP

Professionals can take stocks a long way up, but the time always arrives when a stock runs out of steam and turns down. Identifying the "top" is the second pattern all investors should understand. While it is critical for investors to be able to see the breakout and participate in the ride up, it is also critical for them to see the top and avoid the ride down. In many cases, the ride down is even quicker and more brutal. This is especially true of stocks with the sharpest moves up. Without solid intervening bases, stocks can plummet much faster and further than anyone ever believes.

In many cases, the trading pattern will give Buy signals at the bottom and Sell signals at the top, but investors often ignore these signals. When the stock is at the bottom, investors often wait until the breakout is already in progress before buying. When the stock reaches a top, investors are often so euphoric with the profits they have made that they fail to notice the signal of an abrupt change in direction. Micron Technologies is an interesting example of a stock that took the round trip.

A CASE STUDY: MICRON TECHNOLOGIES

Micron Technologies is a major manufacturer of semiconductors, and one of the most volatile and actively traded stocks in the market. When the stock went up, it went up like a rocket and ran to heights that even its most ardent fans could not have imagined. When it finally petered out and went down, it dropped like a stone, sinking much further and much faster than its most vociferous detractors could have imagined. Look at Micron's trading pattern and ask yourself, *"When would have been the most appropriate time to buy and sell this stock?"*

At the start of 1993, Micron was selling for $3.78. By July 1995, it had surged to $89. In 30 months, its price had increased by 2,278 percent. However, from its peak, Micron headed straight down until it reached $19.50 in July 1996, a decline of 79 percent. In forty-two months, Micron went from $4 to $89 and back to $19 without any major, long-term, fundamental change in its business. It did not invent a new type of chip, put Intel out of business, or get acquired. No amount of "rational" fundamental analysis could have explained this volatility. But the stock market is not always about rational analysis. It is often about momentum. In Micron's case, the chart of the stock almost always foretold its future price direction. Those who used the chart as a tool probably made money. Those who ignored it probably were annihilated.

In the case of Micron Technologies, the word "investor" is highly inappropriate. Most people who bought Micron's stock were trading, not investing. Micron has about 200 million shares. In 1995 and 1996, Micron traded 2.8 billion shares. The shares turned over an average of seven times per year, making the average holding period much less than two months. In 1996, it was the most actively traded stock on the New York Stock Exchange. If the average investor owned the stock for less than two months, most were traders, playing the momentum game. A fundamental investor might look at Micron and be bewildered by its volatility. But that investor would have only two choices: respect the power of momentum or avoid the stock.

MICRON'S CHART CLEARLY POINTED THE WAY

Micron's chart pattern is actually extremely common, with clearly delineated Buy and Sell signals. From December 1992 through May 1993, Micron formed a solid base under $6. In June and July, volume increased as the price went to $8.97. This surge represented the first Buy signal. Volume continued to jump, reaching 146 million shares in October. Unlike Ross, which had a surge in volume followed by a surge in price, Micron had a simultaneous price and volume breakout. This type of breakout always indicates sharp future volatility. With this type of action, investors must be cautious because a month like October 1993 can signal either a continuing breakout or a top.

Over the next several months, Micron formed a base in the $9 range and then traded up to $14 on somewhat lower volume. In some cases, lower volume on the upside would have been a negative, but in Micron's case it was a positive; it showed that despite the 275 percent increase in price, investors were still comfortable with the stock. In March, volume

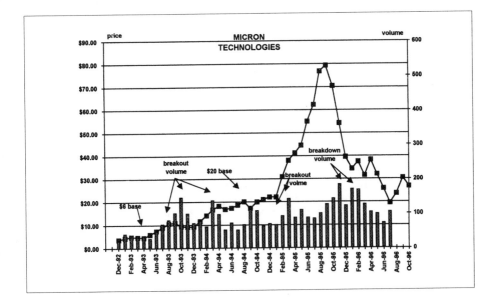

increased again, as Micron surged upward. This was the second Buy signal, indicating that the upside trend was still intact. Micron moved up to $20 and consolidated its base. It remained near $20 for eleven months, trading on lower but consistent volume. This was a very positive sign. The base formed by Micron at $20 laid the foundation for the next move up.

In February and March 1995, volume picked up as the stock surged to $31. This was Micron's third Buy signal. From February to August, the stock almost quadrupled on heavy volume. Many investors sold the stock during this period, but in doing so they were making a mistake. Nothing in Micron's chart gave any indication of a change in direction. Despite the gigantic run up and the huge trading volume, the volume remained relatively consistent and never exceeded the level it reached during the breakout month. If volume is consistent, the momentum of the stock tends to continue.

During September, Micron reached a high of $90 before closing the month at $79.38. As Micron's stock continued its sharp advance to $90, it was sowing the seeds of its own decline. While the stock had formed bases at $10 and $20, there were no bases between $20 and $90. **As a stock moves up, it is critical that it form intermediate bases so that**

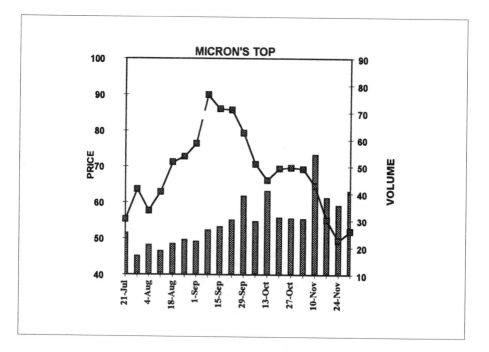

it can consolidate its position. If Micron could not form a base near its top, it could be vulnerable to dropping all the way to $20.

As Micron moved toward its peak, volatility and volume increased, both troubling signs. In the week of September 8, Micron surged from $76 to almost $90, but in the next three weeks, it dropped to $79 ³/₈ on four times the volume. This downside volume was disturbing, because it indicated that the mass of professionals was rapidly switching from buyers to sellers and doing so with conviction.

Just as momentum can support a stock on the upside, so it can destroy a stock on the downside. Volume is a critical component, because it reflects the movement of the army of professionals. In Micron's case, volume continued to increase as the stock price moved down. Micron traded 174 million shares as it went from $55 to $90 and 352 million shares as it went from $90 to $55. (On the chart of Micron's top, note how volume surged as the stock dropped.) The point here is very simple, but it is one that investors continually miss:

- A stock that has been surging upward can only change direction if it meets a greater force.
- That greater force is almost always manifest in higher volume.
- If a stock declines on huge volume, don't wait to read the analysts' reports. Head for the exits.

Anyone who looked at the chart would have sold Micron as it started to trade down. In most cases, this sign will not occur exactly at the top. But if you had bought Micron at $10, you would have been delighted to sell at $79. Giving up $10 at the top was surely better than the alternative of hanging on. Just remember, surging downside volume is a stock's way of telling you there is trouble ahead. Unless you think you have some secret inside information, it is not worth fighting the tape.

This is usually the time when the broker calls urging you to buy. *"Our analysts still love it, and it is 30 percent off the high."* But Micron had no base at which to stop a downward plunge. In the next six weeks, it dropped to $43 on heavy volume. Downside moves can be quick and brutal if there is no base to support the stock.

After a few quiet weeks during the Christmas season, volume exploded. In January and February, Micron traded 338 million shares. In one week, it traded 70 million shares, one-third of its stock. After the peak in February, both the price and the volume continued to decline. In seven weeks, the volume was less than 20 million, and in three weeks, it was less than 10 million. The selling was drying up, but there was no buying. At the end of July, volume again picked up, as the stock sunk under $20. The downside momentum was now broken, and the price could stabilize. While Micron rallied during 1997, it sunk back and in December was again selling just above $20.

The message of Micron Technologies is simple. The stock went up far more than anyone would have expected, and then it cratered. So long as the volume was consistent, the stock kept going up. Once the volume pattern was broken, the stock changed directions. Investors who studied the chart could have seen the breakout and taken the entire ride up. They also could have seen the top and avoided the entire ride down. Those who did not study the charts probably got whipsawed in both directions.

THE MARKET DOES NOT OVERREACT

Charts can not only signal when a stock is going to move up or down, they can also signal when a company is going to face some unusually good or bad news—especially bad news. When stocks plunge on bad news, analysts normally issue reports indicating their surprise at the news, but in many cases the stock itself has already foreshadowed the problem. A careful look at the charts usually reveals the signs of coming difficulties.

Sometimes a minor event, such as a small reduction in earnings estimates, leads to a dramatic revaluation of a stock. An analyst may cut earnings estimates by 5 percent, and the stock may drop 35 percent. When this occurs, other analysts often say, *"The market has overreacted,"* and urge investors to double up their holdings. After all, a 5 percent cut in earnings should not have had such a devastating impact on the stock. Investors should be wary. The market does not overreact. In fact, in many cases when stocks are trashed, future events prove that the earnings reduction was just the tip of the iceberg and that something was radically wrong with the company. Further, the first "overreaction" is rarely the last. Collapses in a stock, like earthquakes, are usually preceded by smaller tremors and followed by aftershocks.

If a stock behaves in a manner that most analysts and you consider to be irrational, the first question you should ask is, *"Why is everyone else panicking when I am not?"* When the masses run for the exits, even if you do not see a fire or smell the smoke, you would do well to listen to the screams. Professional investors do not panic over small items. If they are running for the exits, with no concern for price, it is because they fear that there are greater problems ahead. Think hard before you buy a stock that is being trashed.

A CASE STUDY: DONNKENNY

Donnkenny produces moderately priced sportswear for women. The company went public in June 1993. In December, its president, Richard Rubin, sold 100,000 shares. In April 1994, Rubin sold an additional 330,000 shares, and Merrill Lynch, which had backed the company, sold 1.6 million shares. In July 1995, Rubin sold an additional 100,000 shares. In November 1995, Rubin sold 200,000 more shares. Donnkenny announced that it would distribute Mickey Mouse clothing in China and take a fourth-quarter charge. The stock dropped from $18 to $14 on six times normal volume. Anyone looking at the chart should have been concerned. The company reported good year-end results and said that it would have a strong 1995. The stock moved up to $19. In August 1996, Rubin sold another 150,000 shares. A consistent pattern of sales by management is never a bullish sign.

In September 1996, the company announced that it was changing its fiscal year from November to December. Several analysts reaffirmed their estimates, while one analyst, whose estimates had been the highest on the Street, lowered her numbers by $.05 to be in line with consensus. The stock reacted strongly to the change in the fiscal year and the earnings adjustment, dropping more than 20 percent on eight times normal volume. (Note on the following chart that all of the major increases in volume were accompanied by sharp declines in the stock price.) Another analyst, whose position had been more conservative to begin with, wrote a note with the headline *"Market Overreacts Again."* This analyst happens to be very intelligent, but when analysts write that the market has overreacted, it is they, not the market, who are usually wrong.

The change in the fiscal year and the small adjustment in earnings were not significant, so why did the stock react so strongly? Perhaps someone suspected something, but whatever the reason, the huge downside volume on what appeared to be insignificant news was a decidedly negative sign. The chart was telling investors that there was something more seriously wrong with Donnkenny.

On October 28, an analyst wrote a note indicating that Donnkenny would report its earnings in mid-November, instead of in late October as originally planned. Neither the analyst nor the investors seemed to take much note of this delay, but it was a significant signal. A company's delaying its reporting date is always a sign of trouble. If you own stock in a company that has a material delay in reporting, don't wait around to find out why.

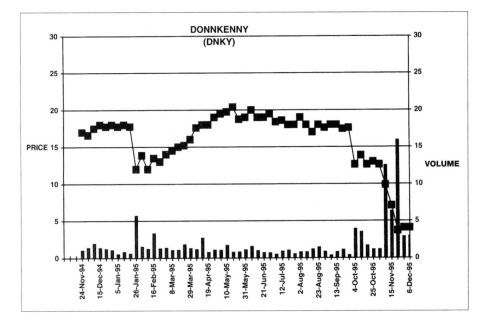

The trouble did not take long to materialize. On November 6, the company's auditors, KPMG Peat Marwick, resigned. The company demoted its chief financial officer and appointed someone new. The company implied that KPMG had been fired. First Call (a company that distributes the investment and corporate research provided by brokerage houses and others) carried a note from an analyst entitled "New CFO a Positive," noting that the new CFO had spent five years at Ralph Lauren. Another firm also praised the appointment. Both talked about the strengthening of the management team. Neither seemed concerned about the change in auditors. But the analyst who had previously talked about the market overreacting lowered her rating, because she believed that the "firing of the CFO and the auditor just before the release of earnings . . . is not positive" (a smart call, but a major understatement).

The stock, which had closed at $12\,^1/_2$, would not open. By midmorning it was selling at $6\,^1/_2$. Two firms downgraded the stock. Donnkenny closed at $8\,^7/_8$ on 9.3 million shares. About two-thirds of the shares outstanding traded. A lot of investors were making bets.

On November 8, Prudential Securities raised its rating to Buy. The First Call note was entitled "Panic Sell-off Overdone." This was the second time that an analyst had said that the tape was wrong. The Prudential analyst noted that investors were concerned about possible fraud, but that the new CFO and a board member had assured him everything was all right. With estimates of $1.38 for 1996 and $1.60 for 1997, Donnkenny looked like a very cheap stock. The Prudential recommendation pushed Donnkenny up to $9\,^7/_8$.

On November 12, Donnkenny released a statement saying that KPMG had resigned, not been fired, and that it had resigned because of poor data access. (Never a good sign: It is difficult for auditors to do a good job if you don't let them look at your books.) On November 14, the *Wall Street Journal* reported that three executives had sold $13.4 million in stock over the past eighteen months. Finally, on November 15, Donnkenny reported that third-quarter earnings would be below analysts' estimates and that it would have to restate its earnings from the previous years. The stock dropped to $4\,^3/_{16}$. Prudential lowered its rating from Buy to Sell. Two other firms also reduced their ratings.

Look at the chart and the volume. All the shares were changing hands. The auditors had resigned. The earnings report was delayed. There was no way that good news could follow. In fact, there is almost never an instance in which good news follows the dismissal of the auditors in the middle of the year. One rule that every investor should remember is never buy a stock if the auditors resign in the middle of the year.

When the stock dropped from $16 to $12 in October, the market was sending a message that something was wrong. From then until the problems fully materialized, two analysts wrote notes saying that the market had overreacted, and investors traded millions of shares as the stock plunged. The lessons of Donnkenny are simple:

- There is almost never a good reason for late reporting of earnings.
- There is *never* a good reason for changing auditors in the middle of the year.
- When a stock acts "sick," the company usually has major problems.
- The market does not overreact.
- Investors who fight the tape do so at their own peril.

In 1997, new management took over Donnkenny, but as of December, the stock was selling for $3.50 a share. Stocks that have broken down and burned investors do not rapidly recover.

WITH CHARTS, THE GREATEST VIRTUE IS SIMPLICITY

In looking at the Price and Volume Charts of Ross, Micron, and Donnkenny, it is very easy for the investor to see when the stock began a major move up and when it began a major move down. The basic Price and Volume Chart has the advantage of simplicity. Any investor can look at it and see when the volume is increasing and how the price is reacting to changes in volume. A breakout volume is always extremely easy to spot.

Upside versus downside volume is also extremely easy to spot. If the volume is increasing as the stock is declining, there is much more downside risk.

The message for the individual investor is simple: When stocks break out or plunge for no apparent reason, it is wise to assume that someone knows something you do not. When people who are closer to the company than you are begin to buy or sell, causing dramatic new patterns to emerge, do not wait around to learn what they know. If the charts tell you that something is going wrong, sell the stock. Do not attempt to fight the tape.

The only complex issue in the Price and Volume Charts is the timeframe. If you are looking at what you believe is a breakout from a base, you must go back to the formation of the base. If you take too short a timeframe, a surge in volume can look like a breakout but not be of sufficient power to move away from the base. A true breakout occurs only on the highest volume. Similarly, if you are looking at a breakdown, you must look at the volume during the stock's entire move up. Most tops require volume higher than the original breakout.

PRICE AND VOLUME CHARTS ON THE WEB

The Internet has made Price and Volume Charts extremely easy to use. All Internet brokers have chart services, as do the search engines (such as Yahoo) and other financial sites for investors. My particular favorite is BigCharts. The on-line brokers tend to have better short-term charts. But for most investors, long-term charts will do. **In many ways, the charts on the Internet are more effective and easier to work with than the charts that the professionals use.** The major advantage of the Internet charts is the ease with which investors can switch between timeframes. Most charts have five-year, two-year, one-year, six-month, three-month, and one-month timeframes. Some of the more sophisticated sites even have one-day charts. On BigCharts, for example, you have the following choices: five minutes; fifteen minutes; five days; one, two, three, and six months; year-to-date; one to five years; one decade; and all historical data.

Pick a stock in which you are interested. Click on the basic chart. You will see choices for different timeframes. Start with a long timeframe. Five years is probably sufficient. Get a picture of the long-term pattern of the stock. Is it in an uptrend or a downtrend? Has it formed a solid base? Watch the battle between buyers and sellers. Look at the spikes in volume. How did the stock perform as volume increased or decreased? Look at the peaks and valleys in price. How did price and volume correlate at these points? Think of the chart as the movement of an army. You can see where it has been, but can you see where it is going?

Click on the next shorter timeframe, such as two years. Does the slightly shorter-term pattern look different? Continue clicking down the time-frame spectrum. Each click will take only seconds, but each chart will give you a different view. Try to focus on the periods in which there were the most dramatic price and volume changes. If the stock has been in a long-term trend, you will need a long-term chart, but if the peaks in volume have recently changed the direction of the stock, you can use a more short-term chart. When you get to the most short-term chart, look up close at the recent trading pattern. Is there a significant change in price or volume? Does the stock seem to be diverging from its basic trend?

Many charts will be largely nondescript, but some charts will show dramatic changes in price and volume. If you see a breakout on the upside, buy or certainly continue holding the stock. Stick with it as long as the trend is in place. If you see a top accompanied by a surge in volume, don't wait around for the bad news. Sell the stock and take your profits. Just remember, the market usually knows more than you do.

INTRADAY TRADING CHARTS SHOW SHORT-TERM DETAIL

Price and Volume Charts are extremely effective in providing investors with a simple overview of the long-term movements of stocks. The tops, bottoms, breakouts, and bases are all very easy to see. But while they are excellent for long-term moves, their very simplicity makes them less useful in understanding shorter-term price movements. For individuals who are more trading-oriented and want to be able to anticipate short-term actions by the professionals, Intraday Trading Charts are useful.

The difference between the Price and Volume Chart and the Intraday Trading Chart is the difference between a photograph taken from a satellite and one taken from the top of a hill. They both show the same battlefield, but the Price and Volume Chart shows more of an overview, while the Intraday Trading Chart shows more detail. If you want to have an overview of the entire opposing army, Intraday charts will be of limited use, but if you want to follow the deployment of a battalion, they will provide rich detail.

The Intraday Trading Chart is similar to the Price and Volume Chart except that instead of using a single point for the price on each day, the Intraday Trading Chart uses a bar for each day. The short horizontal lines on the right and left sides of the bar indicate the opening and closing prices respectively. The length of the daily bars reflects the range of price swings during the day. Short bars indicate that the stock is trading in a narrow price range during the day, while long bars indicate that it is trading in a wide price range. If the length of the bars suddenly increases, it is a sign of sharp divergences of opinion among professionals. When these divergences occur, the stock is likely to enter a period of higher volatility. As a result, these are critical changes for an investor to watch.

The relationship between the opening and closing prices helps to indi-

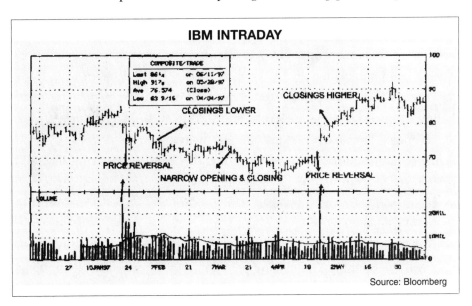

Source: Bloomberg

cate both the trading pattern and the direction of a possible move. If the range between the prices is narrow, the stock will probably trade in an orderly fashion. If it is wide, the stock is likely to be more volatile. If the closings are consistently lower than the openings, the stock will probably trade down. If the closings are consistently higher than the openings, the stock will probably trade up. Price reversals occur when there is a wide intraday trading range—a wide spread between opening and closing prices—and a substantial change in volume.

The Intraday Trading Charts also show the "moving average" of the stock. The moving average, which represents the price action of a stock over a specified period of time, is another key technical indicator. Most technicians believe that a move above or below the moving average line signifies a change in direction of the stock. The most common time periods used for moving averages are fifty and 200 days.

Because the Intraday Trading Charts show much more detailed information, they have to have a shorter timeframe. It is not possible to clearly show every opening and closing price and all intraday price swings on a long-term chart. The optimum time period for an Intraday Chart is six months, and the best use of these charts is in making short-term trading decisions. The chart on the previous page presents a picture of the daily trading of IBM during a six-month period.

As the beginning of the chart shows, IBM was trading up in an orderly fashion, with narrow spreads between openings and closings, but with closings on balance higher. On January 23, 1997, IBM had a wide intraday range. The closing price was about $4 lower than the opening price. Volume tripled off previous levels, and the stock dropped below its moving average. The sharp price decline on heavy volume was a key signal. While bargain hunters stepped in to buy, this trading pattern indicated a price reversal from the increases of the previous weeks. It is never wise to stand in front of a price reversal. During the next six-week period, IBM dropped from $79 to $64.

In the middle of March, the price began to stabilize. The differences between the opening and closing prices narrowed dramatically, indicating a more orderly trading pattern. Then closings began to be higher than openings, indicating a trend up. In the fourth week of April, the trading range widened and the volume tripled, indicating another price and volume reversal. In the next month, the price of IBM jumped from $68 to $90.

In using Intraday Trading Charts, the most important thing that the investor should look for is a price and volume reversal. A price and volume reversal shows that the professionals are changing their stance on the stock. If the stock swings from down closings to up closings on higher volume, it is a sign that professionals are buying and the stock will probably move up. If it swings from up closings to down closings on higher volume, it is a sign that professionals are selling and the stock will probably move down. If these reversals cause the stock to break through the moving averages, the extent of the move is likely to be greater.

Like Price and Volume Charts, Intraday Trading Charts are easily located on the Internet. The best of the charts are available through chart services, the on-line brokers, or specialized financial services. As with the Price and Volume Charts, it is useful to click on the Intraday Charts and play with different timeframes. Most investors will find it easier to use Price and Volume Charts for the long term and Intraday Trading Charts for the short term. Most of the on-line services use Price and Volume Charts for the longest timeframes and Intraday Trading Charts for the rest, so there is no need to worry about which one to pick. The service will give you the best one for the period in which you are interested.

The Price and Volume Charts and the Intraday Trading Charts are early warning systems for the individual investor because they reflect both the past and the future moves of the professional. Charts can never *predict* the future, but they can provide an excellent picture of the short- and long-term price action of a stock. For the individual, who probably knows less about the company than the professional, charts can be critical. When volume starts to increase, it is a sign that professionals are becoming more active in a stock. If volume increases and the stock moves up, it is a sign that the professionals are buying. If volume increases and the stock moves down, it is a sign that professionals are selling.

MOVING AVERAGE CONVERGENCE/DIVERGENCE INDICATOR: DIFFICULT TO UNDERSTAND, EASY TO USE

Of all of the technical indicators, the Moving Average Convergence/ Divergence Indicator (MACD) is one of the most difficult to understand and yet one of the simplest to use. The MACD is one of a number of charts that utilize moving averages as a technical tool. The moving average tracks the average price of a stock over a specified period of time. The MACD uses an exponential moving average, which means it provides more weight to recent data and less to old data.

The complete theory of the MACD is confusing to most people, and I won't explain it here, but using the MACD chart is extremely easy. The chart has two sections. The top section shows the price of the stock. The bottom section has a solid line (the Period Indicator) and a dotted line (the Signal Indicator). A change in trend occurs when the solid line crosses the dotted line at a sharp angle. When the solid line sharply crosses from below, the trend is up and you should buy the stock. When the solid line

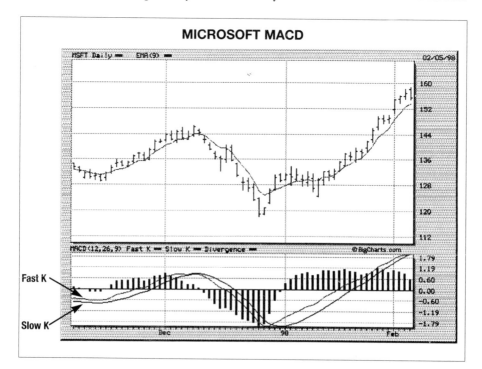

MICROSOFT MACD

sharply crosses from above, the trend is down and you should sell the stock. If the crossing is not sharp or if the two lines continue to move together, there is no change in the trend. The MACD charts are especially useful for tracking short-term moves because the weighting of the lines magnifies changes in trends. All the individual has to do is look for sharp crossing patterns and act.

On the previous page is a MACD chart for Microsoft. While the concept of MACD can be confusing, the predictive value is extremely high and using the charts is incredibly easy. Look at the sharp crossings. There are three during the period. The first crossing was positive, indicating a Buy. It occurred at the beginning of November 1997. Microsoft was selling at about $132. In the next five weeks, it climbed to $146. The second crossing was negative, indicating a Sell. It occurred in early December when Microsoft was selling at $144. The stock promptly dropped to $120. The third crossing was also positive, indicating a Buy. It occurred at the end of December when Microsoft was selling at $120. Microsoft promptly ran to $142. In the three months of the chart, Microsoft went from $136 to $142, an increase of $6, but following the MACD signals on the upside and the downside would have enabled investors to make $60.

What makes the MACD interesting is its ease of use. All you have to do is look for the sharp crossings of the two lines and see if they indicate an advance or a decline. Go to one of the websites that features MACD charts and look at the charts for the stocks in your portfolio. You will be surprised at how often the sharp crossings reflected the best Buy and Sell points. If you cannot find MACD charts, look at other charts that utilize moving averages.

— · —

As the charts in this chapter show, investors can make a lot of money by utilizing technical tools as an early warning system for the actions of the professionals. The Price and Volume, Intraday Trading, and MACD charts present Buy and Sell points in very simple formats. But there are a large number of other charting systems that appeal to various investors. To see which one is right for you, go to one of the charting websites, such as BigCharts, and play with the alternatives. Pick a stock you own and spend some time testing the charts. Look at different indicators, such as money flows, price channels, short interest, stochastics, relative strength, and various types of moving averages. Try different chart types, such as candlesticks and high-low close. See which of the technical systems presents the easiest and clearest picture for you to understand. Then try that system on a few more stocks. There is no single right technical system. You should find the one with which you are the most comfortable.

The biggest challenge lies not in understanding the charts, but in being willing to act when the charts indicate a position that is opposed to your fundamental beliefs. When most investors see a negative indicator in the chart of a stock they own, their first response usually is that the chart is wrong. This is both dangerous and foolish. The chart represents the collective wisdom of all buyers and sellers. It is often foretelling the future on both a fundamental and a technical basis. The investor is almost always better off accepting what the charts have to say. This does not mean that you should buy or sell every time a minor signal occurs. Very often minor technical signals are reversed, and no change in investment status is necessary. But when a major signal occurs, do not wait around for second and third confirmations. Major signals indicate changes in trends, and for the most part, investors should follow them.

CHAPTER EIGHT

Connect the Dots

External events can radically change the field of battle. A monsoon can leave the army mired in position. Or another previously ignored force can enter the fray and change the balance of power. The first general to see the event, understand its full implications, and make the right move usually wins. The key is for him to see the links between external events and his own battle position, and to use them as a weapon of warfare. The same rules apply to the stock market. It is critical to watch the external events that can change the balance of power in the market and to understand the links between the events and the prices of stocks.

Nothing affects the stock market more than real news events. When you turn on the news, you immediately know that some of the headlines are going to directly impact specific stocks, and you very often have a good guess as to the extent and the direction of the impact.

- If the headline says that Mexico is devaluing the peso by 50 percent, you know that the dollar value of Mexican stocks is going to plunge.
- If the headline says that a regional brokerage firm is being bought out by a major bank at twice its current price, you know that the firm's stock price will surge.
- If the headline says that the biggest hurricane in history is

devastating the coast of Florida, you know that the stocks of property insurance companies will go down.

Since you know the news, you know that there are vast sums to be made if you can get your orders executed before everyone else. The problem is that you cannot. You are not the only person who reads the newspaper or watches television. When major news events occur, some stocks have huge influxes of orders. The market makers or specialists immediately adjust the prices to conform to the new reality. By the time you make your trade, the stocks may have already had major moves.

- The Mexican stock that had closed at $20 is now indicated at $10 because of the devaluation.
- The regional brokerage firm which had closed at $20 will open at $36 because of the takeover.
- The insurance company that had closed at $60 will now open at $55 because of the hurricane.

When important news comes out, people rush for the entrances or the exits like a crowd of Latin American soccer fans. Even if you are going in the right direction, you can still get trampled. Besides the fact that the major moves are likely to be made before you have a chance to trade, the heightened volatility brought about by news events always benefits the professionals. They are in a position to understand the news and analyze its implications faster than the average investor.

When the peso is devalued, the professionals know which companies will be decimated and which may actually benefit. You may not. When a takeover is announced, the professionals have an educated view as to whether the deal will go through and whether the bid will be raised. You may not. When a hurricane hits, the professionals know which firms are the most exposed and which have laid off much of their disaster risk.

Making direct investments based on major news stories is often unwise. If you see a news item with black-and-white implications and you own the affected stock, wait until the volatility abates and then reevaluate your holdings. If you do not own the stock, resist the temptation to play. If volatility is high, you cannot afford to be a step behind the professionals.

THE INDIVIDUAL'S EDGE

So can the individual investor ever use news events to his advantage? Yes, but his goal must be to search for the more subtle connections between stocks. When an event occurs that has a major impact on one stock, it usually has an impact, though less direct, on other stocks. While most investors jump on the stock that is the focus of the news, the best opportunities often come in stocks on which the event has a secondary or even tertiary impact. The key for the guerrilla investor is to keep track of the list of companies in which he has, or has developed, home-turf advantage. If he can identify how those companies are indirectly impacted before the rest of the market does, he will be ahead of the game. Here are some examples of subtle connections to watch for if you follow retail, banking, or construction and building stocks:

- If the peso is devalued, American companies that import inexpensive goods from Mexico, such as apparel companies, may benefit, while American companies that sell products to Mexico may suffer.
- If a regional brokerage firm receives a takeover offer from a major bank at a huge premium, stocks of other regional brokerage firms and money management firms that might become takeover targets will also surge. Stocks of other banks could go down if investors thought that the banks might be disadvantaged by not owning a brokerage firm or might overpay to make an acquisition of their own.
- When a disaster such as a hurricane hits, unfortunate as it may seem, there are winners. The insurance funds pouring into the market are a boon to home builders, building-supply firms, and appliance stores. While most people do not look at disasters and say, *"What a great opportunity for Home Depot,"* the reality

is that every house that is knocked down has to be rebuilt, and someone has to provide the supplies.

The stock market is a dynamic environment in which almost everything is interrelated. One of the biggest errors investors make is to ignore the links between events, or else to be swayed into accepting a company's or analyst's spin on the situation. The reality is:

1. Events create ripples that impact a broad range of stocks.
2. Whether the impact is real, causing a change in earnings, or psychological, causing a change in investors' views, it may often be greater than most initially believe.
3. If one company shows a sharp break in its trading pattern, investors should look at related companies. Their moves may not be far behind.

There is one major difference between positive and negative changes. When the change is positive, companies rush to trumpet the good news, but when the change is negative, they put on spin control. Few companies issue press releases stating that a new competitive threat will materially hurt their business, and few analysts, who do investment banking business, will issue a report saying that a company is now toast. Because companies and analysts are more forthcoming about good news than they are about bad news, investors must look more diligently at negative changes in the competitive environment.

Too many investors ignore or even fight the news that they see in front of them if it presents a picture they do not like. But fighting the news, like fighting the tape, is a recipe for disaster. If the news and the tape combine to sound a warning, the negative impact is usually dramatic.

LINKS BETWEEN COMPETITORS

Most industries are a zero-sum game. There is only so much business to go around. When a major competitor, such as Wal-Mart, enters a market, its share must come out of someone's hide. Over the years, I have watched company after company explain that Wal-Mart did not really represent a competitive challenge. These companies had reams of statistics that showed they could compete against Wal-Mart. Some even claimed that Wal-Mart helped their business. One does not have to be a retail expert to understand that Wal-Mart's $100 billion in annual sales had to be taken from someone. Despite the spin control from competing companies, almost all have been hurt by Wal-Mart. If you see a major new competitive threat that could affect one of your stocks, be cautious in accepting your company's spin control.

Be especially cautious if you see a surge of new companies entering a business. A decade ago, there were a large number of fast-growing companies in the convenience-store business. At first they did well, but as competition intensified, margins suffered. Then the oil companies turned their service stations into convenience stores. It should not have taken a Certified Financial Analyst's degree to recognize that when tens of thousands of gas stations stopped repairing cars and started selling milk, the convenience stores would suffer. Price wars developed. Most of the publicly owned convenience-store chains went bankrupt. No matter how good a market seems, it will never be healthy if there are too many new competitors.

The opposite is also true. The consolidation of competitors can help a market, both because the number of competitors is reduced, and because the consolidating companies can leverage their overhead. Banking is currently going through a huge consolidation. When you see banks merging, closing overlapping branches, laying off tens of thousands of employees, consolidating operations, and reducing the number of competitors in a market, it's an easy guess that profits will improve, not only for the banks that are merging but for other competitors as well.

You should always be wary of industries in which the number of competitors is increasing and look for industries in which it is shrinking. There are three good ways to profit from shrinking levels of competition:

1. Buy the consolidators. Look for fragmented industries, such as real estate, in which public companies are buying up small independents. This is currently occurring in the real estate and funeral home industries. The consolidators are usually able to gain pricing and capital leverage.

2. Buy the attractive regionals. Look for consolidating industries in which the largest companies are buying up strong regional companies, such as is currently occurring in banking. When mergers start in an industry, they usually continue until all of the attractive candidates have been bought.

3. Buy the survivors. Look for companies that take up the slack when other companies close their facilities. When airlines like Eastern and Pan American liquidated, it opened the market for Delta, American, and United.

Understanding the level of competition can be a good tool in making investments. If competition is increasing either because powerful firms are moving into the market or because there are too many companies in a niche, the investor should be cautious. If competition is decreasing because of bankruptcies or because a company is consolidating the market, investors should look for opportunities.

LINKS BETWEEN CUSTOMERS AND SUPPLIERS

The fortunes of a large major company will tell you a lot about what is happening to its major suppliers. If you own stock in a manufacturer and one retailer accounts for 30 percent of its sales, it seems logical that you would listen to the reports from the retailer to track how your company is doing. But you would be shocked at how many investors ignore this type of news. Even professionals may miss the connections. Analysts may miss them because they are focused on one industry and the industry doesn't encompass both companies. Busy portfolio managers may miss them because no one helps them connect the dots.

BRIGHT SELL SIGNALS IN THE SUNGLASS BUSINESS

A perfect example of this situation can be found in the story of Sunglass Hut (RAYS), the largest retailer of sunglasses, and Oakley, a major sunglass brand. Sunglass Hut went public in 1993 at $5. The company went on an acquisition binge and became a darling of growth investors. By March 1996, RAYS had soared more than 700 percent to almost $37 and commanded a lofty 45x p/e multiple. As it climbed from $7 to $36⁵/₁₆, Sunglass Hut had only one down month. It never stopped to form a base.

After surging above $36 in March, RAYS was unable to hold the price and started to decline. Downside volume increased. By the middle of April, RAYS was below $30 and struggling to form a base. Then in the last two weeks of June, volume suddenly surged. Many investors were betting that the key summer selling season would be weak. As is so often the case, the news followed the charts. On July 1, Sunglass Hut told analysts that its June comparable store sales would be 1 to 3 percent below plan. Such a shortfall is not the end of the world, but because RAYS's chart was already weak, the impact was quick and brutal. In three days, RAYS dropped from $24³/₈ to $18 on 9.4 million shares. Now the stock was broken. Anyone looking for a sign to sell had one. Analysts tried to rally the stock, but the bottom fell out again. In ten days, Sunglass Hut dropped below $11 because of a minor shortfall in June sales.

Investors often ignore the warning signs of stocks. Despite the huge price

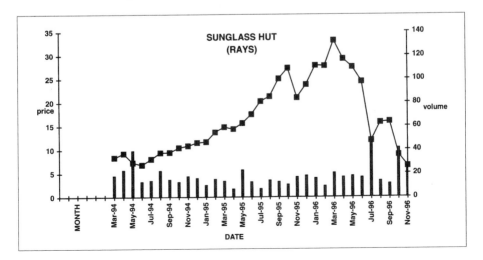

drop and jump in volume, investors began to bid up the price of the stock. RAYS rallied from $12 to $18. But the upside volume was troublingly light. Sunglass Hut was sending a second invitation to sell for anyone who was interested.

Anyone who did not sell did not have to wait long to regret their inaction. In early October, RAYS said that September sales had been weak and that the weakness might continue into the fourth quarter. Ordinarily, September is a meaningless month for sunglasses, but because RAYS had a vulnerable chart, the news set off a panic. In five days, the stock dropped from $16 to $9. By the end of November, RAYS had declined from $36 $^{15}/_{16}$ to $6 $^{3}/_{4}$. In three years, sales had tripled and earnings per share had more than doubled, and RAYS was selling for less than it had in its first week of trading.

Anyone who had been watching the news and the trading patterns of Sunglass Hut should have understood the warning signals. Besides sending a warning to its own shareholders, RAYS was also sending a warning to others in the sunglass industry, especially to shareholders of Oakley, one of its largest suppliers. Oakley was a hot company. It went public in August 1995 at 11^{1}/_{2}$, and by June 1996 it had reached $27. At its high, Oakley was selling for 41x earnings and 9.5x sales, astoundingly high valuations.

It is interesting to compare the charts of Sunglass Hut and Oakley. While Sunglass Hut was declining from $36 to $27, Oakley was rallying

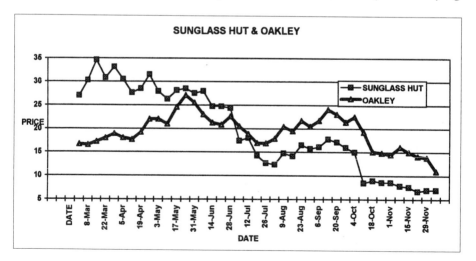

from $16 to $27. It is always *possible* for one company to do well when its largest customer is hurting, but weak retail sales are never a good sign for major suppliers.

Oakley had a secondary offering on June 12. The CEO also sold 10 million shares at about $24. Did he know that Sunglass Hut's comparable store sales were below plan and that its inventories were too high? Did the investors who bought his stock look at the chart of Sunglass Hut and ask why it looked so much weaker than that of Oakley? Did the investors in Sunglass Hut ask the Oakley CEO why he was selling 10 million shares just before the beginning of the key summer selling season? Whatever the answers, this sale by the top executive of Oakley at the same time the stock of Sunglass Hut was weakening should have sent a strong message to investors.

After the secondary offering, Oakley did not hold its price. As Sunglass Hut dropped from $24 to $18, Oakley dropped from $22 to $17. But then an interesting divergence began to occur. Many of the investment banking houses that had handled Oakley's offering recommended the stock. Oakley's stock rallied to $21, while Sunglass Hut's dropped to $12. In May, both Sunglass Hut and Oakley had been selling at $27. Both were in the same business. Oakley and Oakley's CEO had unloaded a huge block of stock, and yet by August, Sunglass Hut had declined to $12, while Oakley was selling for $21.

In the first week of October, when Sunglass Hut announced that its

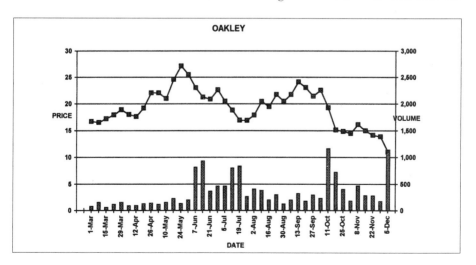

business was weak and its inventories were high, Oakley's stock dropped in reaction, but the next day it rallied. Bausch & Lomb, the largest manufacturer of sunglasses, said that its sales were weak. Investors should have listened. The stock of Oakley was in a downtrend. Its largest customer and biggest competitor had announced that business was soft. Yet Oakley rallied its stock by telling investors that business was still good.

Oakley reported strong earnings and announced a 3 million share stock buyback, but the price still dropped to $16. When a company reports good news and the stock declines, it is sending investors another message. If good news pushes the stock down, what will happen if bad news is reported? Oakley had played its card, but the market reacted negatively. This was another warning sign, but many investors still ignored the obvious.

Then the bomb dropped. On December 3, Sunglass Hut reported more weak sales. Oakley responded by saying that its earnings per share would show a decline of 30 percent. Analysts cut their earnings estimates and ratings, and the stock plunged to $11 $5/8$.

Why was anyone surprised? The chart had been telling investors that something was wrong. Insiders had sold. Customers and competitors had said that sales were weak. **One does not have to be a highly paid analyst to figure out that if the retailers cannot sell sunglasses, the manufacturers will eventually be hurt.** Oakley may be a fine company, but if your largest customer says that business is terrible, there is no point in hoping that you will be the only supplier exempted. The surprise was not that Oakley reported weak numbers on December 3. The surprise was that with all of the signs of problems, it took investors so long to figure it out. (During 1997, both Sunglass Hut and Oakley continued to have weak earnings and depressed stock prices. By December, Sunglass Hut was still under $7, while Oakley was under $10.)

DON'T SEND ROTTEN APPLES BY MAIL!

Another example of how investors can fail to read both the tape and the news is the story of Apple Computer and Micro Warehouse, a company in the mail-order computer business. In February 1996, Micro Warehouse was given a 1.0 rating by every analyst who followed it. It was one of the ten highest-rated stocks. Micro Warehouse had a dynamic record. Its earnings per share surged from $.22 in 1991 to $1.48 in 1995. With this growth rate, it was easy for analysts to value it at 30x earnings. But Micro Warehouse primarily sold Apple products. One does not have to be a computer wizard to remember that Windows 95 was introduced in the summer of 1995 and that its primary victim was Apple. The Macintosh, which had once been hailed as a revolutionary machine, was now an also-ran. Wintel (Windows and Intel) had emerged victorious, and there were even those who questioned whether Apple could survive.

Not surprisingly, Apple's stock was hammered. On July 14, 1995, Apple was selling for $48 3/4. By the end of October, it had dropped to $35. One year later, it reached a low of $16 7/8, a decline of almost two-thirds. Apple ran a large loss. The CEO was dismissed. A new CEO was hired, but he was subsequently dismissed as he failed to get the business going.

The question that investors should have asked was, *"How could Micro Warehouse do well if its major supplier, Apple, was sucking wind?"* While mail order was growing rapidly, it would not appear logical that a company that made its living selling Macs would continue to thrive. Micro Warehouse did take steps to diversify away from Apple, but Macintosh was its bread and butter, and Macintosh was wormy—if not rotten.

Despite the fact that Micro Warehouse relied on Apple for a majority of its business, its stock performed much better than that of Apple. When Windows 95 was introduced, the two stocks were at about $47. By the following March, Apple had sunk to $26, while Micro Warehouse had risen to $50.

While the stock price was holding up, the technical pattern had begun to deteriorate. Volume increased, but the stock price was unable to break through resistance levels. Then it began to decline. Seven insiders sold stock. Perhaps they wondered why their company should do well if Apple was doing so poorly. On May 28, Bloomberg ran a story entitled *"Micro Warehouse Insider Selling May Mean That More Weakness Remains."* Unfortunately, the analysts, who continued to give this stock

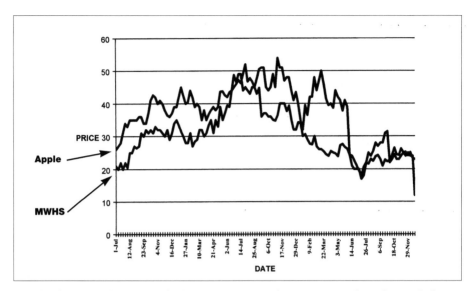

the highest ranking, and the investors, who continued to buy, did not put much credence in this story.

Then the first bomb dropped. On June 5, Micro Warehouse issued a press release stating that net income would be below analysts' estimates. The company attributed the expected lower net income to the continued weakness in its Apple Macintosh business. This statement came as a gigantic surprise to investors. The next day, Micro Warehouse's stock fell 11 7/8 points to $22 7/8, a loss of almost one-third of its value. Most of the analysts reduced their rating on the stock. In the next month, MWHS dropped to $17.

The first question that everyone should have asked is, *"Why was the announcement such a surprise?"* Apple's business had been terrible for months. Even the most casual observer knew that it was in trouble. The trading pattern of MWHS had been deteriorating and insiders had been selling. It was a surprise because even the most sophisticated of investors often do not connect the dots.

The Micro Warehouse story should have ended here with the stock plunging immediately to new lows, but, as in so many other cases, the first major drop is rarely the last. Instead, it is an opportunity for more people who do not connect the dots to lose more money. From July 12 to September 21, MWHS moved up from $17 to $31 1/2, almost doubling in

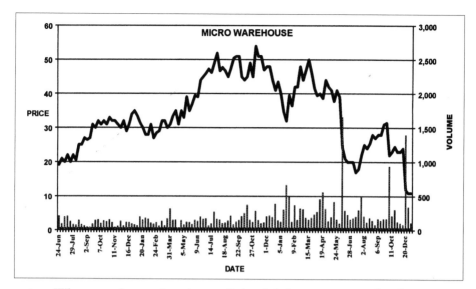

price. Why was the stock going up? Apple's business was clearly not getting better and the volume was light, but the analysts were still bullish, and there are always bargain hunters.

During the week of October 4, the next bomb dropped. Business continued to be weak. Micro Warehouse's stock dropped from $31½ to $22. For the next ten weeks, the stock traded in the low $20s on light volume. The final bomb dropped during the week of December 20, just in time for the end-of-the-year tax-loss selling. Micro Warehouse said that business remained weak. How could it have said anything else? Apple was still losing market share. MWHS dropped to $12 on gigantic volume. Analysts cut their numbers again. The stock that had been loved by analysts at $45 was now hated by analysts at $12.

From the time that Apple started to rapidly lose share, MWHS had three bombs. In June, October, and December, the stock had declines of at least $10 each. During 1997, both Apple and Micro Warehouse had weak earnings and stock prices. In December, both stocks were selling for less than $15. The question is, *"Why in the face of Apple's problems and the chart's weakness did investors continue to jump back into Micro Warehouse?"* The answer should be clear by now: Investors failed to look at the charts and connect the dots. Investing can be very simple if you don't try to fight the tape or the news.

CONNECTIONS WITHIN INDUSTRY GROUPS

Although companies within an industry compete with each other, their stocks have a surprising tendency to move in the same direction at the same time. At first this might seem illogical. It might seem as if some companies and their stocks would do well while competing companies and their stocks did poorly. But in many instances, stocks within an industry move in concert. This occurs for both fundamental and technical reasons.

Fundamentally, companies can be impacted by the same industry-wide conditions. If Microsoft introduces a new operating system or Intel develops a new chip, demand for computers will be high, even though some companies will do better than others. If interest rates go down, financial-service stocks will benefit. But there is more to the common movement than can be attributed to fundamentals alone.

Industry groups, like stocks, have technical patterns. These technical patterns contribute to what is viewed as the "fashion" of investing. An industry group, like a stock, can be sitting relatively unchanged, with buyers and sellers in balance. Then, what seems like a minor event happens. A company reports strong earnings or an industry pundit talks bullishly about prospects. Suddenly, the group breaks out and starts to rally. Analysts jump on it. The biggest stocks may move first, but soon the rally takes the others along with it. It often continues longer and further than most investors would have expected. Then, at some point, the group stops moving up. A top is reached. The news is still positive, but the stocks are no longer rallying. Another seemingly minor event occurs, this one negative. A few months earlier, it would have been ignored by the market, but now it sends all of the stocks in the group plummeting.

The explanation for the behavior of the group is the same as the explanation for individual stocks. When a group is ready to break out, investors tend to focus on the good news. When a group is ready to break down, investors tend to focus on the bad news. In both cases, minor events can be magnified. While there may be underlying fundamental reasons for the move, the technical patterns are often as significant.

The market runs in rhythms, and the rhythms need not have a particular fundamental rationale. For instance, the semiconductor book-to-bill ratio comes in slightly higher than plan, and suddenly all of the technology stocks start to run. You wonder why such a small change should have sent the stocks up by 20 percent. The answer usually is that the group had a technical pattern that was ready for a breakout and the small change pushed it over the top. **Focusing on events that change a group's technical pattern can often give individual investors a great opportunity to make money, because many investors fail to grasp their importance.** They ignore the trading action of the stock and its group, and instead listen to the spin control from the companies and look for rationality in the market.

Running on Empty

An interesting example of such a minor event occurred early in 1997 in the athletic footwear industry. On Thursday, April 17, a company named Footstar, a recent spin-off from Melville Corporation, reported earnings. Footstar operates Footaction athletic shoe stores and leases footwear departments in Kmart. It is a large, but by no means dominant, company in its industry.

The day started well for Footstar. Analysts had been looking for earnings of $.06 per share, but Footstar blew away the estimates and reported $.16. The results were sensational. The stock immediately traded up $2 to $28. An analyst who had recommended the stock called: *"I told you to buy it last week. You better move quickly before it runs away. The stock is at only 10x earnings. With these numbers it can double."*

The early-morning conference call started promisingly, with management detailing the strong performance. Then the company started to talk about sales in the previous two weeks. It said that business since Easter had been a little weak. Inventories were a little too high. Some goods were being returned to manufacturers, such as Nike and Fila, and earnings in the next quarter might be a little below plan. Some companies would have been more aggressive in managing their earnings. They would have reported $.08 rather than $.16 in the first quarter and used the hidden earnings to cushion the next several quarters. (You should never underestimate a company's ability to manage its earnings. A company can play vast numbers of games to modify the earnings in a particular quarter. But Footstar was a new public company. It had little experience with analysts, and its management may not yet have learned how to play earnings games.)

As the conference call continued, the price of Footstar began to drop. Investors scurried from the call to sell their stock. By 10:30 A.M., Footstar had dropped back to $26. By 10:45, it had dropped to $25. At 10:50, it was halted for a trading imbalance. One hour later, Footstar was reopened at $19 (another indication of the advantage of moving fast gained by those on the conference call).

Analysts talked about Footstar's problems. Some undoubtedly mentioned that Footstar was sending products back to Fila and Nike. Those stocks started to take a hit. Nike dropped almost $4. The next day, it dropped another $2. Fila dropped $3.50. The next day, it dropped another $3.25. Investors also sold shares of other athletic shoe retailers. Finish Line, which had reported surprisingly strong earnings the week before, saw the price of its stock plunge from $16 to $12. Even Woolworth, which owns the Footlocker chain, dropped $2.

At the end of the day, most of the stocks in the group had been hit. Holders of the few that remained unscathed must have gone to sleep feeling a sense of relief. They thought they had dodged the bombs. Perhaps they convinced themselves that their stocks had some special fundamentals. But their turn would come, and come quickly.

Reebok had closed Thursday at $45 3/4, down only $.25. But the next morning, it reported weak earnings. The stock dropped $5 5/8. Converse had closed Thursday at $17 7/8, but Friday it sank $3 1/8. Russell, a maker of athletic apparel, also reported weaker-than-expected earnings and plunged $8 1/2 to $27 1/8. The lesson of Reebok, Converse, and Russell was simple: When stocks in an industry are self-destructing, few companies ever remain unscathed. **Before you go to sleep thinking that you alone have avoided getting killed, think again.**

The carnage was complete. Anyone who had listened to the Footstar conference call could have made large amounts of money by selling or shorting athletic footwear stocks. But many who listened to the conference call had no interest in selling. After all, there was no disaster. Or so it seemed. Footstar had reported an excellent quarter, as had Finish Line and a number of other companies. Footstar had not said that business had died. It only said that there was a small slowdown for two weeks. Further, Footstar was not the dominant player in its industry. So why did a two-week slowdown at one retailer cause all of the stocks in the group to get killed?

The explanation has less to do with the news conveyed by Footstar than with the technical trends in the athletic footwear and apparel industries. By the time Footstar indicated possible short-term problems, the companies were already in a weakened technical position. The stocks had already declined sharply and were heading lower. One year earlier, the market would have shaken off this announcement, but now the stocks were ready to drop. Investors seized on a relatively minor comment to punish every stock in the group.

DID EVERYONE GROW A THIRD FOOT?

Look at the chart of the athletic footwear stocks from the beginning of 1995 through April 1997. Most of the stocks had reasonably similar patterns, moving from lows early in the period to their highs during the end of 1996 and beginning of 1997, and then dropping in April 1997. Even though some companies had greater volatility and others began their move later, the technical patterns have a lot in common.

It is easy to understand why stocks in some industries move in concert. Bank stocks may move together because of changes in interest rates. Oil stocks may move together because of changes in oil prices. Telecommunications companies may move together because of changes in the regulatory environment. But what accounts for the similar movement of the athletic shoe stocks? No gigantic macro-economic trend suddenly changed demand. People did not grow a third foot. Nor was there any radical new technology that impacted everyone in the industry. These companies are competitors, fighting with each other for market share. As one company does well, another should do badly.

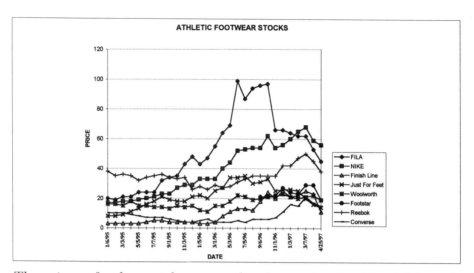

There is no fundamental reason why the stocks should exhibit such similar trading patterns.

Look at the breadth of the moves, especially the moves up. These companies had an unbelievable run. From their lows to their highs, Nike went up by 335 percent, Fila by 472 percent, Finish Line by 733 percent, Just For Feet by 428 percent, Woolworth by 155 percent, Reebok by 100 percent, and Converse by 700 percent. If you had bought each of these stocks at its low and sold them at its high, you would have made more than five times your money in about two years. These are striking moves, especially for a mature industry like sneakers.

Why did the stocks of competing footwear companies have such a dramatic, unified move? The answer relates to the technical pattern of the group and the power of momentum. The group had come from a low base, having been out of favor for a long time. As earnings started to improve, investors jumped on the stocks. Momentum carried them the rest of the way. Even smaller companies with marginal records obtained growth multiples.

Look at the experience of Nike. It parlayed its start with running shoes into a dominant position in both athletic footwear and activewear. From Michael Jordan to Tiger Woods, Nike has more great athletes than everyone else combined. When every kid in your neighborhood started to wear Nike, every picture of every athlete contained a swoosh, and everyone

ATHLETIC FOOTWEAR STOCKS: 1995-1997 HIGHS & LOWS

Company	Low	High	Percent Change
Nike	$17	$74	335
Fila	$18	$103	472
Finish Line	$3	$25	733
Just For Feet	$7	$37	428
Woolworth	$9	$23	155
Reebok	$25	$50	100
Converse	$3	$24	700

wanted to "be like Mike," it was probably the right time to buy Nike. While Nike is clearly a great company, it was also a great company in 1995. While the earnings improved significantly, was it enough to justify the jump in the price of the stock from $17 to $74? A significant portion of the advance was momentum, and while Nike soared, so did most of the other companies in the industry.

Momentum works on the downside as well. By the middle of 1996, the upside momentum for the athletic footwear companies was coming to an end. Just For Feet was the first to crack. After surging from $4 to $37, it ran out of steam. Inventories, which investors had ignored on the way up, suddenly became critical, and its acquisition of a chain of smaller stores did not help. In July, the stock cracked down from $37 to $27 on huge volume, and its run was over.

Fila was next. Fila's pattern resembles that of many other stocks that have surged up without forming a base. There were the two breakouts at $20 and $30, and then an almost straight run to $103. But in October 1996, Fila had huge volume on the downside that broke the upward momentum. (It is not surprising that one year later Fila was selling just near $20, the very price of its major base.)

Nike's turn came in November. The stock traded 31 million shares in two weeks as it dropped from $61 to $57. In March, it dropped again on high volume. Then, on April 7, a very capable analyst from Smith Barney lowered her rating. During the next week, Nike plunged $4 ⅛ on volume of 28.7 million, twice as high as its breakout volume. Despite strong earnings, this volume should have dispelled any doubt that Nike's advance was over. Nike had run from $17 to $74, but now it was on the way down.

Interestingly, the charts reveal that almost all of the stocks in the group had rolled over and were heading down before Footstar's announcement. The conference call announcement was only a reflection of what the charts were already saying. It was not the two weeks of softness in sales that sent the stocks dropping but rather the already declining technical patterns, especially Nike's price decline. Look at the chart of the stocks from February to April 1997. It is easy to see the decline in the making. And once the upside momentum was broken, the athletic footwear stocks continued to decline. By January 1998, Nike, Fila, Reebok, and Converse were all on the new low list, while most of the other stocks were close to their lows. Momentum is always a double-edged sword. Ironically, the only stock that had gone back up was Footstar, the company that seemed to have started the panic.

FIVE WAYS TO PROFIT FROM INDUSTRY NEWS

The question that individuals should ask is, *"How can I use the actions of the groups to make money?"* Some investors like to play the groups

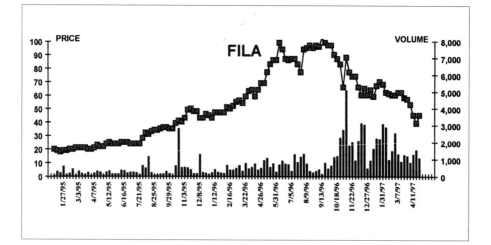

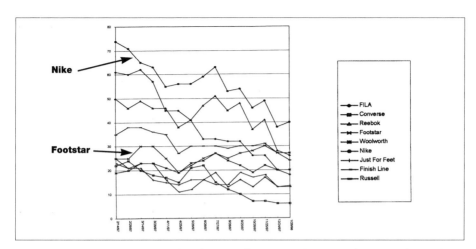

themselves. They look at the charts of groups the way they would look at the charts of stocks. They move into industries that look like they are about to break out, and out of industries that look like they are about to break down. There is nothing wrong with this strategy, but substantial time and discipline are required to follow it effectively. You have to watch events, study the relative strength of industry charts, and be ready to move as fashion changes. If you are not on top of events, you will jump on after the group has already begun its move up and jump off after it has already begun its move down, and you will lose. Individual investors don't usually have this kind of time.

This does not mean you should ignore the actions of a group of stocks or wait patiently until the group in which you have your largest investments has its day in the sun. On the contrary, it is critical to watch the trading action of the competitors of your largest holdings. These competitors may

ATHLETIC FOOTWEAR STOCKS: 1997 HIGHS, APRIL 1997 & JANUARY 1998 PRICES

Company	High	4/25/97	1/26/98
Nike	$76	$56	$40
Fila	$74	$45	$18
Finish Line	$27	$11	$12.50
Just For Feet	$32	$14	$13.50
Woolworth	$26	$19	$20
Reebok	$53	$38	$26
Converse	$28	$15	$6

tell you a lot about the stocks you own. You have to watch the news that affects the companies you are interested in to maintain your home-turf edge, but you need some time-saving strategies to do it. Here are six easy ways to look at stocks that compete directly with those you own:

1. Look at the prices of the largest stocks in the industry to see if they are moving in the same direction as the stocks you own. Larger stocks will tend to move before smaller stocks. If the larger stocks in your industry move up strongly, the smaller stocks will usually follow suit. If the larger stocks have major moves upward and your stock doesn't budge, you may want to revisit your reason for owning it.

When the larger stocks move down, they often put a cap on the group as a whole. If Microsoft and Intel are sinking, it is tough for smaller technology companies to rally. These larger stocks tend to set the psychology of the group. If investors are down on great companies, they often do not want to hear about lesser-quality companies. In addition, the professional investors, such as the mutual fund managers, who have major positions in these huge companies, are getting hammered. Many people invested in these mutual funds are watching the news and redeeming their shares. The fund managers will be trying to sell what they can to meet the redemptions and will have no appetite for buying. Thus, if the industry bellwethers are in trouble, other stocks in the industry will have a difficult time doing well.

2. Chart some of the competing companies against each other. Go to your charting website and create a chart that includes a number of competing companies (like the athletic footwear chart above). Look at the pattern of the group as a whole and of your stocks in particular. This can be a very interesting exercise.

3. Look at a table that shows the "price percentage leaders." These are the stocks that have increased or decreased the most in price during the previous period. (This table is available in every financial newspaper.) Look for stocks competing with those you own. If they have had a major move up or down, try to understand the factors behind this move and discern whether they will also impact your stocks.

4. Scan a related table showing the "volume percentage leaders." These are the stocks that have had the biggest increase in trading volume. Stocks in which major events are occurring often have the highest increases in volume. *Investors Business Daily* lists an extensive number of stocks with volume increases. If you can make the connections between the stocks in these lists and the stocks in which you are interested before the rest of the market, you can frequently win.

5. Look at the "new high" and the "new low" lists. These lists show the types of stocks that are doing very well or very poorly. Think about where your stocks are relative to their own highs and lows. If you see a number of companies that compete with yours on the new high list while yours is mired in the middle of its range, something is wrong. If your stock is not moving up while the competitors are hitting new highs, how do you think it will perform when the competitors start to decline? But if your stock is holding its own while the competitors are all hitting new lows, you may be in a good position when the competitors turn and start to rally.

6. Look at the "relative strength" of various industry groups. The action of your stock should in some way conform to the action of its group. Pay special attention when the relative strength of the industry is increasing or decreasing significantly. If the relative strength of your stock is sharply different from that of its group, study the charts carefully. This could be an interesting opportunity or a significant risk.

In looking at stocks of competing companies or the industry group as a whole, never underestimate the ability of seemingly minor events to have a broad impact. If you can watch the news and understand the technical patterns of the stocks in a particular industry in which you have a home-turf advantage, you can very often beat the overly diversified or too narrowly focused professionals at their own game.

Understanding the links between news and stocks is an art, not a science. There are no exact answers as to how companies will respond to a particular piece of information. If a takeover occurs in a particular industry, some stocks will rise because they also are considered to be takeover candidates, but other stocks may fall because investors worry that these companies will become buyers or be hurt by the new competition. Sometimes stocks in a competing industry will move together, as was the case in the athletic footwear business, while sometimes they will move apart, as was the case with Apple and Microsoft.

It takes judgment to look at the fundamental news and the technical patterns and find the links that can enable you to make money. Fortunately, these links can be relatively easy to see if you are looking for them. Investors could have seen the problems with Oakley and Micro Warehouse if they had simply looked at Sunglass Hut and Apple, and investors could have made money in the athletic footwear companies on both the upside and the downside if they had simply looked for the connections between competitors. The trick is to understand the interconnections between stocks and take action when an event occurs. The ability to anticipate and act on these interconnections separates the winners from the losers.

PART 3

Hostile Territory

CHAPTER NINE

Beware False Intelligence: The Analysts

Accurate intelligence is essential to a war effort. But, too often, the intelligence-gathering arm wants to portray the war effort in the most favorable light. When this occurs, the information it presents to the fighting generals is not completely correct. The rose-colored intelligence can actually work against the invading army it is supposed to help. On Wall Street, analysts are the intelligence-gathering arm of the investor. They are under their own form of pressure to perform. In theory, the analysts' job is to find good stocks for clients. But that theory is wrong. Don't get suckered into the idea that the analysts' first job is to make money for you. It is not. The analysts' primary job is to be a supporter of their brokerage firm's investment banking activities. Their second job is to keep the institutional investors happy. Retail customers like you come in a distant third. That's why a warning against information from analysts introduces Part 3. You are entering Hostile Territory.

Because the analysts support investment banking, they disseminate information that can be a little slanted. Investment banking revenues drive brokerage firms, and investment banking clients want analysts who speak favorably of their companies. When was the last time you saw a company give its banking business to an analyst who said, *"Sell the stock"*? Much of an analyst's compensation comes from investment banking business, so most of them are going to say good things about the firm's clients. The bullishness has gotten so extreme that analysts now praise any company that could potentially be a client. With the current deal flow, most analysts now only know how to say *"Buy!"*

Even when bad news occurs, the analyst is expected to write reports that support the client's spin. Only when they are with key institutional clients can their doubt, which would never find its way to paper, creep into words. Professionals understand the game. They know that the analyst most often maintains a more bullish pose in public, and they have direct access, so they can understand where the analyst really stands. This gives them a substantial advantage over the individual investor. **If individual investors are to utilize the work of analysts, they must learn to read between the lines and understand what the analysts are really saying.** They must also find the analysts' blind side and turn it to their advantage. This is not as difficult as it might first appear. In fact, it is often quite easy to use the analysts' weaknesses to beat the professionals at their own game.

MOST ANALYSTS ARE BULLISH

Have you ever noticed that the analysts at your brokerage firm are almost always bullish on most of their stocks? Most have Strong Buys, Buys, or Accumulate ratings. Very rarely do you see a Sell, much less a Short Sell rating. Because the recent market has gone up so much, many believe that the analysts have been prescient and have correctly predicted the action of their stocks. The reality is: **Analysts are not prescient. They are simply bullish.** Just as a stopped clock is right twice a day, so in a rising market the analysts often look smarter than they are.

One reason for their bullishness is that analysts tend to cover the companies they like. Analysts can cover no more than fifteen to twenty companies, but most industries have many more. While analysts generally follow the largest firms, they have leeway in selecting others to follow. Since covering a company represents a significant time commitment, most select companies they like. Few would waste their time following a small company they believe has no future. If the company is not a key player, an analyst who did not like it would just ignore it.

Analysts like to follow winners. It is more fun to follow good firms. Investors love to receive updates on stocks that are hitting new highs and hate to talk about stocks that have been crushed. When I initiated coverage of Sears, the stock had declined sharply from its high. Everyone hated the company. When they saw the name, they often took out their frustrations from many years of losses on me, even though I had never before had a Buy on the stock. Although Sears proved to be a huge winner, following it for the first few years was not fun.

Good companies are more likely to have investment banking activities, because they are usually growing faster than weak companies are. This can be a key financial issue for analysts. Finally, investors often equate the quality of the analysts with the quality of the companies they follow. If the analyst has a list of first-rate companies, investors tend to think the analyst is smart, while if an analyst has a list of second-rate companies, investors tend to think of the analyst as dumb. Investors have often lost money in second-rate firms and are hostile to anyone who would follow, much less recommend, them. In actuality, the quality of stocks on the analyst's list may say little about his stock-picking ability. In fact, the analyst with the list of lousy stocks may be making much more money for his customers.

Analysts try to keep winners and prune out losers. When a company has performed poorly, the analysts begin to mistrust everything that it has to say, and the investors begin to hate the analysts for putting them in a "dog." Often, when a company has a major disaster, the analysts quickly downgrade the stock to protect their record. The stock may have closed at $30, but it is clear from the news that it will open at $20. The analysts write a note, downgrading the stock before it can open. On their record, it says that they downgraded it at $30. It does not matter that none of their clients was able to sell at that price. Sometimes they might even discontinue coverage, dropping the stock off their list. Thus, by keeping winners, dropping losers, and selecting the best companies to follow, analysts tend to reinforce their general bullishness.

The communication between companies and the analysts generally makes them more bullish. Companies are usually bullish about their prospects. It is difficult to spend a large amount of time talking with the managers of a company and not begin to believe the promises. This is especially true if there is a strong personal relationship between an analyst and the executives in a company. Human interaction and even friendships can have a powerful influence on analysts. Thus, a symbiotic relationship often develops between an analyst and a company.

COMPANIES SHOW FAVORITISM TO ANALYSTS THEY LIKE

Analysts live for scooping their competition. They are the tabloid television correspondents of the investment world. If an analyst can obtain exclusive information or an interview with management, that analyst will have an edge on the competition. Companies are keenly aware of the importance of this type of information and hand out tidbits judiciously. *"Don't publish this,"* the chief financial officer might whisper to an analyst, *"but the sales of our new division are 40 percent above projection."* After the conversation is finished, the analyst will undoubtedly call many of the largest investors and share this confidential piece of information. (Sharing the news with major institutional shareholders is obviously different from "publishing" it, especially if you are a major institutional shareholder.)

Companies may show favoritism in something as simple as returning phone calls. When a company makes a major announcement, the analysts will call immediately. Those who receive the first return calls will have a substantial advantage. Most companies will return calls selectively, talking first to the analysts who will put the most positive spin on the news. Analysts who are less positive may not receive a call for hours. By the time they do, the information will have already been disseminated, and they will have been shut out. Controlling the order of phone calls may seem like a very minor issue, but it can be extremely significant in a time-sensitive market.

Some companies may actually decide to freeze out analysts they do not like. I once put out a Sell recommendation on Sports & Recreation (now called Jumbo Sports). Management was furious with my report. The company mobilized other analysts against me. Then it removed my name from its fax list and refused to talk with me. Without any access to information, it became very difficult to follow the company.

Companies can also give a favored analyst special access. They can offer private meetings with the CEO to an analyst and selected institutional shareholders. Or, they can agree to participate at one of the many conferences sponsored by an analyst's brokerage firm. The success of a brokerage firm's conference depends on the strength of the presenters. A conference with top speakers, such as Bill Gates, will have a major advantage in attracting the best institutional investors. It is the responsibility of the analysts to deliver top management from companies they follow for their firm's conferences. Top executives choosing where to speak and whom to send naturally tend to favor those brokerage analysts who have the most positive view of their company's future.

Companies also invite analysts to special events. In 1996, many firms sponsored analyst meetings at the Olympics. In many cases, the analysts were flown down on private jets, lodged in deluxe hotels, and given tickets to the best events. The Olympics are not the only boondoggle offered to analysts. Cruise lines sponsor meetings at sea. Movie companies give analysts private screenings, and some companies even put the analysts' quotes in their annual reports. None of these actions directly compromises an analyst, but in subtle ways they can modify the analyst's views. The question that investors should ask is, *"Can an analyst who is sitting in the front row of the basketball venue watching the Dream Team be truly impartial?"*

So the symbiotic relationship between an analyst and the company develops on a number of levels. There is a personal relationship, friends talking to friends. There is an information relationship, giving the analyst the scoop. There is a perk relationship, allowing the analyst to sponsor, or attend, meetings. Each of these ties the analyst and the company together and makes it difficult for the analyst to be truly impartial. In the end, the power of the company, if utilized, may be strong enough to limit the independence of many analysts. This, of course, is a significant issue for investors, who believe that the analysts employed by their brokerage firms are objective observers whose primary goal is to make money for them.

INVESTMENT BANKING COMPROMISES ANALYSTS

As we have seen, while conventional wisdom holds that analysts are employed by brokerage firms to provide good research for investors, the economic reality is that investment banking, not stock trading, drives the profits of Wall Street and the compensation of analysts. The profitability of trading stock is lower than most people think. The annual commissions from trading a stock with 100 million shares might be $5 million. If ten analysts follow the stock, and if the firms for which they work trade 50 percent of all shares, these ten firms will receive an average of $250,000 each. By the time the firm pays the salesperson, the trader, the stock exchange fees, the costs of distributing the reports, and its own overhead, there is relatively little left for the analyst. In a stock with many fewer shares, the direct costs of covering the company could be more than the commissions. With these economics, it is easy to see why analysts do not follow smaller companies that do not have investment banking business.

Compare this scenario with the economics of a company doing a stock offering. In trading stocks, the fees are about $.05 per share on each side of the transaction. In a stock offering, the fee might average $2 per share. If the company with 100 million shares decides to sell 10 million more shares, the fees could be $20 million. If there were four lead underwriters, these firms might split 80 percent of the fees, or $4 million each. This is sixteen times what they would have received from trading the stock during the year. In both cases, someone has to analyze the stock, sell it, and trade it, but in the latter case, the fee is much higher. (It is not uncommon to pay the analyst who brought the offering to the firm a bonus of 10 percent of the fees—in this case, $400,000.)

How do these fees impact the independence of the analyst? It does not take a rocket scientist to calculate that the analyst who can snare major underwriting business is going to make much more money than the analyst who concentrates on trading the stock. Some analysts see themselves as seekers of wisdom and truth, but given these economics, it is obvious why many analysts will focus on investment banking.

The problem for the investor is that the skills needed to be a good stock-picker are often sharply at odds with the qualities that make a good investment banking analyst. Good stock pickers should be independent. They should look at management objectively, question when its strategies seem wrong, and ferret out information that others miss. But few companies will pay large investment banking fees to brokerage houses whose analysts probe too deeply or write too critically.

Companies want analysts who will tell their story in the way they want it told. If the company wants analysts to carry earnings estimates of $1.50, that is the estimate that they should have. The analyst with the estimate of $1.40 is too low, but the analyst at $1.60 is equally problematic for the company. If one analyst has too high an estimate, it will be much more difficult for the company to "surprise" the Street. While the analysts can shade their views, independent thoughts are neither desired nor welcomed.

Analysts are "punished" even when they suggest a future company direction at odds with that desired by management. Suppose an analyst wrote a report saying a company had been mismanaged and the stock might be worth three times the current price if the company was broken up. Even if the report was responsible for the stock's going up, and even if members of management were large shareholders, the analyst's firm would probably not be hired to help in the restructuring. Few managements will reward analysts who force them to restructure their company. While other investment banking firms would receive huge fees for selling off the pieces, the analyst who started the process would be a pariah.

Companies like analysts who are not controversial and who will introduce them to a large number of investors. The chairman of a very successful company once told me that he hired a particular firm for his offering because the firm's analyst ran good fieldtrips. *"He may be a dope,"* the chairman said, *"but he brings hundreds of the most impor-*

tant investors into my stores. I can't do that for myself." The question is whether the customers of this analyst realized that he was a dope, and that he was making more than $1 million per year because he was a good tour guide, not because he was a good stockpicker.

While analysts are supposed to follow their companies closely, it is often "advisable" not to follow them too closely. Looking closely at the numbers of a company is like looking at an eclipse of the sun. They can blind the analyst, at least as far as getting any scoops in the future. Companies often have questionable ways of accounting that can have a material impact on their earnings, and they do not want the analysts to look too closely at these policies. There is no reason to stir up a hornets' nest on a complicated accounting problem, especially when such a problem would have a negative impact on the price of the stock. Fortunately for the companies, when analysts have to follow fifteen companies, work on investment banking projects, and travel extensively on marketing trips, they have little time to read the financial documents. Analysts often rely on management to point out the issues on which they should be focusing, and management is often selective in the topics it chooses.

EXECUTIVE PAY

One subject that is definitely off-limits for any analyst whose firm is looking to maintain an investment banking relationship is executive compensation. Imagine how management would react to an analyst who wrote, *"The CEO is way overpaid."* Even if it were true, such a statement would not only cost the analyst banking business with that company, it would also probably scare off other companies. The CEO of a competitor might agree with the analyst's comment but would never do business with the analyst's firm. After all, he could be the analyst's next target. As long as investment banking drives the economics of Wall Street, few analysts will question the compensation policies of the companies they follow, any more than companies will question the compensation policies of the investment banks.

Investors should be cautious about buying stocks pushed by analysts who work for the brokerage firms doing the stock's investment banking. Suppose that the analyst of a firm slated to be one of the lead bankers in an offering thought that the business was slightly less robust than planned. What would the analyst do? You would like to think she would reduce the earnings estimates and lower the rating on the company. But if she were to do this, the firm would lose the offering and she would forfeit a huge bonus, possibly more than $500,000, and potentially risk losing a job. Put yourself in the analyst's position. You have two kids in private school and a summer home in East Hampton. Besides, you are not 100 percent certain that the earnings will fall short. What would you do? Bonuses of $500,000 and jobs paying $1 million don't come along every day. In most cases, the analyst will point out the potential risks in a guarded fashion but leave the estimates and rating unchanged.

Analysts rarely lower their ratings on their investment banking clients, but they often subtly put their opinions in their reports. J. P. Morgan was one of the underwriters for Intimate Brands, the owner of Victoria's Secret and Bath and Body Works. In the third quarter of 1996, Intimate indicated that earnings would be below plan. The analyst from J. P. Morgan lowered her earnings estimates, but instead of lowering her rating, she wrote: *"We maintain our Buy rating, but expect the stock to remain dead money in the near term."*

With thousands of stocks available, it is difficult to understand why anyone would buy a stock that is "dead money." So while the analyst may have maintained her Buy rating, anyone reading her note would have realized that she no longer thought the stock was a Buy. This is the fine line that analysts have to walk in order to do their job, but as an investor, you do not have to accept what they say as gospel. (Of course, as luck would have it, Intimate Brands had excellent results in 1997 and was one of the best stocks in its group.)

While you should be cautious about buying a stock recommended by the analyst of an investment banker, you should not be cautious in selling a stock if the analyst says something negative about the company. If after an IPO, an analyst for the investment banker initiates coverage with a rating lower than

Strong Buy or a Buy, it is usually a sign of problems ahead. If an analyst selects a less positive rating, such as Long-Term Attractive, it means that she is sufficiently concerned about the prospects of the company to resist the strong pressures from her employer and company management. Since taking this stand will often cause the analyst considerable grief, investors should take note. **This is an analyst's way of tipping off investors.**

Sometimes analysts have more subtle ways of indicating their concern with investment banking clients. Morgan Stanley was one of the lead underwriters for Designer Holdings, the manufacturer of Calvin Klein and other brands of jeans. Several months after the very successful IPO, Josie Esquivel, a capable analyst for Morgan Stanley, held a seminar entitled *"War for Market Share in the Jeans Business."* Josie never said anything negative about Designer Holdings, but by holding the conference she allowed investors to explore the issue of excess competition in this industry. Someone must have figured it out. Shortly before the conference, Designer Holdings was selling for $32. Two months later, it was selling for $16. **If you see an analyst for an investment banking firm say anything that could be construed as negative about a company that has recently had an offering, sell the stock.**

Analysts understand that much of their compensation comes from investment banking. While they do not necessarily "shill" for the companies, they make sure that their earnings estimates and reports reflect the views that the company espouses. Like it or not, these are the rules of the game.

BEWARE OF BROKERAGE-HOUSE RATINGS

The report comes from your broker. You look at the headline. The analyst has a Buy on the stock. You assume that this means that the analyst wants you to buy it. Not so fast. You look at another report. It has a Hold rating. You assume that the analyst wants you to hold it. Again, not so fast. Analyst ratings can be misleading. At many firms, "Buy" may not mean buy. At most firms, "Hold" certainly does not mean hold.

THE THREE-RATING SYSTEM

There is no consistency among brokerage-house ratings. A few firms make it easy for investors. They have three ratings—Buy, Hold, and Sell. It is, of course, reasonable to question why they need even these three ratings. Buy and Sell should probably suffice. The meaning of a Buy or Sell rating is clear. The meaning of Hold is more problematic. If a stock is no longer good enough for you to Buy, why should you continue to hold it? There are probably some good reasons, such as not having to pay taxes. **But in most cases, the analyst does not really want you to hold Hold-rated stocks.** The analyst normally uses a Hold rating to maintain a neutral position on a stock.

While the three-rating system is pretty straightforward, most brokerage firms have four or five ratings. The four ratings might be: 1. Strong Buy, 2. Buy, 3. Hold or Market Perform, and 4. Unattractive or Sell. The five ratings might be: 1. Strong Buy, 2. Buy, 3. Accumulate or Long-term Attractive, 4. Market Perform, and 5. Sell.

THE FOUR- OR FIVE-RATING SYSTEM

A Strong Buy in a four- or a five-rating system is like a Buy in a three-rating system. It is the highest rating available to an analyst. Not surprisingly, companies much prefer the analyst to have a Strong Buy rather than a plain Buy, because it sounds more positive. When I worked for a brokerage firm with only three ratings, companies would always ask why I did not have a Strong Buy on their stock. I responded that the Buy was my top rating. This rarely satisfied them. They liked the sound of Strong Buy more. Sometime after I left, the brokerage firm changed to a five-rating system.

Since the Strong Buy indicates the analyst's best ideas at a firm with a four- or five-point system, the Buy rating is a place where many analysts choose to hide. When you see a stock in a five-point system rated Buy, you should ask why it isn't good enough to be a Strong Buy. Or, to put it another way, *"Why should I purchase a stock rated Buy when I could just as easily purchase one rated Strong Buy?"* The difference between a Strong Buy and a Buy is simple: Strong Buy means buy the stock. Buy does not. Buy is often a rating used by analysts for investment banking clients. It says, *"We really don't think this stock is the greatest buy in the world, but we led their last stock offering, so if we don't keep saying something positive, the management will kill us."*

Rating a stock a Buy instead of a Strong Buy enables analysts to avoid rocking the boat. Many analysts hate to cut ratings even if the stock price has moved up dramatically. I knew a top-rated analyst who lowered a stock that had doubled in price from a Strong Buy to a Buy. The stock dropped 20 percent on the downgrade. The CEO of the company was so infuriated that he stopped doing business with the analyst's firm, even though the firm had always been the company's investment banker. The message to competing analysts became crystal clear: The company would punish anyone who downgraded the stock. So the other analysts did the intelligent thing: They kept the company permanently at a Buy. Because they never raised it to a Strong Buy, they never had to worry about downgrading it.

The key to looking at an analyst's Buy in a five-point system is to see if the analyst ever changes the rating. If the analyst has maintained the rating for years, it's worthless. In these cases, the only way to tell if the analyst actually likes the stock is to read between the lines. Analysts often find subtle ways to distinguish between one Buy and another. They may use "price objectives." If the stock is at $28 and it has a price objective of $30, it is not really a Buy. They may also talk about the potential for upside surprises (a Buy) or about downside risks (not a Buy). Or, like an analyst from J. P. Morgan, they may actually tell you, *"The stock is dead money."*

The third rating in a five-point system, Accumulate or Long-term Attractive, is the most inane. **If the analyst has stocks that are Strong Buys and stocks that are Buys, why would you ever want to purchase a stock that is rated Accumulate?** Besides, what is the difference between accumulating a stock and buying it? If you accumulate, you still have to put up the same amount of money to purchase a share. So what does Accumulate actually mean? Accumulate is a euphemism that means, *"This stock is not good enough to be a Strong*

Buy or a Buy, but we still want to be able to talk to management and we would like to participate in the company's next offering, so we have come up with a rating that allows us to sound positive without being positive."

Long-term Attractive is another term that is like kissing your sister. (It is a little better than kissing your mother-in-law, but that's about it.) The first question you should ask when you see the rating Long-term Attractive is, *"Why should I buy a stock that is not attractive in the short term?"* Long-term Attractive means, *"This stock is not cheap, and we see no reason for rating it a Buy, but the company is decent and we like the management. Perhaps the stock will come down in price, and we will have an opportunity to raise our rating. If you already own it, don't panic. At some point in the distant future, you may actually get your money back."* In other words, Long-term Attractive means, *"We are sorry that you own this dog, but you'll make out in the end, if you live long enough."*

The fourth rating might be Hold, or Market Perform. Both of these ratings sound pretty good. An analyst would obviously not want you to hold a stock that is going to go down, and many analysts would be happy to have you own a stock that performs as well as the market. The problem is that while the terms sound good, their meaning is not. In most cases, Hold usually means, *"If you hate money, hold this stock!"* Market Perform usually means, *"If the market performs as badly as this stock will, you are in big trouble."*

There are two exceptions to the Hold rule. Often there are important companies in an industry that the analyst has never really followed. To comment on the company, the analyst needs an earnings estimate and a rating. The Hold is the analyst's way of saying, *"I don't know much about this company."* It is relatively easy to find out if a company fits into this category. If the analyst has never published a report on the company, it's a good bet that Hold means the analyst really does not know much about it.

The second exception to the Hold rule occurs when a group of stocks in the analyst's universe has a big move up before the analyst can initiate coverage. Last year, most of the Internet stocks started to fly before many of the software analysts even knew what www.com meant. Somewhere during the move, the director of research and the head of investment banking at the brokerage firm probably approached the firm's software analyst and said something like, *"Don't you realize that we're losing out on all this Internet banking business because you don't follow these stocks?"*

The analyst looked down at his neatly polished Gucci loafers and replied, *"I've been working on the group for three months. My report is almost ready."* Of course, the truth may be that the analyst missed the significance of the Web or was scared to jump on stocks that had already run up. But that is hardly something you can tell your bosses.

"I want that report out next week," the director of research strongly suggested. *"We're making a pitch to three potential IPOs and I need to show that we cover the group."*

The analyst is now in a quandary. The stocks have already quadrupled. If he initiates coverage with a Buy, everyone will accuse him of having "missed the group," which in fact he has. But if he does not speak glowingly about the prospects of the industry, his firm will never receive investment banking business. It is here that a Hold rating comes in very handy. The analyst initiates coverage with a Hold rating. This allows him to talk as an expert about the industry. He writes a report that speaks glowingly about the future, which the investment bankers can use in marketing to potential IPOs. In his report, he indicates that he is waiting for the stocks to decline by 10 to 20 percent before raising the rating to a Buy. By holding out the possibility of raising his rating, the analyst can partially cover himself with the sales force that is still furious about his having missed the group. Of course, what this rating really says is, *"I screwed up and missed the stocks. I hope they go down a little, so that I can raise my rating and not look so stupid."*

This type of Hold rating is always easy to identify. It is used in the initiation of coverage for a group of stocks that has had a huge upside move while the analyst sat on the sideline. It is easy to judge how much the analyst has missed the group. Look at the size of the report. The more the analyst believes he has screwed up, the longer will be the report, as if length compensates for lack of strength.

The final rating that most firms use is Sell. Sell is a very simple rating. It means sell this stock. However, Sell is a rating that is not often used. Investors may find the limited use of the Sell rating perplexing. After all, there is a lot of selling going on. The amount of selling is equal to the amount of Strong Buying, Buying, and Accumulating combined. Since every transaction has a buyer and a seller, one would think that the analysts would spend as much time finding Sells as finding Buys. But the reality is: **Analysts have more than one hundred Buy recommendations for every Sell recommendation.**

Companies do not like analysts who have Sell recommendations. Since investment banking fees drive the business and since companies rarely give banking business to negative analysts, the analyst who wants to eat well and have a co-op on Park Avenue will probably not issue a lot of Sells. In addition, many portfolio managers do not like analysts who issue Sell recommendations, especially when they own the stocks. Since the Sell rating is rare, its use often results in a stock being trashed. Even if the reasons are valid, the owners of the stock are unlikely to be pleased. So, faced with a negative reaction from both companies and investors, most analysts avoid the Sell rating and stick with euphemisms, like Dead Money or Significant Risk, to describe stocks they do not like.

My favorite euphemism is Source of Funds. By using the term Source of Funds, the analyst is saying, *"If there is a stock you want to buy, sell this stock and use the proceeds as a source of funds."* In other words, Source of Funds means sell.

One final investment rating, Short Sell, is almost never used. In a short sell, investors "sell" a stock they do not own, betting that the stock will go down. A short sell is more than a sell. It is a bet against a company. Obviously, you very rarely see a Short Sell recommendation, but that does not negate the legitimacy of this rating, nor should it discourage you from shorting. In the final chapter, we'll discuss when it's appropriate to short a stock.

Some brokerage firms have created a more complicated system by using both short-term and long-term ratings for each stock. A typical rating might be 1/1, which means Short-Term Buy/Long-Term Buy, or 2/1, which means Short-Term Hold/Long-Term Buy. In theory, this is a good way to look at stocks. The short-term rating reflects the analyst's view as to how the stock will perform in the immediate future. The long-term rating reflects the analyst's view of the long-term strength of the company. In practice, analysts tend to use the short-term ratings for their real views and the long-term ratings to appease banking clients. At one firm, for example, 37 percent of the stocks were rated Short-Term Buy, but 86 percent were rated Long-Term Buy. By carrying a Short-Term Hold and a Long-Term Buy, the analyst can tell the management of the company that she still rates them a Buy, while telling investors that the company is a Hold. The system works fine, so long as you understand the game.

ANALYSTS NEVER MEET A STOCK THEY DON'T LIKE

Ratings inflation is absolutely rampant, far beyond "irrational exuberance." Many of the ratings are at best misleading and at worst meaningless. In order to demonstrate the ratings inflation, I picked seven firms at random and used their ratings from early July 1996. Stocks with no ratings were excluded from the calculations.

- At **Montgomery Securities**, 368 stocks, or 72 percent, had Buy ratings, and only one stock had a Sell rating. It is interesting to speculate what that one company must have done to the analyst to merit a Sell. It is also reasonable to ask where investors would find the money to buy 368 stocks while only selling one.
- At **Robertson Stevens**, 316 stocks, or 79.4 percent, had bullish ratings. The remaining 20.6 percent were rated as Market Performers. Thus, of 398 stocks, Robertson believed that 316 would outperform the market, 82 would perform even with the market, and none would underperform the market. Since half of all stocks, by definition, underperform, it is incredible that Robertson's analysts have the ability to completely avoid stocks that will underperform.

- **Robinson Humphrey** uses a system that has both short-term and long-term ratings. For the short term, 37 percent were rated Buy, but for the long term, 86 percent were rated Buy and only one stock was rated Sell.
- At **Needham**, 72 percent of the stocks were rated Strong Buy or Buy, and 28 percent were rated Hold. There were no Sell-rated stocks.
- At **Gerard Klauer**, 64 percent of the stocks were rated Buy, and 35 percent were rated Hold. There was one Sell.
- At **Wheat First**, 197 stocks had ratings of Outperform or better, and only nine stocks had ratings of Underperform—a pretty impressive batting average. Wheat had no Sells.
- At **Alex Brown**, 65 percent of the stocks had the firm's top ratings—Strongest Overperformance or Overperformance; 35 percent of the stocks were rated Market Performance; and most impressive, no stock was rated either Underperformance or Substantial Underperformance. In other words, Alex Brown had 401 stocks that it believed would outperform the market and none that it believed would underperform the market. Amazing! Of course, skeptics might ask why Alex Brown has five ratings if it only uses three, but then perhaps this firm really can pick only winners.

It is pretty clear that the analysts were giving the customers little guidance. Seventy percent of the stocks were Long-Term Buys, so it must have been difficult for the investor to select the best Buys. More significant, only three out of 1,559 stocks were rated Sell, so the analysts were giving investors almost no help on what to sell. The reality is simple: Analysts' ratings are of little use in picking stocks.

EIGHT RULES FOR DEALING WITH ANALYSTS

The analysts do not make it easy for investors to decide what stocks to buy and sell, but still, as we have seen, the analysts have some tendencies that can be useful in picking stocks. Follow these eight rules that summarize how to work with analysts, and you'll be ahead of the game:

1. Analysts who initiate coverage of a company when a stock is at a new high may just be pitching investment banking business. This is especially common among firms that follow growth stocks. If the stock has previously not had much of a growth profile, it may continue to go up as new momentum investors jump in, but investors have no way of knowing whether the analyst believes in the company or is just looking for a payday. (If the analyst's firm does not get the business, watch out. A drop in ratings can trash a stock.)

2. Take note when analysts lower earnings estimates on their favorite stocks. All analysts have favorite stocks. Not only have they built strong relationships with the managements of these companies, but their reputation is often tied to these stocks. They have probably put many of the current shareholders into them. Lowering the rating could have a huge impact on the price of the stock and alienate investors, management, and the analyst's own sales force. As a result, analysts often maintain Buy ratings on the stocks with which they are most closely identified. I have known analysts who maintained Buy recommendations on individual stocks for more than a decade. The longer the rating was maintained, the harder it became for the analyst to change it. Instead of changing the rating, these analysts often communicate problems by lowering the earnings estimates. When an analyst who is closely associated with a company lowers estimates, investors should start writing Sell tickets.

This is especially true when the company has recently done a stock offering. When companies do an offering, they usually "guide" analysts to the "right" earnings estimates. Because companies and investment bankers are concerned about lawsuits, they are very careful to make sure that analysts have the right numbers. If an analyst lowers an estimate shortly after an offering, it is a sure sign of trouble, even if the analyst continues to say good things about the company.

3. Beware of analysts "fine-tuning" their estimates. When analysts have a Buy on a stock and they decide to change the earnings estimates from $1 to $1.04, they typically say that they are "raising" the estimates. But when they change their estimates from $1.04 to $1, they typically say that they are "fine-tuning" their model. Fine-tuning is a euphemism that in most cases means lowering. Fine-tuning can be especially worrisome when analysts lower the current quarter but leave their annual estimates unchanged. If the consensus for a quarter is $1, most of the analysts probably received guidance from the company, and the company probably planned to earn $1.05. If the company finds that business is more difficult than expected, its first step may be to tell the analysts to fine-tune their models. Companies do not like to tell analysts to lower estimates unless it is absolutely necessary. The analysts do not like to lower estimates either. So they drop this quarter by a few cents and hope that the company can pull a rabbit out of its hat before the year ends.

When analysts fine-tune a quarter but leave the year unchanged, they are actually raising their estimates for subsequent quarters. Given the weakness in the current quarter, this significantly increases the likelihood that the company will disappoint investors. I have seen analysts fine-tune estimates three quarters in a row, only to find that the fourth quarter ended up a disaster. While there may be instances in which fine-tuning is appropriate, in most cases investors should recognize it for what it is—a reduction in the earnings estimate—and assume that subsequent quarters will also have to be fine-tuned, unless you hear a very convincing argument otherwise.

4. Beware of changes in the target price for no good reason. When analysts issue recommendations, they usually have target prices for the stock. The target price is the goal that the analyst has for the stock within a particular timeframe. The target price and the timeframe are usually detailed on the cover of the research report. A funny thing often happens when the stocks reach their target: Because analysts like to keep their winners, they merely change the target price. Changing the target price may be entirely appropriate if earnings have come in above expectations or if a long enough period of time has passed so that analysts can start looking at next year's earnings. If the analyst can really make a case that the growth rate has increased, he can justify a higher multiple and hence a higher price target. But in many cases, the analyst is adjusting his target prices without changing either the projected earnings estimates or the projected growth rate just so he can continue his Buy. When this occurs, it is a good time to start looking at the chart for a Sell point. If a stock exceeds the analyst's initial projected target without any change in the estimates, do not fall for the analyst's new price target and continued Buy. Ask yourself if it's time to sell.

5. Look for analysts with Sell recommendations. If nothing else, analysts who issue Sell recommendations are independent. By issuing Sell recommendations, the analyst is almost certainly giving up investment banking business and making a determination that picking the right stocks is more important than generating banking fees. This is a position that analysts do not take lightly. Wall Street is not overpopulated with analysts who prefer truth to money. The seven brokerage firms cited earlier had only three long-term Sells. But a few analysts do issue them. I once worked with an oil analyst named Mark Gilman who always had Sell recommendations on about half of his stocks. Gilman was also one of the few analysts who would openly challenge the managements of his companies. Gilman was not always right, but he was always independent.

Sell recommendations make life easier for investors. There is no hiding behind a euphemism like Market Perform. In the following cases, Sell recommendations are particularly significant:

- Try to find analysts who have Sell ratings on stocks that everyone else loves. When one analyst has a Sell and all the other analysts have Strong Buys, that analyst usually has an opinion that, right or wrong, is worth noting.
- Try to find analysts with Sell recommendations on companies currently doing investment banking business. When a company does an offering, there is a payday for most of the analysts. The analyst with the Sell rating is walking away from that pay. Investors would do well to listen to what that analyst has to say.
- Try to find analysts with Sell recommendations based on accounting issues. These recommendations are especially interesting, because most analysts do not look closely at accounting

issues. Analysts who have gone to the trouble of studying them may be onto something.

- Once in a very long while, an analyst may actually have a Short Sell recommendation. Such a recommendation is worth looking at because it is such a rare and radical step against a company. This is not to say that you should short the stock, but you should look at the argument the analyst is making.

6. Pick a few analysts and stick with them. Think of analysts the way you would think of athletes. Shaquille O'Neal and Yinka Dare are both seven-foot centers, but their performances are hardly comparable. The performance of analysts can differ as much as the performance of athletes. If you can identify the Shaquille O'Neals instead of the Yinka Dares, you will make money. The easiest way to begin is to ask your broker which analysts are the best money-makers. In every brokerage firm, there are a very few great money-makers, a few consistent losers, and many who are just average. Most brokers have a pretty good sense as to which are the best. Ask them which analysts they use for their own investments. Most will use only three or four. Stick with the best analysts, even if they are not in the hottest groups. The easiest way to lose money is to rely on a bad analyst in a hot group.

7. A consistent loser can be as good as a consistent winner. Every once in a while, you may find analysts who are always wrong. They are consistent money losers. But these analysts can be of great use because they are perfect contrary indicators.

An institutional salesman told me a story about an analyst who was almost always wrong. If the analyst said that a stock was going to go up, it usually went down, and vice versa. It was difficult trying to sell this analyst's research, but the salesman tried his best. There was, however, one portfolio manager who wanted to know everything that this analyst said. The portfolio manager told him, *"I'll pay you $100,000 per year, but I want to get the first phone call on anything that this analyst says."* The salesman never understood why, but he was happy to make the commission, so he always promptly called the manager with any news from the analyst.

One day, the analyst recommended the stock of a large industrial company that appeared to be having severe financial problems. The salesman could not understand what the analyst liked about the stock, and thought that the recommendation could backfire, so he did not call any clients. Within two days the stock had dropped by 50 percent. While others were fielding angry calls, this salesman was feeling pretty smug.

Then the portfolio manager called, enraged: *"Why didn't you call me about the recommendation?"*

"I thought it was a dumb idea," the salesman replied. *"Besides, it dropped from $12 to $8 in two days."*

"I own the stock," the portfolio manager screamed.

"Then I saved you from buying more," the salesman replied.

"Don't you get it?" the portfolio manager snapped. *"If I knew this idiot was recommending the stock, I would have sold every share. I've known this bozo for fifteen years, and he's always wrong. He is the perfect contrary indicator! If he says 'Buy,' I sell. If he says 'Sell,' I buy. He is never right! Do you know how much money I can make betting against him?"*

My friend was dumbfounded. It had never occurred to him that someone would actually use the analyst as a contrary indicator, but analysts who are always wrong can make you as much money as analysts who are always right, as long as you remember to bet against them. So, in addition to asking the broker which are the best analysts, it is also sometimes useful to ask which are the worst.

8. Try to identify what an analyst does particularly well. Some analysts are good at finding value stocks, but terrible at growth or momentum stocks. Some analysts can spot trends, but cannot make earnings estimates. Some are good at a certain part of their industry, but weak in other parts. David Goldsmith, an analyst at Buckingham Research, had an uncanny ability to figure out the breakup value of media, cable, and cellular companies. During a decade in which many of these companies were taken over, Goldsmith made a huge amount of money for his clients. There have been few analysts who were ever better. However, when Goldsmith attempted to focus on more mundane issues, such as whether a movie or a TV series would be a success, he was only average. The trick was to use him for what he was great at, not to rely on him for everything. You do not need an analyst who is a jack of all trades. You need an analyst who is especially good at a few things. If you can figure out what those things are, you can use that analyst to make a lot of money.

— . —

The analysts are the intelligence-gathering arm of the brokerage houses. It is easy to read their glowing reports and rush out to buy the stocks. But before you do, remember that the analysts are overwhelmingly bullish, that their bullishness is augmented by the fees from investment banking, and that brokerage house ratings are of extremely limited value. If you follow the rules listed above, you can use the analysts to your advantage and eliminate some of the advantages of the professionals.

CHAPTER TEN

Pitfalls (and Opportunities)

Throughout this book, we've covered general attitudes and actions the guerrilla investor should take in order to defeat the Street's professionals. Before we get to the final chapter, where we'll develop an actual investment strategy, it would be useful to look at a number of critical pitfalls and opportunities that every individual investor should watch for while trading in Hostile Territory. These common, easy-to-miss situations frequently tell a lot about the future direction of the price of a stock. Individual investors who avoid these pitfalls and capitalize on these opportunities can greatly enhance their performance.

WATCH THE REVOLVING DOOR

In a seemingly strong company, too much management turnover can be a bad sign. If managers resign, they are sending a message about their view of the future of the company's stock price. Most managers have unvested stock options which they forfeit when they leave. Suppose a manager has 200,000 shares of options that would be vested in two years, and the stock is currently $20 per share above the option price. The manager's options are already $4 million in the money. Further, suppose the analysts say the stock will go up another $30 in the next two years. If the analysts are right, the options will be worth $10 million when they are vested. By leaving, the manager is walking away from a potentially huge payday. Perhaps money is not important to the manager, or perhaps the manager has a different view of the future than the analysts do.

Watch which managers are leaving. If the CEO of a fast-growing company resigns "to pursue other interests," long-term fundamental problems are likely. CEOs usually don't leave businesses if everything is booming. In May 1996, the president of Aetna resigned so that he could spend more time with his family. At the time of his resignation, Aetna's stock was at about $95. In the next several months, the price increased to $120. Besides the resignation, there was also heavy insider selling. (One director dumped almost $130 million of stock.) But investors did not seem to care. Several months later, Aetna announced that it was having more problems than expected in integrating a recent acquisition. The stock tumbled to less than $70. Perhaps the news should not have been such a surprise. If everything was running smoothly, insiders would not have been dumping $130 million of stock, and the president could probably have found a way to keep his job and still spend quality time with his family.

When the chief financial officer suddenly leaves, look for potential accounting issues. CFOs often leave companies. In most cases, their departure is not a cause for concern. However, if the company has a reputation for being aggressive, the CFO could have had conflicts with the CEO over accounting policy. In almost every case, the CEO wants to report the higher numbers. A number of years ago, the CFO of Intelligent Electronics resigned and refused to sign the financial statements. Because Intelligent Electronics had a reputation for aggressive accounting, the stock dropped by 50 percent and never recovered. The firing of managers can also indicate hidden problems. A company doing well should have little reason to fire a number of key managers.

While too much turnover is not positive for a successful company, it may be positive for a company that has been doing badly. Then, the resignation or firing of a top executive could foretell a sale or a corporate restructuring. If a new CEO is brought in or if the company is beginning a turnaround strategy, you can expect—and even want—a high level of management turnover. Otherwise, however, it's a bad sign. The company will always put the best spin possible on it, but you should treat this spin with skepticism. Just remember, managers who resign leave lots of money on the table. Perhaps you should as well.

BEWARE OF COMPANIES THAT REPORT INFORMATION LATE

Some companies report their earnings ten days, twenty days, or even thirty days after the end of the quarter, but they report according to a reasonably regular schedule year in and year out. All companies must report within forty-five days after the end of the quarter. At year-end, they are allowed ninety days, so they can prepare the required audited financial statements. On occasion, companies will delay their earnings report. Sometimes there is a good reason. If a company has made an acquisition or is taking a major write-off, accounting issues may require additional time. But in many cases when companies report late, they do so because they have bad news which they want to delay as long as possible. As a rule, companies like to release good news as fast as possible and delay bad news as long as possible. They also like to release good news at a time when most investors will see it, and postpone bad news until a time when fewer investors will notice.

THE GOOD FRIDAY EARNINGS REPORT

One trick companies often use if they have bad news is to wait until Friday afternoon to report it, preferably after the market has closed and most investors have gone home. The Friday before a long holiday weekend is especially effective. One sneaky company used to report weak earnings on Good Friday, when the stock market was closed. Perhaps the hope was that no one would notice, or that by the time investors returned to work, there would be other issues to worry about.

One year, I was rushing out of my office before the Jewish holiday of Yom Kippur when a company I followed made a very disappointing announcement. Since I was late for synagogue, I had no time to call the company. By a twist of fate, I happened to walk into synagogue with the seventy-five-year-old chairman of the company. *"How could you have issued this disappointing news at 4:00 when many investors are leaving for the Jewish holidays?"* I asked.

"I'm sorry," the chairman replied, *"The announcement was a mistake. The news wasn't supposed to be released until 5:30."* With many investors spending the next day atoning for their sins, they might miss this company's disaster entirely.

If you hear that a company will report after the close on a Friday (or on one of the Jewish holidays), be wary. The surprises are not likely to be on the upside.

Especially beware of companies that have not filed by their regulatory deadlines. When a company requests a filing extension, it usually signals serious accounting complications. A company called Greenman (now called Noodle Kiddoodle) had been an extremely hot stock. An analyst who had been recommending it noticed that more than ninety days had passed since the end of the fiscal year. When he called the company, the CFO cavalierly told him that everything was fine, but the company wanted to wait a few more days before reporting. The analyst immediately reduced his rating. One week later, Greenman reported that it would have to take a major write-off. The stock fell by half. The moral is simple: **If you see a company ask for an extension, sell first, ask questions later.** Forty-five days after the end of a quarter and ninety days after the end of a year is sufficient time to report results, unless something is seriously wrong.

WATCH OUT FOR COMPANIES THAT CHANGE THEIR AUDITORS

Companies may change their auditors because the CFO and the auditors don't get along. There might be a conflict with another client of the auditor, or the company might feel that the auditors were not doing a good job. There are many excellent reasons for changing auditors. But there are also many not-so-excellent reasons. Often, a company changes auditors because of a disagreement over accounting policies. These differences usually concern earnings, and often the amount at issue is substantial. In a dispute between a company and its auditors, it is usually the company that wants to report the higher numbers. The executives of the company own stock and often have performance bonuses. The auditors are paid a fee and have professional reputations to protect. When in doubt, pick the side of the auditors.

If an auditor resigns during the middle of the fiscal year, don't wait around to find out why. The chances are good that something is seriously wrong. Not only will the auditors forfeit their fees, but they could also potentially become the subject of a lawsuit from either the company or the shareholders. Mid-year resignations will occur only if the auditors and the company have reached an impasse over a very serious issue. It would be nice if the company would explain the reason for the termination, but can you imagine a company saying, *"Our auditors quit because they thought we were cooking the books"*? Companies are never this forthright. At Donnkenny (one of the case studies in Chapter 7), the most to which management would admit was that the auditors complained about a lack of access to information. Of course, a few weeks later, it admitted that it would have to restate its sales and earnings. Don't be swayed if the company announces that it has immediately hired another auditor. There are always accountants willing to accept a fee, and the new auditor may not accept the company's view, either. If there is a change in auditors during the year, sell your stock and let someone else worry about it.

A number of years ago, Regal Communications, a leader in infomercials, had just bought the company that ran the psychic infomercials and was about to report its year-end results. One day, the company released a short statement saying that its auditors had resigned and were immediately being replaced by another firm. On the conference call, the company assured investors that the resignation was due to a personality conflict. Some time thereafter, the new auditors indicated that there was a problem with the financial results. In the end, the acquisition was voided. Regal Communications went bankrupt and was liquidated. (I always wondered why the management of the psychic company did not see the problems coming. Perhaps it should have called its own hotline.) The rule is simple enough: If the auditors can't stomach the numbers, neither should you.

MANAGEMENTS DON'T ALWAYS WANT THEIR STOCKS TO GO UP

Almost every statement in this book is based on the concept that managements want the best stock price for their company. This is true 99 percent of the time, but there are a few exceptions. These situations can give investors an interesting buying opportunity.

Management will often want the price of the stock to remain low if the company is having a huge stock buyback program or if the managers themselves are buying. If management or the company is buying stock, it is obviously in its interest to pay less. This is not to say that management will attempt to trash the price of its own stock, but it may delay or soft-pedal a bullish report until it is finished buying. If you see a company or its executives aggressively buying stock, it is a good bet that bullish pronouncements may follow the buying.

Management would also prefer a lower stock price when it receives its options. Since options are priced as of a particular day, the lower the stock price on that day, the more valuable the options. Most companies will not jerk around their stock price in order to get a marginally better price on a small number of options. But if the amount of the options is sufficiently large, a few companies may play some games. I remember going to an analyst's meeting at which the CEO stood up in front of hundreds of investors and said he was concerned about future business. In the next three days, the stock dropped 10 percent. I happened to run into a director of the company whom I had known from Harvard Business School. I mentioned the meeting and the subsequent action of the stock. He smiled slyly. *"Go look at the company's chart,"* he suggested. *"We always do something stupid in July. That's when we price the employee options. If we can get the one million options priced $6 lower, we can save $6 million in compensation. By the middle of August, all the shareholders will have forgotten about it."* I looked back at the chart for twenty years, and sure enough, there was almost always a decline in the middle of July. Few companies engage in this type of behavior, and those that do will not admit to it. **However, if you see a company making a huge option grant, it is always reasonable to ask about the date on which the options are priced. Everything else being equal, this may not be a bad date on which to buy the stock.**

Another situation is easier to track—the spin-off of a subsidiary from a parent. When the company is spun off, the executives of the spin-off are granted options. While the selling company wants the highest price it can get for the business, the executives of the subsidiary would rather see a lower stock price so their options will be more valuable (remember, the more a stock moves up during the option period, the more money you can make). The executives of the subsidiary normally conduct the road show.

I remember talking to the CEO of a company that was being spun off by a large retailer. I told him that I thought his stock could sell for $30. *"I'll be happier with $25,"* he replied. *"If the price gets too high, the options will be worthless. We've spent years building this business, and my people deserve something. Besides, what's a few million dollars to [the parent company]?"* The CEO was just being honest. He wanted the offering to go off at a slightly lower price so that his options and those of his employees would be worth something. Your strategy should be: Because executives of companies that are being spun off often soft-pedal their prospects in order to get a better price for their options, consider buying stock in spin-offs right after the options are priced.

WATCH FOR INSIDER BUYING AND SELLING

Perhaps no clue is more useful to the individual investor than signs of insider buying and selling. When insiders buy, they are making a bet for the future of their company, but when insiders sell, they are making a bet against their company. In looking at insider trading, three factors are important: the amount of stock being traded, the amount relative to insider ownership, and the people involved. The quantity of the transactions is obviously critical. If insiders are buying or selling large rather than small amounts of stock, they are making a more definitive statement. The relative quantity is also important. If executives are selling their entire position, these trades should raise more of a red flag than if they are selling only 10 percent of their stock. Finally, the number and identity of the people making transactions are critical. If large numbers of key executives are buying or selling stock, they are making a broad-based statement about their company's future.

Insider buying can be a good sign that a company is turning around. When executives take their own money and buy stock in their companies, they are significantly increasing their reliance on the financial success of the companies. If something goes wrong, they may not only lose their job, they may also lose the money they have invested. Because of their focus on the fundamentals of the business and restrictions on their purchases and sales, insiders tend to be early buyers. It is very common for stocks to sit at the same price after insiders buy. But massive insider buying is a sign that the insiders regard the company more bullishly than the analysts do.

When Jim Halpin and his team joined CompUSA, the stock had been decimated. The former growth stock was now ignored by most analysts. It did not take management long to realize that the underlying business was strong and that the company could be turned around. Sixteen insiders made at least one purchase of CompUSA stock, and eleven made multiple purchases. All told, these sixteen insiders invested about $4 million of their own money, a dramatic vote of confidence that also proved to be extremely profitable when the stock soared.

Heavy insider buying in a stock that analysts hate sets up an interesting dichotomy. The analysts are betting that the stock will go down, while the managers are betting that it will go up. **In almost all cases, you would be wise to bet with the managers.** One company that fits this dichotomy is Crown American Realty Trust. Although Crown was the largest REIT to have gone public at the time, many investors did not like the company, and the stock performed poorly. At the end of 1994, after the sale of a related company, Crown announced a dramatic upgrading of its malls, with May, Sears, JC Penney, Wal-Mart, and others either moving in or expanding their stores. But Crown faced a serious problem: To accommodate the new tenants, it had to do construction, and for that, it needed money. With its restricted capital structure and low stock price, management decided that the only potential source of capital was to cut the dividend. In August 1995, Crown cut the dividend from $1.40 to $.80 per share. This reduction caught the analysts by surprise. Almost every analyst reduced the rating to Sell or Underperform. By the end of the quarter, Crown had the eighth worst rating of the thousands of stocks rated by analysts. The stock dropped to $6 1/2. Despite a yield of 12 percent, few wanted to buy it.

The insiders started buying. In the ten months after the dividend cut, fourteen insiders, including the president, the chairman, all of the trustees, the CFO, seven vice presidents, and one corporate officer, made twenty-eight substantial purchases of Crown's stock. The stock moved back to $8 1/2. With the dividends, the return to those who bought at the bottom was more than 33 percent. In most cases, when there is heavy insider buying in a stock that the analysts hate, the insiders end up being right.

If insider buying is a sign that business is improving, insider selling can be a sign that it has reached a peak or is heading down. (Remember the director of Aetna who sold $130 million of stock shortly before it plunged and the insiders of Rainforest Café who bailed out?) Investor relations usually has good explanations for each sale. *"The CFO needed to pay for his kid's college. The CEO is building a new house, and the chairman is endowing a foundation."* You may be pleased that these executives are all realizing the American dream, but do their sales make you eager to buy their stock? **If the stock is not good enough for many of its executives, why should it be good enough for you?**

From August 11 to August 14, 1997, Michael Cowpland, the CEO of Corel, a Canadian software company, sold $14.5 million of stock at more than $6 per share shortly before the company announced disappointing earnings and the stock declined by 33 percent. By December, the stock had dropped to $3 and the CFO had resigned. (The CEO received more than $13 million more than he would have if he had waited until December to sell.) The CEO claimed that he had no advance knowledge of the earnings. While I am sure that this is true, the CEO certainly must have had a better "feel" for the quality of the business than did other shareholders. Insiders do not always know everything. Nor do they always sell at the top. But they probably know more about the business of the company than you do.

WATCH FOR THE HYPE WHEN INSIDERS SELL

Be especially cautious if you see large insider selling in a company that has been hyping its stock. You can always tell the level of hype by the number of press releases and bullish analyst statements. If a company keeps issuing bullish press releases and encouraging analysts to raise earnings estimates while management bails out, you could be facing serious trouble. The question that investors should always ask is, *"If business is so great, why is the management selling?"* There is rarely a good answer to this question.

A Canadian toy company named SLM International offers a good example of insider selling coupled with hype. SLM had three businesses: CCM hockey products, Buddy L plastic toys, and an above-ground swimming pool business (which was purchased from Coleco in bankruptcy). SLM's financial record was modest. In November 1992, it was selling for $11. Then, in the next ten months, the stock almost tripled. One of the main drivers was a licensing agreement for a new process that SLM claimed revived dead batteries. SLM licensed this process from a small company in Alberta, Canada, which in turn had licensed it from a company in Atlanta.

The concept of a charger that would recharge ordinary alkaline batteries is one to which everyone can relate. On the day of the announcement of this process, the stocks of other battery makers were trounced. Duracell, for instance, initially plunged 14 percent before closing down 6 percent. Some skeptics did question why the developer of the process was unable to market it, why it had given the license to the small company in Canada, and why this company had licensed it to SLM, but many bought into the dream that they would soon be able to recharge their batteries.

While the stock was running up, management was unloading large blocks. Between July 27, 1992, and October 12, 1993, while the stock went from $12 3/4 to $29 1/3, the following insider transactions took place:

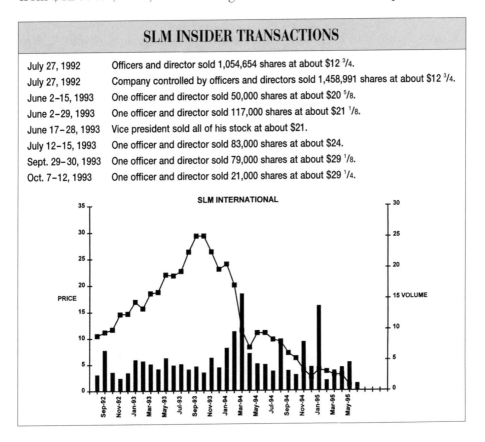

SLM INSIDER TRANSACTIONS

July 27, 1992	Officers and director sold 1,054,654 shares at about $12 3/4.
July 27, 1992	Company controlled by officers and directors sold 1,458,991 shares at about $12 3/4.
June 2–15, 1993	One officer and director sold 50,000 shares at about $20 5/8.
June 2–29, 1993	One officer and director sold 117,000 shares at about $21 1/8.
June 17–28, 1993	Vice president sold all of his stock at about $21.
July 12–15, 1993	One officer and director sold 83,000 shares at about $24.
Sept. 29–30, 1993	One officer and director sold 79,000 shares at about $29 1/8.
Oct. 7–12, 1993	One officer and director sold 21,000 shares at about $29 1/4.

In one year, three officers and directors of the company sold $40.4 million of stock. While the stock was hitting new highs, inventories were backing up. In the fourth quarter of 1992, SLM announced that sales had been much less than plan, inventories had increased sharply, and the company had lost $.50

per share. Did the managers know when they sold their stock that revenues would be much less than plan? It is difficult to say. Perhaps they saw signs that made them nervous, or perhaps they were just lucky. The price of the stock tumbled from $29 in October 1993 to below $3 by December 1994. SLM reported a loss of $112 million for 1993.

The moral of SLM is simple. There is nothing wrong with developing a product that can recharge ordinary alkaline batteries. Sometimes revolutionary products do work. But while people were focusing on the hype of the batteries, inventories were growing out of control, and the company was self-destructing. The managers were lucky enough to sell $40 million of stock, while the investors were left in the dark. (Literally and figuratively, because the battery charger never really worked.) Management did not try to hide their sales from investors. But investors did not have to buy the stock they were selling. Obviously, no one took the time to ask, *"If SLM is such a great company, why are all of the insiders selling?"* While there are examples to the contrary, a good rule of thumb is: Avoid hyped stocks with a large amount of insider selling.

SOMETIMES INVESTORS NEVER LEARN . . .

This would have been the end of the SLM story, except that SLM sold its Buddy L division, plus the pools, to Empire of Carolina, a small toy company. Empire had gotten itself the deal of the year, or so its management told investors. Acquisitions are often a good way for a company to build its business and increase its earnings. But there are two issues that investors should watch. First, lousy businesses tend to remain lousy businesses, even if they are in the hands of new owners. Second, when management makes an acquisition and raves about the potential while simultaneously selling large amounts of stock, investors should be extremely cautious.

The businesses acquired from SLM were very large, relative to the size of Empire of Carolina, and had extremely checkered financial histories, but Empire was confident that it could turn them around. From the time of the acquisition, the price of Empire's stock surged. Although they believed that Empire was going to have a fantastic year, top managers and some of the key investors in the company decided to sell stock. The insiders believed in the future of their company, but they probably needed to diversify their holdings or build new houses.

Empire's secondary offering did not go as well as hoped, and the size had to be cut back. On June 25, 1996, the company sold 1,400,000 shares and insiders sold 1,723,908 shares at $12. The stock started to drift down. Three weeks later, it was at $9. When a stock drops after an offering, investors should take notice. The company has already taken its best shot on the road show. It has told its story to any investor who would listen or who wanted a free lunch. Finding new investors afterward is difficult. Besides, many investors were now underwater. They were just hoping for a chance to get even, and with each day they were becoming increasingly nervous.

On August 7, Empire dropped a bombshell. Its second-quarter loss was higher than the loss in the previous year, while its third and fourth quarters would be hurt by three problems: Several new blow-molding machines were not fully operational. The senior vice president of operations had cancer. And Hurricane Bertha caused the plant to be closed for several days.

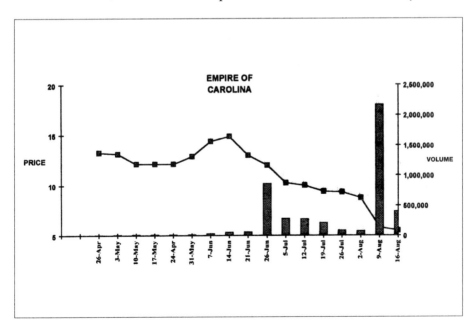

The timing of these announcements was interesting. Insiders had unloaded huge blocks of stock on June 25, so all these events had to have occurred immediately afterward or the company would have had to inform investors on the road show. The hurricane was an act of nature, but the problem with the machines and the illness of the senior VP must have been discovered in the days after the offering. The stock of Empire plummeted. Within the next year, the stock had declined to less than $1.

There are a few key lessons for investors to take from Empire:

- Beware of a minnow trying to swallow a whale. In many cases, acquiring a larger company is much more difficult than it looks.
- Beware of companies buying lousy businesses.
- Watch when insiders are selling while they are hyping their stock. If they believe business is so good, why are they selling?

The management of SLM raved about the potential of Buddy L while it was selling stock, and then saw its stock price plummet as the business disappointed. Two years later, the management of Empire raved about the potential of Buddy L while it was selling stock, and then saw the price of the shares plummet. As the saying goes: Fool me once, shame on you. Fool me twice, shame on me.

AN UGLY DUCKLING CAN BECOME A SWAN OR REMAIN A DUCK

Companies can be much like people, always trying to change their image to make themselves more appealing. People go to gyms to get in shape, to the finest stores to buy new outfits, and even to plastic surgeons for an entirely new look. While the changes may have some impact, they are still the same person they always were, just in a slightly different package. Companies have their equivalents of a makeover. The stakes can be substantial. If a company can convince investors that it is a rapidly growing telecommunications company rather than a stodgy producer of frozen fish, the expansion of its p/e multiple can be significant. But the game is tricky: If in the end the company is really nothing but a manufacturer of frozen fish, it will smell funny to anyone who buys it on a telecommunications play.

The simplest changes are purely cosmetic. A company takes a small, rapidly growing division and asserts that the division is the key to its future and that, as a result, the company's stock deserves a growth multiple. Don't ever buy into this game. If it looks like a duck and quacks, it is a duck, even if it says it is a swan!

A slightly more substantial makeover involves a name change. It is entirely appropriate for a company to change its name if it disposes of the business that was formerly its marquee. It would be foolish for it to sport a name that now belonged to someone else. Zayre changed its name to TJX after the Zayre division was sold. There is talk that Woolworth will change its name now that the Woolworth stores are closed.

Companies can also change their name if they burn enough investors or are looking for a fresh start. When the stock of Sports & Recreation moved to the New York Stock Exchange, the management, with pure chutzpah, selected the ticker symbol WON. Unfortunately, WON lost. As the stock plunged from the mid-$20s to $1 per share, few appreciated the meaning of the ticker symbol. After the stock collapsed, a new management team changed the name of the company to Jumbo Sports and the ticker symbol to JSI. But just because a company changes its name does not mean that all of the old problems will suddenly disappear. This is often the corporate equivalent of the witness protection program.

Finally, some companies create new names to reflect their new identities. As a rule, subtle changes are usually appropriate. Vanity Fair changed its name to VF Corporation after jeans became more important to the company than intimate apparel. Dramatic changes, however, are often worrisome, especially if the company embarks on a whole new image campaign. Creating a new name and identity is one of the more useless things that a company can do. It confuses employees and stockholders, costs money, and it takes management's focus away from running the business. Does anyone remember when United Airlines became Allegis? I never was able to find the Allegis terminal at the airport.

Watch for hokey names that are supposed to mean something, like Unisys. Most great companies stick to their core businesses and have simple names that employees, customers, and stockholders can understand. Think of some of the best stocks—Dell Computer, Compaq Computer, Intel, Microsoft, Wal-Mart, Costco, Toys 'R' Us, Coca-Cola, Citibank, J. P. Morgan. There is not a funny name in the bunch. **Obscure names are for managers who don't know what business they are in.**

Some changes are more fundamental. A company may make major acquisitions in order to reposition itself. General Motors bought Hughes and EDS in order to become a technology company. Sears bought Allstate, Dean Witter, and a number of other businesses in order to become a financial services company. Kmart bought Sports Authority, Office Max, Builders Square, and PACE to become a growth specialty retailer. United Airlines bought Hertz (so did Ford) and hotel chains in order to become a travel services company. The problem is that, in the end, these companies remained what they always were: a car manufacturer, two retailers, and an airline. The argument that they were being transformed into new growth companies just never held water.

Companies also make divestitures to reposition themselves. General Motors sold Hughes and EDS to return to its core—automobile manufacturing. Sears sold Allstate, Dean Witter, Coldwell Banker, Homart, and Prodigy to return to its core—retailing. Kmart sold Sports Authority, Office Max, Builders Square, and PACE to return to being a discount store company. Allegis sold Hertz and the hotels and became—surprise!—UAL Corp. (At least, now you know it's an airline.) Ford also sold Hertz to return to being a car company.

Have you noticed anything interesting about the picture? A company can make huge acquisitions and divestitures, only to end up the same as it started. Along the way, the investment bankers won, because they received fees on all the transactions, but anyone who bought into the "transformations" lost, because there were no transformations. Except when divesting their core, few companies have ever been able to change their basic businesses. If you cannot decide whether the duckling is going to become a swan or remain a duck, assume that it will remain a duck.

WATCH OUT FOR EGO TRIPS

Companies sometimes embark on ego trips which will impress even the most casual of observers as a waste of shareholder's money. If you see such ego trips, avoid the stocks. Sports tie-ins are extremely popular now. Companies have put their names on football games (the Insight.com Copper Bowl), sports stadiums (the Delta Center), and golf tournaments (the Kmart Greater Greensboro Open). These are often intelligent marketing moves. Retailers and airlines deal with millions of consumers and probably gain excellent exposure. But some tie-ins seem to make less sense. 3Com Park comes to mind (I still call it Candlestick). Does the association with a sports stadium help the sales of 3Com's technology products or is it more of an ego trip?

My favorite, which is unfortunately ending, is the Corel Women's Tennis Tour. (I guess when you lose $232 million, something has to go.) Even if Corel had not sustained such losses, and even if its stock had not plunged from $19 in November 1995 to $1.71 in January 1998, do you think that sponsoring women's tennis tournaments could really help it to beat Microsoft? Or do you think that this type of sponsorship was really just an ego trip for the company?

Much the same applies to huge corporate headquarters that reek of an edifice complex. Sears built the tallest building in the world, and its stock sank. (It then moved out of the building, and its stock rallied.) The Pan Am building in New York survived long after the airline was history. If you see companies spending large amounts of shareholders' money for ego trips that you do not think will help their business, avoid the stocks.

BEWARE OF THE INFORMATION SHUFFLE

Be careful if you see a company start to shuffle information. Companies often change the way they report a piece of information in order to pretend that everything is still the same. If you ask about market share for the company as a whole and investor relations talks about market share for selected products, there is a problem. If you ask about backlogs and investor relations talks about the reaction of customers to the new product lines, something is wrong. The changes may be subtle, but the chances are very good that the company is trying to hide something.

A number of years ago, a few retailers such as The Limited started to build larger stores. To make their inventories seem lower, they started to give inventories per square foot rather than inventories per store. There was nothing wrong with this, except for the fact that they continued to give sales per store. Comparing inventories per square foot with sales per store was simply a way of shuffling information so that investors would not realize that the inventories were too high. They fooled investors, until the day of reckoning arrived and their earnings were disappointing.

Just remember, companies give out the information that they want you to know, not the information that you should know. Their job is to market themselves to customers and investors. They often do not want the rest of the world to know certain things, and no law says they have to always be forthright. If you sense that a company is beginning to shuffle information, be extremely cautious.

DON'T BUY WHAT STOCKBROKERS ARE SELLING, BUY WHAT THEY ARE BUYING

If you are using a stockbroker, you probably assume that your broker knows something, but what your broker knows and what you think the broker knows may have little to do with each other. The broker is the financial equivalent of directory assistance. Think of all the calls the broker receives during the day. Someone may call about a mutual fund, someone else about a tax-free bond, a third person about a convertible debenture, while a fourth might want to know about an emerging market. Finally, you call asking about a particular stock. **It is virtually impossible for any broker to stay up-to-date on all information.**

Most brokerage firms receive hundreds of pages of research on stocks every day as well as prospectuses for corporate offerings. It would take the broker half the day to read this information, and it only covers equities. The broker must also read the reports sent out by mutual funds, fixed-income analysts, and international analysts, as well as newspapers and magazines. The analyst can focus on twenty stocks, but the broker is expected to know 27,000, or rather, the one of the 27,000 that you are asking about, in addition to knowing about bonds, treasuries, mutual funds, and international markets. It is obvious that no broker can know all of these things.

In most cases, the broker knows how to look things up. When you ask a question, the broker taps out the symbol and tells you what the analyst has to say. There is nothing wrong with this process, just as there is nothing wrong with calling directory assistance. In each case, the person you are asking goes to a computerized database and reads you the information. The difference is that you assume that the telephone operator is merely parroting back information, while you assume that the stockbroker is analyzing and interpreting the information. In most cases, the stockbroker is no more likely to interpret the information than the directory assistance operator is likely to tell you which restaurant has the best Chinese food.

To make the situation worse, directory assistance charges you for the information you receive, while the broker can only charge you if you make a transaction. The broker can talk to you five times a day, but if you do not make a trade, the broker does not get paid. It is thus in the broker's interest to get you to sell one stock and buy another. If you own one stock that has performed well and ask brokers for advice, most will suggest selling it and buying something else. This is not to suggest that brokers want to churn your account. But their interests and yours are not the same, because they get paid only when you make a transaction.

The most important transaction for a broker is to sell you the brokerage firm's own underwritings. It is around these underwritings that a firm builds its investment banking and makes the lion's share of its profits. Not only do the brokers receive a much higher fee for selling an underwriting, but there is often considerable pressure on the broker to produce, especially if the underwriting is going poorly. While hot deals are easy to sell, it is the cold deals in which the retail brokers really prove their worth to the company.

This is the heart of the conflict between the broker and the client. **With the Internet and on-line brokerage, the traditional brokerage firm may no longer be the best vehicle for getting stock information or buying mutual funds. It is more expensive and less complete.** Instead of calling a broker, check the Web for up-to-date stock prices, news, and earnings estimates. Various sites, such as Motley Fool or Street.com, provide excellent commentary. Zacks, Morningstar, and others have good tools for screening. Mutual fund information is also more readily available on-line. In fact, the only proprietary information that your broker has is the work of the firm's analysts. This is not to impugn your broker. Your broker is there to serve you. But there is no reason to bother the broker if you can just as easily find the information for yourself.

The major advantage of traditional brokerage firms is a strong calendar of underwritings, which clients can purchase. But since most of the hot deals go to institutions, the calendar that is offered to individuals may not be worth the trouble.The reason that many people keep accounts at major firms is so they can participate in underwritings, most of which they should probably avoid.

This is not to say that brokers do not have good ideas. Most brokers know which of the firm's analysts are the best. Listening to the broker in this regard can be extremely useful. In many cases, it is worth having an account with a major firm if the broker can help you distinguish between the good and the mediocre analysts. In addition, most brokers also have their own favorite stocks, often the ones they are buying for their own account. If brokers are putting their own money in the stocks, they have done their homework. They are, after all, professionals. The problem is that you may never find out about these stocks unless you ask directly, *"What are you buying for yourself?"* Even then, they may not tell you. Most firms do not want their brokers freelancing.

A broker from Bear Stearns called me last year. He ran through two of the firm's recommendations. Then I asked him what he was buying for himself. He started to tell me about some hot bank that was involved in litigation with the government. *"It's a $2 stock, but it could be worth . . ."* he stopped in mid-sentence. *"Can't talk now,"* he said and hung up the phone. I guessed that his supervisor must have walked by while he was explaining this nonapproved idea. The broker called back the next day and spun a wonderful story, which he had thoroughly researched. No analysts were following the stock, but he was on top of all the details. *"You understand,"* he told me, *"this isn't the type of stock that I should be selling you. Our firm doesn't cover it, and it's not a quality name, but I've bought a lot for myself."* The stock tripled in a year. If brokers are buying a stock for their personal account, at a minimum you know that they will stay on top of the information. The only caveat: If you decide to buy one of these stocks, you should remind the broker to keep you informed about it.

The rules with brokers are simple:

- Do not assume that brokers know any more about most subjects than directory assistance operators.
- Do not use brokers for quotes or information gathering. Use the Internet.
- Recognize that brokers get paid only when you make a transaction.
- Watch out for the "deals" that brokers push the hardest. These deals could be trouble.
- Ask brokers what they are buying for themselves. Your best shot is buying and selling along with them.
- Use brokers to guide you through the maze of the firm's own analysts.

If you assume that brokers are experts on every subject, you will lose. If you keep pestering them for information that is easier to get on your own, they may lose your phone number. But if you concentrate on what they know and what they are interested in, they can be of real use.

WOULD YOU BUY A STOCK FROM MORTIMER SNERD?

Be extremely cautious when you see "talking heads" recommending stocks on television, in periodicals, or in chat rooms on the Web. Many have excellent records and good ideas, but some are dummies. Even if you can tell the good from the bad, you still have two problems. While these talking heads may tell you when to buy, they do not come back on television to tell you when to sell. The next time you see them, they may not even mention the stock, or they may say, *"It reached my price objective, and I sold it."* That may be of little comfort if you have bought the stock and it has since declined.

Of even greater concern is the fact that most talking heads have an ax to grind. Portfolio managers rarely recommend a stock they do not already own, and often have large positions in the stocks they are pushing. For all you know, they may be trying to get the price up so that they can sell. There are a number of aggressive hedge fund managers who use their appearances on television for just this purpose. The people watching television hear the exciting story and then rush to buy the stock. The portfolio manager then sells into the buying. This may not be the most moral thing to do, but morality has never been a long suit on Wall Street.

The rule about talking heads is simple: Don't follow their advice just because they say they like a stock. If you do, you will always be one step behind. If you hear an idea that you like, check it out for yourself. Use your own judgment, and trade it on your own terms. Just remember, the fact that someone is on CNBC or in a chat room does not make him or her smart per se. Talking heads may have good ideas, but like Mortimer Snerd, who sat on Edgar Bergen's lap, they may be dummies. You would not buy a stock from a dummy, so don't buy one from a talking head, unless you check it out for yourself.

CHAPTER ELEVEN

Trading with the Enemy: Buying and Selling

To defeat the enemy, individuals need to devise a strategy for investing and to adopt an investing style consistent with that strategy. A strategy is a battle plan that describes how the investor intends to marshal resources and attack the enemy. Some people say that their strategy is to outperform the market. But this is a goal, not a strategy, and it is a goal shared by every investor. How many people do you know who say that they want to underperform the market? Everyone wants to win.

Most investing strategies are built around specific investment philosophies:

- An **earnings surprise strategy** is based on the concept that companies with upside earnings surprises will outperform the market.
- A **growth strategy** is based on the concept that growth stocks will outperform the market.
- A **value strategy** is based on the concept that stocks with low price/earnings or high price-to-book ratios will outperform the market.

- A **contrarian strategy** is based on the concept that investors can win by betting against the consensus.
- A **technical strategy** is based on the concept that charts can show the future direction of stocks.

Each of these strategies can work, but all have the same shortcoming for the guerrilla investor: They focus on the market and are not tailored to the skills of the individual. Each may have produced great results for the professionals who follow them, but if they do not utilize *your* strengths and avoid *your* weaknesses, they will not work for you.

The strategy of Guerrilla Investing works differently from these other strategies. Instead of starting with a system of investing and the assumption that all investors have the same skills, Guerrilla Investing starts with an understanding of the field of battle and with a specific investor. Guerrilla Investing assumes that each investor has different skills and predispositions and allows investors to create individualized investing strategies that maximize their own strengths and minimize their own weaknesses. The basic concept of Guerrilla Investing is that you will never win a battle unless you first understand your own strengths and weaknesses and those of your enemy.

For some individuals, laying this groundwork may seem a needless step, but it is absolutely critical. If you are a casual investor who wants to own a few stocks and does not have time to follow the market actively, you cannot utilize a strategy that works for an active trader. If you know nothing about technology and are uncomfortable with high volatility, you cannot utilize a strategy that requires you to invest in momentum stocks. **No matter how good a strategy may be for someone else, it will not work for you if it does not fit your abilities and needs.**

A professional may make billions by trading international currencies, playing options, or engaging in risk arbitrage, but that does not mean you will be able to do the same. Following the guidance of someone else will work against you if you do not share that person's knowledge and skills. To win, you must find a strategy specifically geared to work for you.

Again, suppose that you were the general of a small guerrilla force fighting in a jungle against a modern army. Would you use the strategies of great generals like Hannibal and Genghis Khan? Probably not. These generals fought in vastly different times, with different weapons, against different enemies. Hannibal used elephants and Genghis Khan used horses against foot soldiers. Their ancient experience would be of little use in fighting a modern army.

Would you use the strategies that General Schwarzkopf used against the Iraqis? Probably not. The Americans fought in the desert and had vast military superiority. His strategies would be of little use to an under-armed guerrilla in a jungle. You could learn a considerable amount by *studying* his strategies, but to *use* his ideas you would have to adapt them to your own military situation.

Think of another activity that requires a strategy. Suppose you were the coach of one of the small schools that the football powerhouses schedule for fodder at the beginning of the year. You are playing Michigan. Before the game, you might look at the strategies of Bill Walsh. Walsh's "West Coast Offense" may be a great concept, but it was not written from the perspective of a forty-five-point underdog. Spraying passes around the field may not be a realistic option against a much more powerful team that is blitzing on every play.

Think about your power position relative to the professionals in the stock market. Is the hypothetical football team more of an underdog than you would be if you were playing against George Soros or Warren Buffett? If you faced one of these investors one-on-one, what do you think the point spread would be?

If the odds are so against you, how can you compete directly against a powerful football team or a great investor? The answer is, you can't. No matter how much advice you receive from all of the greatest coaches in history, your second-tier school isn't likely to defeat a powerhouse. And no matter how many books you read by the greatest investors in history, it is unlikely that you will ever defeat Soros or Buffett at their own games. The best strategy to avoid losing to Michigan is: Don't schedule the game. And the best strategy to avoid losing to Soros or Buffett is: Don't compete directly against them.

This may not seem like the macho thing to do. Many people have the attitude, *"Bring on the competition!"* But this is foolhardy. Most rational people would not get into a boxing ring with Mike Tyson, especially if they like having two ears. Nor would they try to stop a speeding freight train, unless they believed they were Superman. Trying to defeat a much stronger enemy head-on is suicide. If you try it in the stock market, you may not lose your life, or even your ears, but you will lose your shirt. The purpose of investing is to beat the market, but you will never do this if you play into the professionals' strengths.

Fortunately, because of the size and complexity of the stock market, it is usually possible to avoid fighting the professionals head-on. If you can avoid their strengths, attack their weaknesses, and find niches in which you have home turf, you have an excellent chance of winning. The essential first step is to utilize the strategy of Guerrilla Investing: Understand your strengths and weaknesses and those of your enemy.

FIND AN INVESTMENT STYLE

Once the strategy of Guerrilla Investing has been adopted, the individual needs to develop an investing style to implement it. Many investing strategies professionals use can be used in Guerrilla Investing as long as they are applied in ways consistent with guerrilla principles. To be compatible with Guerrilla Investing, the strategies must be applied in a manner that maximizes the strengths of the individual investor and minimizes the strengths of the enemy. For example, a strategy of buying large-capitalization stocks will work within Guerrilla Investing if you buy and hold but not if you actively trade.

A strategy of buying smaller-cap stocks can work more effectively as a style in Guerrilla Investing because small-cap stocks are less well followed, more illiquid, and easier to find a home-turf advantage in than large-cap stocks. The strategy of buying undervalued and underappreciated stocks works well for the same reasons. A strategy of following the trading patterns of insiders also fits within Guerrilla Investing, because it minimizes the advantages of the professionals and even puts their main advantage, their research capabilities, to work for you.

Guerrilla Investing can also work with more growth-oriented strategies. Buying stocks with high relative strength and earnings strength, called momentum investing, can work for individuals so long as investors check the charts for changes in momentum and find home-turf advantages in most of the stocks they own. That's also true of the strategy of earnings surprises. The projected earnings estimates and reporting dates are available on the Internet. If the individual is willing to spend the time to check out the estimates and actual earnings as they are reported, an earnings surprise strategy can be used as a style in Guerrilla Investing.

Technical strategies can also be used within the framework of Guerrilla Investing. Individuals now have access to the same charts the professionals have. If they discipline themselves to check the charts on a daily basis, they can spot both breakouts and tops and use these technical patterns as an investing guide.

There are some styles that will never fit within the rules of Guerrilla Investing because they pit the individual's weaknesses directly against the professionals' strengths. Individuals will never win with a strategy of playing arbitrage deals, because the information is too complex. They will never win with a strategy of playing options, because the timing is too fast. Nor will they win investing in emerging markets, because the information is too far from home turf. But the Guerrilla Investing framework is sufficiently broad for most other investing strategies to fit within its rules.

No STYLE WILL WORK FOR ALL INVESTORS

The effectiveness of various styles is hotly debated, but the reality is:

- Every major investing style works some of the time.
- No one style works best all of the time.
- No style works for all investors.

In strong markets, growth styles may outperform. In down markets, value styles may outperform. In fact, it is usually the success of a style that is its own undoing. When a style becomes "in," investors bid up the stocks that fit the style's parameters and dump the stocks that do not. At some point, the valuations become too extreme. No more upside is left in the stocks that fit the style, but huge upside is in the stocks that do not. At this point, investors use some seemingly minor event as an excuse to jump off one style and jump on another.

Even if a style is working for the market as a whole, it will not work for all investors. Some investors may not have the time or resources to implement the style. Others may not understand it or feel comfortable with it. An investor who does not understand or feel comfortable using a style will never succeed with it no matter how good the style may be.

If you are not comfortable with high multiples, you will never succeed in using the **momentum style**. If you are not patient, you will never be comfortable using the **takeover style**. If you do not have the time to study earnings, you will never succeed with the **earnings surprise style**. If you do not feel comfortable reading charts, you will never succeed in using a **technical style**. There is nothing wrong with this. Don't worry if you don't feel comfortable with the style currently in vogue. Just because a style works for a professional does not mean it will work for you.

YOUR INVESTING STYLE SHOULD FIT YOU

Think about fashion. Each year, the designers come out with the new styles. You look at them in the magazines. They look smashing on the 5-foot-11-inch, 105-pound models, but that does not mean they will look smashing on you. They may not fit your personal style. Their attitude may be too young, too old, or too hip and trendy. The style may not fit your needs. You may be looking for serious clothes to wear to work, not frivolous clothes to wear to a nightclub. The designer may be hot, but if the clothes do not fit your style and your needs, you will not buy them.

Investing in the stock market is much like fashion. Some investing styles are popular and some are not. But it is not the popularity that counts. Rather it is how those styles fit you and your lifestyle. Bare midriffs may be in, but a first-grade teacher would probably not wear an outfit revealing her midriff to school. Three-piece suits may be in, but a plumber would not show up at your house wearing one. Investing styles, like clothes, must fit the individual. Most people want to be a hip and trendy investor. They want to think they can play in the fastest and hottest investing games. But most people can't. The reality is: These games are no more suited to most people than the hippest of clothing styles are. In selecting a style, you must look at yourself honestly. No matter how fast and exciting a style may seem, it will not work for you if it does not fit your personality and abilities. Only you will know what fits and what works for you.

BUILD YOUR STYLE STOCK BY STOCK

How do you find your investing style? You do it just like you find your clothing style. Few people start with a given clothing strategy. They rarely say, "*I think I'll go for the preppy look.*" Instead, they go with what they need and what appeals to them. You may need an outfit for work. You know where you work and what clothes are appropriate. When you see an outfit you like, you try it on to see if it looks good on you and is right for your needs. The next time you go shopping, you might buy something similar or you might make small adjustments as seasons and trends dictate. Over a period of time, your personal style will evolve. You may never articulate it, but if you look at your wardrobe, you will see that you have developed your own style.

It is much the same in investing. Just as you start with picking clothes you like and evolving a style, so in investing you should start with picking stocks you like and see if they lead you to a particular style. The following exercise should help you to understand your style:

1. Pick your favorite stocks that you have owned—ten, if possible. These should not necessarily be the stocks that performed the best. Rather, they should be the ones you were most comfortable owning. Write down why you bought them and why you liked them.

2. Next, pick ten current stories describing a stock from your broker, business newspapers, a website, or any other sources. The stories should appeal to you. Write down why you like them.

3. Pick the stocks you've owned that you did not like—ten or fewer—and write down what was wrong with them.

4. Look at your answers. See if they form a pattern. Don't worry if your answers do not sound sophisticated or if more than one pattern emerges. You may like growth stocks in companies in which you have home turf, stocks with insider buying, and spin-offs.

5. Look at the stock picks or market commentary of ten professionals. CNBC and *Barron's* are good sources for this step because of their in-depth interviews. The *Barron's* "Roundtable" is excellent because it presents many prominent investors together. *Forbes* and *Wall Street Week* also have excellent commentary. Some websites have strong investing styles. Write down your best description of each expert's style. Pick the experts with whom you are the most comfortable. Write down why you liked them.

6. Compare your reasons for liking the professionals with your reasons for liking particular stocks. There should be a consistency between them. If there is, you are ready to move forward. If there is not, rethink your answers. If the stocks you like best are stodgy blue chips, you should not be gravitating toward a commentator who prefers technology.

7. Define your style in your own words. It does not have to sound fancy, but it has to be something you can understand. For example, you might write, *"My style is to buy undervalued, small-cap stocks in businesses I know something about."* Or, *"My style is to buy stocks that are growing by more than 20 percent per year and have price-earnings ratios under 20x."* Or even, *"My style is to buy and hold blue chips and to trade smaller stocks I know well."* There is no right style. There is only the style with which you are the most comfortable. Your style

does not have to match a specific professional's any more than your clothing style has to match a particular designer's. The only critical element is that it is consistent for you.

8. Pretend you are buying a portfolio of stocks using your style. Are you satisfied with what you would own? If you are not, go back and look at how you arrived at your style. When you finish this exercise, you should have a style with which you are comfortable and a portfolio of stocks that fit the style.

STICK WITH YOUR STYLE

Many people are tempted to jump from style to style as the investing fashions of the moment dictate. When growth is in, they buy growth. When value is in, they buy value. When tech stocks are hot, they buy techs. The problem with jumping from style to style is that you have to be able to judge when styles are changing and feel comfortable using different styles. Jumping from style to style works about as well as jumping on each new fashion craze. You will end up the investing equivalent of a "fashion victim."

Focusing on one core investment style gives an investor a framework for approaching the game. Investors who stick to a particular style know how to read its signs. They know when to buy and sell, when to feel comfortable, and when to panic. **Investors who jump from trend to trend may feel like they are in the middle of the action, but they are often simply chasing ghosts.**

If you are a value investor, you understand what value is. When you see a cheap stock, you buy it. When it becomes fully priced, you sell it. If value stocks are out of favor and you decide to jump to a momentum style, you will lose your grounding because your head will still be stuck in a value mode. When a momentum stock disappoints, you will decide that it is a good value after all and continue to hold it. When this occurs, you are lost, all because you will be trying to manage two styles at the same time.

The most successful investors usually stick to one style in all markets. They know that if they switch in midstream, they will get whipsawed.

Beau Duncan of Duncan Hurst is one of the most successful momentum investors. He has a discipline of buying only stocks with high relative strength and earnings strength. Over the years, I have talked to Beau about a large number of stocks I thought were great investments. But the first question he always asks is, *"What are the earnings and relative strength ratings?"* No matter how good the story, he would not touch it if it did not meet his ratings requirements. Beau does not understand value stocks, but he is a great momentum investor. In the last five years, Beau has ranked in the top 10 percent of all money managers. His secret is simple: He found a style that worked for him and stuck to it.

Other great investors are the same. Warren Buffett buys great companies at moderate price/earnings multiples. Mike Price is a brilliant value investor. His definition of value may fluctuate with the times, but he always buys strong companies that are out of favor. Peter Lynch was the consummate stockpicker. Lynch buys thousands of companies, one stock at a time, and always outperforms the market. Each of these investors has built a great record because they stuck to their styles, no matter what the market was doing.

Investing styles may also relate to types of stocks and industries. Jonas Gerstl of EGS Partners is one of the best investors I know. Jonas is a value investor who specializes in buying consumer stocks. When consumer value stocks are in, no one beats Jonas. When they are out, he is an average performer. But Jonas never strays from his discipline because, over the years, it has given him one of the best records on Wall Street.

The hardest part of having a style is that it will sometimes be out of favor. If you are a value player in a bull market or a small-cap player in a big-cap market, your results will lag. It can be difficult when your style is underperforming. You look at the money other people are making and feel like an idiot. You look at the growth or the big-cap stocks hitting new highs, and finally, you decide to jump to a new style. This will invariably be the wrong decision. Most people tend to jump just when fashions in the market are getting ready to change.

Bob Martorelli, who runs the Phoenix Fund at Merrill Lynch, is a superb investor. As the name of the fund connotes, Bob buys stocks that are down and out. Over the years, Bob has built a fine record, but in growth markets, Bob's stocks are often out of phase, and he can underperform. In these markets, it must be tempting for Bob to junk his style and find something that is temporarily working better. But Bob hangs tough because he knows that markets change and that, over the long term, he will outperform.

If your style in investing goes out of fashion, you can rethink whether it remains right for you. Styles do change, and sometimes you must change with them. If you are still waiting for your Nehru jacket to come back into fashion, you are in trouble. Still, most styles tend to repeat themselves, so junking one you feel comfortable with may be a mistake. If your style or the groups of stocks you prefer are temporarily out of phase, don't panic. It is fine to make subtle updates in your investing style, the way you would with your wardrobe. But avoid radical makeovers. They are usually a disaster.

An investing style need not be set in stone. It should evolve over time as experience and conditions dictate. Like a good general, you must be willing to seize opportunities as they present themselves. But the essential first step is for you to find an investing style to use as a base. The style should be easy to describe, comfortable to live with, and successful in the market. There is no magic to a style. It must simply fit your personality and lifestyle.

FIND A CORE OF STOCKS

Create a list of stocks that you will monitor on a regular basis. It should include any stock you own, have home-turf advantage in, or have successfully traded. If you want to build a portfolio of twenty stocks, you should monitor fifty or sixty in order to find the best opportunities.

Monitoring fifty or sixty stocks sounds like a daunting task, but it is actually quite easy. All professionals monitor the stocks in which they are interested. When they see a major price change or a news item on one of their companies, they check the news or the charts to see what is going on. You should do the same.

The Web provides the easiest and most efficient way to monitor stocks. You merely find an on-line investing service, type in the ticker symbols, and the website creates a custom monitor. I use My Yahoo!, a website offered by the Yahoo search engine, to follow stocks. My Yahoo! allows me to see the prices and news stories on all my stocks. Other search engines are also excellent, as are the on-line brokers, and many of the specialized investment services. Every time you click onto your custom monitor, you will see your stocks, their prices, and a list of news stories about the companies you are following. You should be able to scan sixty stocks in less than five minutes. **In fact, it will take you far less time to scan the stocks and look at the news than it would take you just to read the prices in the newspaper.**

Click on your customized portfolio on a regular basis. Look at the news. The news is easy to see, because stocks with news are always marked with an asterisk. Watch how the stocks react to particular events. Check the earnings estimates and the analysts' ratings. Again, this is easy because the analysts' actions are always prominently shown. Watch to see how the stocks react to upgrades and downgrades in ratings. Look at stocks that have major changes in price. See if the trading volume is changing as well. Look at the charts at least once a week. Clicking through charts is easy. You do not have to study them all in detail. Instead, focus on those stocks nearing a breakout or a top.

If you get a new idea that interests you, whether it is from a business periodical, an interview with an expert, an on-line chat room, a recommendation from a broker, a tip from a friend, or from your own direct experience, add the stock to your list.

See if you can get a feel for particular stocks. Do not worry about missing a good chance to buy one. There will be thousands of others, and most stocks will usually give you more than one opportunity to buy. It is more important to get comfortable with the way a stock acts than it is to buy it the first time around.

In some cases, you will never feel comfortable with the way a stock acts. You may not like the chart. The earnings multiple may not fit your style. You may not like the volatility or understand the way it reacts to particular events. If you do not feel comfortable with a stock, drop it from your list. You should not focus on stocks you are uncomfortable with, no matter how great the opportunity seems.

Don't worry about monitoring the most popular stocks, unless they perfectly fit your style. These stocks will always be written up in the newspaper and talked about on television, making them easy to follow. Try to pick stocks in which you think you can develop some home-turf advantage.

If you feel comfortable with a stock, do a little more work. Check out the company's website. Look at its annual report. Get some analysts' reports on the stock and study the investing thesis. See if it fits your investing style. If it does not, drop it from your list. If you feel comfortable with it, monitor it a little more closely. Think of it like a date. **The time to get to know a stock is before you buy it, not after you are married to it.**

The more you watch a stock, the better you will understand it. You will be able to see how it trades in strong and weak markets, how it reacts to earnings and ratings changes, and how it moves compared with other stocks in its group. The more experience you have with a stock, the better will be your chances of making money on it. Don't feel under pressure to buy it immediately. You are just trying to build a base of knowledge.

Drop from your list any stock that you have traded wrong in the past. Every investor will always trade some stocks wrong. Some will even trade great stocks wrong. I know I have. Even if it is a great pick for others, it may not be a great stock for you because you may find yourself buying at the high and selling at the low. Stocks are like people. You won't get along with everyone, and some of them won't get along with you. Unless you are very disciplined, you should bury your mistakes. Watching them will irritate you, and it is unlikely you will do much better the next time around. Never waste your time on a stock with which you are clearly out of phase.

Keep on your list any stock which has ever made good money for you. The best opportunities will almost always come in stocks you have successfully played before. If you bought a stock three years ago and sold it after it doubled, do not forget about it. Even if it is not the greatest company in the world, it may work for you because you already understand something about its business and you have the confidence to trade it.

When you see a convergence of events that reminds you of your original purchase, you will know that it is again time to buy. But you will never notice the events unless you keep the stock on your list to monitor.

PICK A FEW INDUSTRIES

As you look at the stocks on your monitor list, see if they fall into industry groupings. Most people will tend to gravitate toward specific industries in which they have home-turf advantage. Some groups of stocks may relate to their professions. Others may relate to their personal interests or geographic locations. Almost everyone tends to feel more comfortable with some industries than with others.

If you are gravitating toward a few core industries, focus on them in building your knowledge base. Learn as much as you can about companies in these industries. Check the news and charts. Go to websites like Morningstar.net and look at the site's comparisons between stocks in the industry. You may find names of new companies that interest you. If you have a number of competing companies on your list, monitoring may actually become easier. You will have time to watch more of the interactions.

If I am really interested in one company, I always put the names of its closest competitors on my monitor list. Not only can these become attractive stocks for me to buy, but they can also give me critical information about the stock in which I am the most interested.

Look at the key ratios for these competing companies, such as price/book, price/sales, price/earnings, return on equity, etc. Your goal should be to see how similar companies compare. You should not necessarily buy the stocks that look the cheapest on any measurement. In fact, there is often something wrong with stocks that look too cheap. But you should use these ratios as guidelines in evaluating companies.

See if you can find what makes stocks in a specific industry move. In retailing, the monthly comparable store sales are critical. In banking, interest rates and industry consolidation are key. In the oil industry, petroleum prices are vital. Try to understand how these factors impact the companies in which you are interested. If you can relate to the industry and understand what makes its stocks move, put a few more of the stocks on your list. **In investing, as in war, you need solid bases of strength. There is nothing wrong with having one or two core industries in which a substantial number of your stocks are located.** It is better to have two industries that are somewhat different from each other, so that they do not move in tandem. But even if the two are closely related, you are better off having developed a solid base than you would be if you invested all over the place.

Diversifying a portfolio is very easy. You can always buy mutual funds in the areas you do not understand to limit your risk in specializing. Building a solid base of knowledge is worth the effort, even if it limits your diversification.

— . —

Once you have built a monitor list and found a few key industries on which to focus, you will have a good group of stocks from which to select. Remember, try to find stocks in which you have some home-turf advantage, with which you feel comfortable, and which fit your style. Before plunging in, get to know them a little. The time you spend before actually investing should significantly help your performance.

PICK A FEW SOURCES OF INFORMATION

Along with picking a group of stocks and a few industries, investors must pick a few sources of information. There are many good stock brokers and investment banking firms, but no one is right all of the time. However, it is more important to build up a rapport with one broker, who understands your needs, than to be jumping from one to another. There are also many excellent websites. You could spend twenty-four hours a day checking out on-line financial information. But there is no one website so critical that every investor has to use it. I like Zacks.com because I am a fundamental investor who actively looks at earnings estimates. I do not actively use Silicon Investor because I do not own many high-tech stocks. This is not to say that Silicon Investor is not an excellent site. It is.

It is just not an excellent site for me because of my investing style.

Treat gathering information the way you would gathering stocks. When you start investing, pick a very small number of sources. Then, slowly check out new alternatives. Experiment with them. See which is the easiest to use and understand. Don't worry about missing news. You will miss news just as you will miss stocks. **The key for every investor is to find sources of information that are comfortable to use, efficient, and fit your style and time constraints. Don't overload yourself with information.**

BUYING, SELLING, AND SHORTING

After articulating an investing style, building a base of stocks, and selecting your sources of information, you are ready to begin trading. The first action, buying a stock, is easy. You call your broker or click on the broker's website, and, in an instant, your money is deployed. But buying can be perilous unless you understand why you are making the purchase, how you will react to events, and when you will sell. You should never buy unless you have thought through the entire process.

Think about buying a stock the way you would about deploying troops. Before engaging the enemy, you must have a plan of attack based on your view of the battlefield. But this plan cannot be made in a vacuum. You must think through how the enemy might respond and what countermeasures you might take. No general would attack without having a plan of retreat, and no investor should buy without having a plan for selling. In the stock market, as in a battle, your troops can get annihilated unless you have thought through the potential consequences.

There are lots of good reasons to buy a stock:

- A friend told you that the company will get acquired.
- Your broker said that the company will beat the Street's earnings estimates.
- The stock has high relative strength and earnings strength.

- An analyst said that the new management would turn the business around.
- The chart shows signs of a breakout.
- You think the company's new products will be a big success.
- You believe that the company is selling for much less than its growth rate warrants.

No one of these reasons for buying is necessarily better than the others. Just make sure you know exactly why you are buying a stock, because that is the only way you'll be able to track its performance.

As we have discussed, the best strategy is to buy a stock for reasons that fit with your investment style. **Think of your style as your native language.** You understand its nuances. Think of another style as a foreign language. Even if you study it, you will not know it as well as you know your own tongue. Sticking with your own style, like speaking your native tongue, offers you the best chance of fully understanding what is happening. If you are a momentum player, you know how stocks behave when there are upside surprises or disappointments. If you are a value player, you know when a stock is selling for a low price relative to its intrinsic value. If you are a technician, you know when a stock is breaking out of its base.

Even when using your own investment style, you should find a confirmation for your decision. Look at how the stock appears from the perspective of a complementary style. Confirmation can come from technical measures. If you are expecting upside surprises in earnings and the chart looks weak, it means that most investors do not share your view. This should not necessarily stop you from buying, but you should ask what you know that the rest of the Street does not. Confirmation can also come from fundamental information. If you believe that a new product line will spur earnings, you will probably find at least one analyst who has already raised estimates. If you think that the company could be a takeover candidate, you will probably be able to find similar companies that are being taken over. If every other piece of information appears to run counter to your investment thesis, you should be wary. It is fine to bet against the Street, but you should only do so if you are relatively certain of your knowledge.

Over time, you will get to know certain companies very well and gain an appreciation for their businesses and trading characteristics. In these cases, you may develop a home-turf advantage significant enough to allow you to slightly modify your style. As a value investor, you may have bought a stock because you thought it was cheap. As you study the company, you may gain more appreciation for the abilities of management and still believe that the company's opportunities have not been fully recognized even though the stock may have tripled. You decide to keep the stock, not because you have become a momentum investor, but because you have home-turf advantage and still think that investors underrate the company. This is fine as long as you don't get suckered into thinking that the company really is a momentum play. Make sure it continues to represent a good value, or you will find yourself lost in the fast lane with the momentum investors.

While you usually will be better off sticking to what you know, there will be times when you buy a stock for reasons at variance with your basic style. If you do take a flyer, be sure that you understand why you are going against your own style, and be ready to sell at the first sign that the stock is not going to work out the way you hoped.

Don't Plunge In

When an opening appears on a battlefield, the wise general will not sit on the sidelines agonizing. Nor will he send all his troops on the offensive unless he is absolutely certain of his position. Instead, he will first send out a scouting party to test the strength of the enemy. Then, if the reports are positive, he will begin his attack. But in most cases, he will not deploy all his troops. Instead, he will keep some in reserve in case the opening turns out to be a trap or in case the enemy counterattacks.

It is the same in investing. When some investors see a stock they like, they plunge in and buy all they want, while others sit on the sidelines, agonizing over whether they should buy. Neither of these is usually the right decision. Unless there is a very clear buy signal, the wise investor, like the wise general, should make an initial purchase, and then build a position a little at a time.

If your goal is to own 300 shares in a company, start by buying 100. Buying a partial position is a much easier decision than buying a full position, since you are deploying a smaller part of your funds. This puts less pressure on the initial purchase and gives you the opportunity to get comfortable owning the stock. If the stock shoots up, you will only make one-third as much, but at least you will be involved. Watch the stock. See how it acts. Study the news. Get comfortable with it. If it still looks attractive, buy another 100 shares. Continue the process until you have a full position.

If you start getting nervous about your holding, no matter what the reason, don't agonize over whether you should sell your entire position. This type of decision can paralyze investors. Sell 100 shares. If you have a gain, you will have locked in some of your profit. If you have a loss, you will have limited some of your risk. Selling a portion of your holdings will take some of the pressure off. If the stock returns to your buy price, you can always buy the 100 shares back. If it moves to your sell price, you can always sell another 100 shares. With the low commission rates currently available, there is almost no penalty in buying and selling smaller lots.

STICK WITH STOCKS THAT WORK

If you have successfully traded a stock, you probably have some feel for the company. The more you successfully trade a stock, the better your chances of successfully trading it again. If a stock has worked for you in the past, go back to it as often as seems appropriate. Look at the times you bought and sold it. See if you can find useful patterns. If you see these patterns reappear, jump on them. **Nothing will work better for you than a stock you really know.**

If you have a choice of two stocks, one that you have never traded and one that you have traded successfully on a number of occasions, go back to the stock you know. It may be more exciting to buy a new name, but you will usually make more money in a stock that has worked for you before.

Think about how you select a restaurant when you are driving on an interstate far from home. There are four restaurants at the exit: three that you have never seen before and Denny's. As you turn into Denny's, you think to yourself, *"Known mediocrity is better than unknown mediocrity!"* You know the food is not the greatest, but you have been there before, and you are comfortable with it.

If you would not take a flyer with the food you eat, why should you take one with the stocks you buy? It is great to find new ideas, but before you invest, you must be comfortable with them. If you do not have the time or resources to thoroughly research a new idea, there is nothing wrong with returning to a stock you have played before.

Recently I saw a story about a stock I had traded successfully more than a decade ago. The stock had been in a long-term funk, trading for less than half its previous high. I had not owned the stock for years because I thought that the management was inept, but I had always kept it on my list of stocks to monitor because I thought it had a good franchise and would eventually be taken over. When I saw that the board of directors had thrown out the old management, I immediately checked to see what the analysts were saying, but no analysts were following the company. The situation was perfect for me. The company was making needed changes and had fallen through the cracks. I did my homework and bought the stock. It may not have been a great company, but I understood what made it tick.

TRADE AROUND A CORE POSITION

When professionals find a stock they really like, they often trade around a core position. They always have a small amount of the stock in their portfolio. When the stock looks particularly attractive, they buy more. When it becomes less attractive, they pare back. You can and should do the same if you find a stock you really like.

The rationale for trading around a core position is simple: As we've already seen, the more you trade a stock, the better you will become at trading it. By keeping a core position, you will be constantly looking to add or pare back your holdings. Since each action is incremental, it is easy to buy and sell as the stock moves up and down. If you have been successful with a stock, trading around a core position will often improve your performance.

BUY BASKETS OF STOCKS

Wall Street loves themes. Investors love to find a group of stocks that will benefit from the same condition. When airfare wars abate, most airline stocks go up. When markets in the Far East crashed in late 1997, investors immediately began to look for companies that would benefit from lower import prices. The connections between stocks may be based on real fundamentals, on technicals, or even on market fashions. But whatever the reason, stocks usually move in groups. Most investors will be well served if they can exploit these themes and connections.

As you watch a stock you like, ask yourself if other stocks in its industry will benefit from the same fundamentals:

- A chain of stores that caters to teenagers is picking up share because many of its competitors have closed. You follow the chain because it's based in your hometown. Find out if other stores in other markets will benefit from the same factors.
- A bank in your market is acquired by a super-regional at a huge premium. Ask what other banks could become takeover candidates.
- Yahoo and AOL keep surging to new highs because of the potential of Internet commerce. Ask what other companies are positioned to gain from the new technology.

Don't be worried if the connections you discover between stocks are not perfect and direct. The best investors are often those who find links that others have missed. Neal Miller, who manages the New Millennium Fund at Fidelity, is the consummate theme investor. Neal may read a small story in the newspaper that gets him thinking about a particular trend. He will start calling analysts and salesmen, but his questions will be different from those of other professionals. Many don't even understand what he is driving at. But Neal is smart. He is like a detective, trying to find the next trend and the stocks that will benefit from it before his competitors do.

When most investors find a theme that connects a group of stocks, they try to buy the best stock in the group on the assumption that the best stock will give them the best return. But in most cases, investors will be better served if they buy a basket of stocks that could all participate in a move. **Instead of buying 300 shares of one company, buy 100 shares of three companies in the same group.**

Buying a basket of stocks limits your risk without materially jeopardizing your upside. In most cases, if the trend develops as you believe it will, all of the stocks in the group will participate and you will get a good return. By diversifying your investment, you will be able to limit the risk that your favorite company will do something foolish or will have special problems that outweigh the trend.

Suppose you decide that all of the regional banks will get acquired. You look at the companies and decide that one bank is the most attractive. Then, while other banks are taken over, this bank you picked makes acquisitions of its own, paying a huge premium for a brokerage firm and a money manager. You feel pretty bad because you correctly figured out the trend and then bought the one stock that does not participate in it.

Dick Keim and David Wilson of Keim Wilson are among the best small-cap money managers. Dick and David keep their portfolio extremely broadly diversified. But most of the time, about half their stocks will fit a theme they want to play. In 1995, Dick went to an oil-service conference in New Orleans. He decided that oil-service stocks would be winners, so he built a position of fifteen stocks in this group. As these stocks surged, Dick recognized that their success would also benefit other local companies, so he bought a package of banks in the oil patch. These banks, in turn, surged.

Even if you have a small portfolio, you can still buy a basket of stocks. You will just have to keep the quantity of each stock small. It is well worth the effort. Playing a basket of stocks will usually minimize your risk and improve your performance.

MAKE OWNERSHIP AN ACTIVE PROCESS

While buying is an active process, owning normally is not. Each morning when you open the newspaper or click on the Web, you check the prices of your stocks. You are usually doing this to measure your performance. If your stocks have gone up, you are happy. If they have gone down, you are not. But just looking at your holdings is passive, unless it convinces you to take some sort of action.

While you do not have to take action every day, you must be in a mode in which you are ready to act. Like a general with troops deployed in battle, you cannot leave your stocks in position without understanding the changes taking place on the battlefield. You must constantly reevaluate your positions and always act when the news or the charts warrant.

The first step in turning ownership into an active process is to revisit your initial analysis of each stock on a periodic basis. Take a step back and start from scratch. Ignore the fact that you may have profits or losses. Look at the fundamentals, the charts, the news, and competing companies. Would you buy this stock now? If you would not buy it now, you should sell it. There is no reason to hold a stock that you would not buy.

If you would buy the stock, make sure that your reason for buying today is as good as your reason for your initial purchase. It should not be a rationalization to justify inaction. It is fine to say that you would buy a stock today because it is undervalued relative to its growth, but it is not fine to say that you would buy it today because it is too cheap to sell. By going back and revisiting your analysis, you should better understand when you no longer have a reason for owning a stock.

Unless you are a short-term trader, don't worry about small price movements. The key to making money is to spot changes in the trend. This is the investing equivalent of spotting major changes in the balance on the battlefield. To do this, you should focus on:

- earnings or other corporate announcements,
- major price movements that break through resistance points,
- unusual changes in trading volume, and
- any unusual trading in the stocks of competing companies.

When companies report earnings, their fundamentals and the expectations of investors often change. This is a crucial time to reevaluate your reason for owning the stock. It is especially important when the stock reacts to the report differently from what you would have thought. If you thought the news was good and the stock price still drops, take a fresh look at why you invested. If the stock goes down on good news, how will it react on bad news?

Major price and volume changes can set a new pattern for a stock. When there is a surge in volume, forces on the Street are changing their positions. When the stock breaks above a resistance point or below a support level, a new direction is often set. Try to understand what is behind major swings in price and/or volume.

A few weeks ago, I saw Paul Harris Stores' stock price plunge from $27 to $20 on huge volume because a very smart analyst named Janet Kloppenberg cut her ratings on the stock. When Paul Harris later reported good earnings, a number of investors criticized Janet for acting too quickly. But the stock continued to sink. Three weeks later, Paul Harris reported weak November sales, and the stock price dropped to $15. One month after that, it reported weak December sales and the stock price declined below $10 as all the analysts rushed to cut their estimates. I do not know how Janet knew that business was going to be weak, but I do know that the huge downside volume should have been a warning to all investors. If you see a stock break down on huge volume, don't assume that the market is wrong.

Watch especially for warning signs. Sales or earnings come in below plan. Analysts reduce their estimates. Inventories are too high. Management is dumping stock. The chart is topping out. Volume has expanded on the downside. The prices of competing stocks are dropping. Each of these are warning signs which you should heed. Most people who own stocks focus on the good news, but watching the bad news can be far more critical. Unless you incorporate the impact of these negative events into your thinking, you will lose.

Don't fall in love with your winners. Investors tend to love stocks that have performed well. If you own a big winner, you will often brag about how much money you have made, and you may even feel an alliance with the company. If something goes wrong, you will try to look on the bright side, maybe even create your own spin control. But it is not your company. You are just a shareholder. The better a stock has performed, the more attached you will be to it, and the harder it will be for you to see the warning signs when business starts to change. When a stock has performed well, keep reevaluating your reasons for owning it.

Don't panic if a stock goes down. A stock will often go down for no particularly good reason. A lower price does not necessarily mean that something is wrong. Everything else being equal, a stock at $40 should be more attractive than a stock at $50. When you go to a store, you look for bargains. If you see a $50 shirt marked down to $40, you are more likely to buy it, but in the stock market, the system often works in reverse. Most investors are more likely to buy a stock at $50 than they are to buy the same stock when it drops to $40. The reason: When the stock drops, they become worried that it is no longer exactly the same top-performing company or the same solid market.

At times there is something wrong, but often there is not. A minor shortfall in earnings may not be the end of the world. Momentum players should be concerned, but for most investors, it could signal a bargain. When a stock drops, reevaluate the fundamentals. Look especially at the chart. If the stock has not dropped on huge volume and broken below key support levels, the decline in price could make it more attractive.

You should, however, beware of stocks that have gotten trashed. When a stock gaps down on gigantic volume and investors run for cover, something is usually seriously wrong. Don't feel comforted when analysts write that the market has overreacted. Take a long look at your holding. Not only will more downside often come, but, once the chart has been destroyed, the upside is usually a long way away. Unless you really understand the company, don't try to be a hero by holding onto your stock.

Do not be worried about the amount of time that you hold a stock. Your holding period will depend on your investing style and on the action of the stock. If you are an active trader, you may turn over your position in a day.

If you are a long-term investor, you may keep the stock for years. There is really only one rule that you should follow: **As long as your reason for buying a stock is still valid, keep it.**

Only one factor should influence you to keep a stock a little longer than usual. If you have substantial profits and are very close to the eighteen-month holding period in which the capital gain shifts from short term to long term, you should take another look at the charts and the fundamentals. If there is no compelling reason to sell immediately, you may want to hang on until your tax basis changes. But be careful. Many investors ignore clear sell signals while waiting for better tax treatment. If the stock is volatile and you are worried about the downside, don't be too greedy. Paying taxes on a gain is better than watching the gain evaporate as the stock sinks.

DON'T SELL ON EMOTIONS

Most investors have a good explanation for why they are buying, but fewer have a good explanation of why they are selling. List the reasons why you bought your last ten stocks. You probably have a number of well-thought-out ideas. Now list the reasons why you sold your last ten stocks. What do you have in the sell category?

- The stock was a dog.
- I got sick of looking at it.
- It dropped 15 percent.
- I wanted to take my tax losses.
- I made a lot of money and decided not to get greedy.
- The stock went up so fast that I got scared.

None of these sell reasons apply to the fundamentals and the technicals of the specific stock. You see no discussion of earnings, valuations, management, or technical patterns. Saying that the stock was a dog is not the same as saying that it had broken down on the charts. Saying that the stock went up so fast that you got scared is not the same as saying it was overpriced or topping out. Further, none of these reasons relates to your investment style. Most are emotional reactions to the performance of the stock. It is natural to get sick of stocks that have performed badly and to want to take profits in stocks that go up, but these are not good reasons for selling.

The only sure way that you can tell when it is appropriate to sell is to look back at your reason for buying. If the reason for buying is no longer valid, you should sell. Sometimes your reason for buying does not work out from the beginning. You may have bought a stock because you expected that earnings would come in better than plan, and they came in below plan. You may have bought a stock because you liked a new product line, and the line bombed. You may have bought a stock because you thought it was breaking out of its technical pattern, but the stock retraced and broke down.

Sometimes, your reason for buying materializes, but countervailing trends more than offset it. The earnings did surprise on the upside, but the company said it was worried about the next quarter. The new product line was a success, but there were significant weaknesses in the older product lines. The stock initially broke out, but all of the other stocks in its group got trashed. At other times, your reason for buying materializes but, after a period of time, stops being valid. A stock that was once undervalued doubles and is no longer undervalued. A stock that broke out and ran is now forming a top and breaking down.

It does not matter if your reason for buying failed to materialize, if it materialized but was offset by other factors, or if it materialized but stopped being valid over time. If the reason is no longer valid, you should sell, because you will never be comfortable with the stock again.

One of the biggest mistakes investors can make is finding a new justification when their original reason for buying proves invalid. Suppose you bought a stock at $20 because you believed that earnings would surprise on the upside. Then earnings came in below plan, and the stock dropped to $16. The temptation is to look at the stock and say, *"I'm going to hold it because it is too cheap to sell."* This is a mistake. If you bought a stock because you expected upside earnings surprises and the earnings do not come through, sell it. The stock may be a good value at

$16, but if you are not comfortable being a value investor, you will constantly be looking to sell this stock.

Think about driving on a highway. Just because other cars are ahead of you does not mean you are going in the right direction. When I was a boy, my family was driving to Florida. We were not sure which road to take. My father looked at the car in front of us, and said, *"Let's follow him. He looks like he knows where he's going."* He probably did. But the road he turned onto headed to New Orleans, and we wanted to go to Miami. Ten miles later, we turned around and retraced our steps, while everyone in the car ragged at my father for going the wrong way. The road may have been right for the car ahead, but it was wrong for us. In investing, as in driving, not everyone is going to the same place.

Your own reason for investing, rather than the price of the stock, should be your guide. If you bought that $20 stock because you believed that the company had high intrinsic value and would be taken over, you would not be nervous when it dropped to $16. Your reason for buying the stock would still be intact, and you might even be comfortable buying more.

It might seem contradictory to suggest that one investor should sell a stock at $16 while another should buy more, but it is not. A fallen stock is fine for a value investor, who understands its intrinsic worth. The same stock is not fine for a momentum investor, who is angry at the company for disappointing. In order to win, investors must know why they are buying a stock and have a road map for understanding where they are trying to go. Once the stock no longer fits your road map, you will be lost. There is nothing wrong with making a mistake. Nor is there anything wrong with losing money. But there is something wrong with holding a stock for the wrong reason.

Be willing to admit your mistakes. A stock is not like a child. It is not yours for life. A stock is like a soldier in your investment army. In a war, soldiers sometimes get killed. In the market, so do stocks. If you are a general, you will be sad when one of your soldiers is killed, but you will also accept it as part of the price of war. It is much the same in the stock market. You will not always be right, and you cannot be wed to your stocks. If one of your stocks gets killed, bury it and go on to the next battle.

DON'T BE AFRAID TO SHORT STOCKS

Shorting is not the same as selling. It is the opposite of buying. When you short a stock, you are putting money at risk, betting that the stock will go down. That's a legitimate bet. It is just as appropriate to bet that a stock will go down as to bet that it will go up, but it is tougher to win. Because the stock market usually goes up, the odds are much worse in shorting, and because the short is open-ended, your risk is unlimited. If you buy a stock and the price goes to zero, you could lose your investment, but if you short a stock and it quadruples in price, you could lose four times your investment. It is much more difficult to make money on the short side than on the long side, but it does not mean that you should never short.

Companies have given short sellers a bad name by claiming that they disseminate bearish information in order to push down the price of a stock. Of course, these same companies will never complain when they, or the analysts who work so hard for them, issue bullish information to push up the price of their stock. Companies spend billions of dollars to tell their stories in the way they want them told. Analysts are paid huge sums and know that part of their job is to push the stocks of their investment banking clients. No one is paying the short sellers. Yes, they want to see their stocks go down, but the owners want equally as much to see them go up.

Nothing is wrong with believing that a stock is overvalued, the balance sheet is deteriorating, the accounting is too aggressive, or the company will not meet earnings estimates. Nor is anything wrong with shorting and betting against a company. However, an investor should recognize a few rules before selling short:

- Your reason for shorting should always be better than your reason for buying.
- Only short stocks on which you have some special home-turf knowledge.
- Don't short just because a stock looks overpriced. Overpriced stocks can still go up. Find a catalyst that will push the price of the stock down.

- Get a confirmation, an additional reason, before shorting.
- Short stocks that are breaking down on the charts. It's best when stocks of competing companies are also breaking down.
- Don't short stocks that have large short positions. While these may be the most overpriced, they also have the biggest risk. Short sellers eventually have to cover (buy). If a stock has a large short position, this buying can create a "short squeeze" that can send the stock soaring. Few investors will want to absorb this type of punishment.
- If the reason that you shorted is no longer valid, cover at once. Maintaining a short position when the rationale is no longer valid is a good invitation to lose money.

With these caveats in mind, there is no reason why individuals should not have some shorts. But don't use shorts as a way of timing the market. Instead, treat shorting a stock the way you would treat buying a stock. If you think that the price is going to decline, take a chance and short it.

DIVERSIFY YOUR PORTFOLIO

How diversified should your portfolio be? The answer is not as simple as it might at first appear. Conceptually, it is better to be diversified. The more diversified you are, the less risk you will have. The dilemma for guerrilla investors is that, in order to gain home-turf advantage and defeat the professionals, they will have to stick with what they know. Since most people's knowledge is limited and specialized, most people will tend to focus on a relatively narrow number of stocks and industries.

But investors should never put themselves in a position in which the success or failure of one stock or group can change their standard of living. It is not the purpose of this book to serve as a guide to financial planning. Nevertheless, before investing, you should take a hard look at your assets and liabilities, your standard of living, and your long-term obligations. As a rule, the closer you are to retirement and the more obligations you have, the greater your level of diversification should be. If you are young, have a good job, and few obligations, you can be less diversified and take more risks. Above all else, you should never put yourself in a position that jeopardizes your home or your long-term well-being.

You should also look at all your liquid assets, including those in your retirement plan. If your retirement plan is in the stock of your employer, the remainder of your portfolio should be more diversified. If it is in a mutual fund, the remainder of your portfolio can be less diversified.

Even if you have a large amount of liquid assets and are broadly diversified with mutual funds, it is still important to diversify your stock holdings. In this case, the reason for diversification is not financial, it is psychological. If you concentrate your portfolio in a limited number of stocks, your risk increases dramatically. Even if a decline in these stocks will not impact your standard of living, it will impact the way that you invest. If your portfolio is crushed, you will be gun-shy about making your next investment.

How can you diversify your portfolio while sticking with companies in which you have home-turf advantage? There are a number of ways you can accomplish this seemingly contradictory goal:

1. Don't let any one position become so large that its performance controls your portfolio.

2. If you like a particular industry or group, buy a selection of companies within it so that the performance of one stock in the group will not have as great an impact on your returns.

3. Find a second industry with different fundamentals for balance. If your largest group of holdings comes from your profession, develop a second group of holdings from your experience as a consumer.

4. Look for a few stocks outside these two industries in which you can acquire home-turf knowledge.

5. Use mutual funds to buy stocks in fields that you do not understand. If you are buying mostly small-cap growth stocks, buy mutual funds that focus on large-cap stocks, real estate, utilities, or foreign stocks. Small holdings in a number

of mutual funds outside of your core strength can offer you strong diversification.

6. Finally, make sure that your retirement plan is invested differently from your portfolio. If you have major investments in equities, put some of your pension fund in bonds, even if the short-term return is lower. If you are buying small-cap stocks, put some of your retirement plan in a more conservative, large-cap fund. If your pension plan is in your company's stock, put a larger percentage of your assets in mutual funds.

You must use your head to invest in what you know and remain diversified. For most investors, the best solution is to focus on what you know and let professionals make investments for you in other areas.

DON'T PLAY HEAD GAMES WITH YOURSELF

In trying to outperform the market, the biggest pitfall most investors fall into is playing head games with themselves. The stock market is an intensely competitive game, and, in playing competitive games, nothing can "do in" a person faster than the head. Once you begin to second-guess yourself or have emotional reactions to the stocks you own, you are dead.

Your head can cause you serious trouble at two critical times: when you are losing big or when you are winning big. When you are losing big, you tend to question all of your decisions or even panic. When you are winning big, you begin to think you are invincible. In either case, you open yourself up to the possibility of making major errors.

The following key rules will help you avoid being trapped in your own head games.

DON'T WORRY IF YOU MISS A STOCK

As you look at recommendations that friends, brokers, or experts have made, you tend to focus on the successful ones you failed to buy. This is a critical mistake. There are tens of thousands of stocks that you can buy, but you will only own a few at a time. For better or worse, you will miss most stocks.

Sometimes you will miss a stock because you do not understand the company's business or because the stock does not fit your investing style. In these cases, missing the stock is for the best, no matter how well it performs. You would never have been comfortable with it.

People are always telling me how they missed Microsoft, Intel, Wal-Mart, or Home Depot. But the reality is that value investors would have dumped these stocks after their first move up even if they had found them the first time, while momentum investors would have dumped them the first time they broke down. Unless you are the rarest of long-term investors, it is unlikely that you would have held any of these stocks for their ten- or twenty-year move up. Looking back on a great stock you could have bought will never help you.

Sometimes you will miss a stock because you are simply too busy. A friend may have told you about a great stock, but you were involved in a problem at work or with your children's education. By the time you had a chance to focus on the stock, it had already moved up 20 percent. Sorry! Missing stocks is a fact of life. It happens every day, even to professionals. If you get upset about it or start thinking about what could have been, you will be crippled as an investor.

Sometimes you will know that buying a particular stock is the right move and you will have the time to focus on it, but for one reason or another you delay making an investment. If this stock is a winner, it will really hurt. You knew to make the investment but could not pull the trigger. Whatever the reason, the worst thing an investor can ever say is, *"I should have bought."*

If you missed a good stock you were monitoring because it did not fit your investing style, dump it off your list. If you missed it because you were too busy, put it at the bottom of your list and look at it again in a few months. Don't chase it now. If you do, you will be buying on emotion. If you missed it because you could not pull the trigger, try to figure out why you could not move on it. You will probably have another chance if you don't psych yourself out.

Too Early or Too Late? Don't Second-Guess Your Sell-Date

While many investors will rue missed opportunities to buy, almost all investors will second-guess themselves when they sell a stock. Because stocks are always in motion, investors will almost always sell too early or too late. Even if you are the consummate technical investor, you will not be able to perfectly pick the top on a consistent basis. No matter how much you may have made, if the stock goes up after you sold, you will say to yourself, I should have held on a little longer. If it went down before you sold, you will curse yourself for not selling earlier.

Second-guessing yourself on an action you have already taken is a waste of time and energy. When you took action, you did so based on the best information you had at that moment. In almost all cases, your decision will not be perfect. Don't be a Monday-morning quarterback. You cannot go back and replay the trade.

Instead of second-guessing yourself, review the process you went through in deciding to sell. See if you can learn anything. If you stuck to your investing style and sold for reasons you thought were appropriate at the time, you are in good shape, no matter what the stock did afterward. There is no way to predict the future, so the fact that some unexpected event transpired after you sold should not cause you to question your reason for selling. If you sold for reasons that conflicted with your investing style or if you sold on emotion, make a note of why you took action so that you can avoid it the next time.

Don't Beat Yourself Up over a Bad Investment

All investors sometimes make bad investments. A bad investment is a stock that not only goes down, but it goes down because your analysis was wrong. You bought it because you thought the new product line would be a success, and it was a dud, or you bought it because you thought that the company would get taken over, and instead it went out and made a foolish acquisition of its own. A bad investment can also be one in which you saw the sign to sell but could not pull the trigger.

Bad investments make investors feel stupid. Either your initial analysis was wrong, or you knew to sell but did not. In either case, you screwed up. I can tell you the name of virtually every really bad investment I have ever made. I am not talking about the stocks that went down 5 or 10 percent, I am talking about the real bombs. And I can remember every stock that I round-tripped. (I bought the stock at $10, planned to sell it at $40 but held on when it only got to $36, and rode it back to $10.) I can close my eyes and see the ticker symbols. And if I did try to forget them, one of my customers would be more than pleased to remind me, *"You're the one that put me into . . ."*

While there is no way to feel good about making a mistake or losing money, you should never beat yourself up over a bad investment. Instead, review your analysis. If you can see how you went wrong, perhaps you will avoid the same mistake the next time. If you cannot see how you went wrong, take the stock off your list. If you do not know why you got blindsided the first time, you will never know when you are about to get blindsided again.

DON'T WAIT FOR THE MARKET TO UNDO YOUR MISTAKES

The hardest mistakes to live with are those you knew to avoid. You saw a stock break down on the charts or the earnings come in less than plan, and you knew to sell. But you waited, in the hope that the stock would rebound a little or even get back to your original purchase price so you could get out whole. Unless you have an investing style that gives you a good reason for believing the stock will rebound, do not wait for the market to undo your mistakes. It will rarely happen. If the stock is going against you, never try to get whole. If you made a mistake, accept it, and go on to the next stock.

DON'T KEEP STOCKS YOU HATE

When investors make big mistakes, they often begin to hate the stocks in which they have either lost money or given back money that they had previously made. Yet ironically, many investors tend to hang on to stocks they hate and sell stocks they love. It is as if they feel they must do penance for making the mistake.

When stocks go down, people often say, *"I hate that stock. As soon as it gets back to the price I paid, I am going to dump it."* They must have some subconscious idea that if the stock returns to its purchase price, the mistake will be erased. This is no way to invest. While you should not sell on emotion, neither should you hold on to stocks you hate. If you really hate a stock, you will never be able to make a rational decision about it. It is like a bad marriage, except with stocks the divorce laws are simple. Life is tough enough without having your money invested in a stock you hate.

DON'T PANIC IF YOUR STYLE OR GROUP IS OUT OF FAVOR

Because the stock market runs in cycles, there will be times when your style or group is out of favor. You may like small-cap companies in the Rust Belt, but the fashion of the day may favor technology companies. Unless you have an extreme style, such as buying only micro-cap stocks, most cycles will be relatively short. The worst thing you can do when your group is underperforming is panic. Most people panic just before their group is ready to turn.

If your group or style is underperforming, review your analysis. Sometimes the fundamentals turn out to be different from what you had thought. If your strategy was to buy stocks in the emerging markets of Asia, the events in the fall of 1997 should certainly have caused you to reappraise the opportunities. Other times, macro-economic issues can change the outlook for an entire industry. If OPEC doubles its production, you would certainly want to reappraise your view of oil stocks. But these types of changes are almost always easy to see and react to.

In most cases, investors panic when their style is underperforming even though nothing is happening in the news. It is often easier to deal with a company that has reported disappointing earnings than with a company that produces good results but is ignored by the market. You look at the fundamentals and can't understand why the rest of the market does not appreciate the company or the industry. *"The market is dumb,"* you curse to yourself.

Finally, after months of watching, you give up. If the market is not interested in Rust Belt stocks, you'll switch to technology stocks, you decide. Of course, within a very short period of time, the technology stocks will crater and the Rust Belt stocks will start to outperform, but by then you will have switched your strategy and lost on both sides.

The moral is simple. It is fine to review your analysis. It is even fine to modify your investing style, but you should never panic. If you panic, you are lost. As long as your investing style continues to make sense, stick to what you know. If you know about the Rust Belt, you have a chance of winning when you buy companies based in it. If you jump to technology stocks, you are likely to get creamed.

DON'T TRY TO HIT HOME RUNS IF YOU ARE UNDER-PERFORMING

If you are well behind the market, do not try to hit home runs. Getting the big hit on an investment is always difficult, and mostly it is a matter of luck. If you press and start trying to catch up to the market quickly by buying options or other risky investments, you are likely to compound your mistakes and get even further behind.

DON'T THINK YOU ARE SMART JUST BECAUSE YOUR STOCKS ARE OUTPERFORMING

While panicking when stocks are underperforming is bad, thinking that you are a genius when your group or style is outperforming can be worse.

For months, you watched as other stocks in the market moved. Then, your stocks caught fire. Suddenly, you were outperforming the market. Every day, your stocks were atop the "new high" list. You start thinking to yourself that the game is easy and you are smart. You are in deep trouble.

Like a stopped clock, which is right twice a day, all investors have times when their stocks outperform. One of your companies might get taken over, or your industry might come into favor. You may be outperforming the market, but you are no smarter than you were a few months ago when you were underperforming. The risk is that you may begin to think you are invincible, and you may start making foolish decisions. Groups and styles will come and go, but the minute you believe you can always win, you will become more aggressive and start taking unnecessary risks. You may have figured something out and be able to outperform the market, but in most cases, people get suckered when they mistake the rotation of the market for their own brilliance.

If a guerrilla force was advancing on a battlefield and saw no sign of the enemy, would the general think that the enemy had fled and the war was over? If he did, he would be in for a rude awakening when the counter-attack came. The guerrilla can always win a small battle, but if the guer-rilla takes the experience of that battle and decides that it can now defeat the enemy head-on, the guerrilla is in deep trouble. The same is true for an individual investor. When your investments are doing well, be thankful and stay humble. Go back to basics and take a long-term view. Look at periods in which you outperformed and periods in which you underperformed. Look for warning signals. Try to figure out what could go wrong. Remember, you are still an individual competing against professionals.

Beating the professionals in the stock market is never easy, but it will become much harder if you let your emotions get the better of you. The best investors are those who remain cool and stick to their investing style. It is often difficult to remain cool, especially if you are losing, but it is essential that you do so. If you are not doing well, take a step back and look at your strategy and your style. Learn from your mistakes, but do not let them haunt you. If you are winning, keep it in perspective. You may be smart, or it may just be your turn to outperform. The day you think you have figured out how to win is the day you will begin to lose.

During the late 1960s, I had great success investing in stocks. I did not know much about investing, but I bought stocks in companies I liked and sold them when it looked like something was going wrong. Then I started to work at Harvard Business School. All my friends were professors or doctoral students at Harvard. When one of them gave me an idea, I bought the stock. If it went down, I decided we were right and the market was wrong. After all, who should know more than someone from Harvard Business School? Of course, just because they had business cards that said "Harvard" did not make them right. I got killed thinking I was smarter than the market. It is a mistake I will try to never make again.

GUERRILLA INVESTING SUMMARIZED

Investing in the stock market is like fighting a war. The person on the other side of the trade is your enemy and only one of the two of you will win. If you are to defeat your enemy, you must have better information and be able to act on it more quickly. Unfortunately, if you are an individual investor, the odds are against you. For the most part, your enemy is a professional investor who has more resources, experience, and knowledge than you do. If you attempt to attack such an investor head-on, you will be defeated. The only way to defeat an opponent who is better armed is to follow the strategy of Guerrilla Investing. You must:

- Know yourself and know your enemy.
- Avoid attacking the enemy's strengths.
- Fight on your own turf by investing in things that you understand.
- Find niches that your enemy misses, primarily by investing in small or under-followed stocks.
- Adopt a buy-and-hold strategy, thus nullifying your enemy's advantages in trading.
- Use your enemys' strengths against them, focusing on their inability to change directions rapidly and capitalizing on their need for short-term performance.
- Consistently bet against the consensus. If your enemy is united in one direction, go in the other. The consensus will always be wrong.

In order to win, you must arm yourself with the right weapons, both fundamental and technical:

- Use the analysts' work as a base, and then try to find where the consensus is wrong.
- Use common sense and your own direct experience.
- Look at the company's financial statements. Watch especially for unexpected changes in the numbers. See if the growth rate and the price/earnings multiple are consistent.
- Use charts as an early warning system. Watch for breakouts and tops. The professionals always show clear signs when they are getting ready to move in one direction or another.
- Look for connections between suppliers and customers and between companies in the same industry. Stocks of related companies often follow similar patterns.
- Don't get suckered in by what the analysts say. Read between the lines. See if a Buy recommendation is really a Buy or just an attempt to keep an investment banking client happy.
- Remember, the market rarely overreacts.
- Watch for pitfalls and opportunities, especially when insiders are buying or selling or companies are shuffling information.

Once you have a battle plan and the information needed to implement it, you are ready to attack. But before you do so, you must:

- Find your own investment style that fits within the strategy of Guerrilla Investing.
- Don't try to chase the movements of the market. Instead, stick with a style that works for you.
- Before you commit your resources to any stock, get to know the company.
- Understand why you are buying the stock and when you plan to sell it.
- Make ownership an active process. Constantly reevaluate your positions, and watch for signs that something is going wrong.
- Don't fall in love with your stocks. Like soldiers in a war, they

sometimes get killed. You should not fall with them.

- Don't play head games with yourself. Keep cool and stick to your style. If you do, you will almost always win in the long run.

Use the Internet, both for information and for on-line investing. Whether you are an active trader or a long-term investor, the Internet provides a quantity and quality of information that rivals what is available to professionals. For the first time, individuals can now receive information with the same timeliness and detail as the professional can. The democratization of information will continue to have a dramatic, long-term impact on the workings of the stock market, and most of the impact will benefit the individual investor.

Finally, and most importantly, never underestimate the power of your enemy. Remember, your enemy is the well-trained army. You are the guerrilla force. You cannot overpower your enemy or win in head-to-head combat. You must approach your enemy with great respect. Capitalize on the opportunities you find, but do not overreach. Above all else, remember the dictum of Sun Tzu as he stated in *The Art of War*, "Know yourself, know your enemy. In one hundred battles, there will be one hundred victories."